THE MAKING OF THE CELTIC ...

During his twenty-five years in public life **Ray MacSharry** served as Minister of State at the Department of Finance and Public Service, as Minister for Agriculture, and as Tánaiste – Deputy Prime Minister – and Minister for Finance in 1982 and again in 1987–8 when the foundations were laid for the Celtic Tiger. He left the latter ministry to become European Commissioner for Agriculture and Rural Development. He left public life in 1993 and joined the private sector. He is Chairman of Eircom, Coillte, Green Property and London City Airport, and a director of a number of other major public companies including Bank of Ireland and Smurfit.

Padraic White, a native of Kinlough, County Leitrim, joined the new Industrial Development Authority of Ireland (IDA-Ireland) at its foundation in 1970 and rose to become its Managing Director from 1981–90. IDA-Ireland became one of the world's most successful investment promotion agencies, attracting some of the world's leading companies to make Ireland their European base. From 1987, he led its pioneering work in establishing the International Financial Services Centre in Dublin as part of a national initiative. He is a director of Irish and international companies and a member of the Board of Trustees of the Eisenhower Exchange Fellowships Inc. He maintains his life-long interest in linking job creation to the unemployed through his role as Chairman – since 1991 – of the Northside Partnership Ltd, Dublin, a pioneering local area-based approach to placing the long-term unemployed in jobs.

Joseph O'Malley has spent a lifetime career in the national print media, writing on political and economic issues. He joined the *Irish Press* in 1963 and in 1968 became Associate Editor of *Business and Finance* magazine. Between 1969 and 1972 he was Editor of *This Week* magazine. Since 1973 he has been the political correspondent of the *Sunday Independent*.

Dr Kieran Kennedy is a distinguished economist. For twenty-five years he was Director of Ireland's Economic and Social Research Institute, the country's premier independent research centre. He is the author of authoritative analyses of many aspects of the Irish economy, including the pioneering study *Productivity and Industrial Growth, The Irish Experience*, which has been recognised as a classic.

Praise for *The Making of the Celtic Tiger*

'I would strongly recommend the recent book on the Celtic Tiger by Ray Mac Sharry and Padraic White, which is a well-informed and authoritative guide for anyone who wants to look back over where we have come from and how our position has been transformed'
An Taoiseach, Bertie Ahern

'This book represents a unique contribution to the historical record and will be required reading for future students of the period'
Conor Brady, *The Irish Times*

'It is an excellent read and a well-told history of public life in Ireland since independence, written by two of the protagonists . . . the retelling of political, social and cultural events by Ray Mac Sharry and Padraic White is a refreshing reminder of how far we have come'
Eddie O'Connor, the *Sunday Business Post*

'The authors have done us a service in writing it, because as players they were able to bring a particular insight to what it was like at the coalface'
Ruairi Quinn, the *Sunday Independent*

'An "I was there" book, a good example of the genre, and an enjoyable read'
Colm McCarthy, the *Irish Independent*

First published in 2000 by
Mercier Press
PO Box 5 5 French Church St Cork
E.mail: books@mercier.ie

16 Hume Street Dublin 2
Tel: (01) 661 5299; Fax: (01) 661 8583
E.mail: books@marino.ie

This paperback edition 2001

Trade enquiries to CMD Distribution
55A Spruce Avenue
Stillorgan Industrial Park
Blackrock County Dublin
Tel: (01) 294 2556; Fax: (01) 294 2564
E.mail: cmd@columba.ie

ISBN 1 85635 336 2

10 9 8 7 6 5 4 3 2 1

A CIP record for this title is available from the British Library

Cover design by Penhouse Design
Printed in Ireland by ColourBooks,
Baldoyle Industrial Estate, Dublin 13

THE MAKING OF THE CELTIC TIGER
THE INSIDE STORY
OF IRELAND'S BOOM ECONOMY

RAY MAC SHARRY AND PADRAIC A. WHITE

IN ASSOCIATION WITH JOSEPH O'MALLEY

CONSULTING EDITOR: DR KIERAN KENNEDY

MERCIER PRESS

To my wife Elaine, without whose support, commitment and dedication it would not have been possible to meet my public duties.

Ray Mac Sharry

I dedicate this book to my wife, Mary, who gave so much of herself to promoting Ireland at countless business functions during my twenty-year career with IDA-Ireland, and to our daughter, Clionadh, who as a child and teenager became very familiar with the IDA 'world' described in this book.

Padraic A. White

Preface

The stimulus to write this book came from our common experience of encountering many people of all ages who wondered how Ireland became such a boom economy and, as it seemed to them, so suddenly. Those with vivid memories of the 1980s can scarcely believe the dramatic reversal of fortune with unemployment and emigration being replaced by job vacancy signs and substantial immigration. Both of us were direct participants in the crucial policies and decisions which led to this economic take-off and we believe it worthwhile and of public interest to put on the record our experiences of those events. This is a personal account based largely on our recollection and conversations with colleagues. It is not an academic study, and we did not seek access to original files.

We owe a debt of gratitude to many people who have helped with their support, advice and encouragement to ensure that this book was transformed from an idea into a finished product. It represents our attempt to chart the course of the Celtic Tiger phenomenon, not merely in terms of the past decade or so, but also to set that economic achievement in a broader context. For the foundation of Ireland's remarkable success at the end of the twentieth century lies as much in the wise decisions taken many decades ago in the fifties and sixties – in abandoning protectionism, encouraging foreign investment, opting for membership of the EEC and investing in education – as it does in those made in more recent times. Without the foresight shown by an earlier generation of innovating politicians from all parties and by visionary public servants, much of what has been accomplished today might never have been realised.

In particular we would like to thank all those who provided both insight and assistance at various stages of this work. We benefited greatly from conversations with former colleagues from our respective pasts in national politics, government, the EU Commission and the Industrial Development Authority – or Agency, as it has now become. These contacts proved helpful in refreshing memories of past events and in supplying helpful insights and observations. We would like to thank the former Secretary General of the Department of Finance, Sean Cromien, and Pádraig Ó hUiginn, a former Chairman of the National Economic and Social Council, for their interest in the project from the outset and their willingness to help where at all possible. In addition, David Duffy, Assistant Research Officer at the Economic and Social Research Institute, provided invaluable assistance in preparing a background historical analysis of the Irish economy, in assisting with the preparation of the graphs and in his comments and observations on the draft text. There were many current and former IDA-Ireland staff who assisted in responding to our requests. Kieran McGowan, who retired as Chief Executive in December 1998, cooperated generously with the project, including his personal reminiscences. His successor, Sean Dorgan, ensured a continuity of cooperation – we wish him every success during his tenure. Colm Donlon, Manager of Press and Public Relations, was our reference point in IDA throughout the project, and we are deeply indebted to him and his staff.

Many others with an IDA connection assisted, including Ted O'Neill, former Executive Director; Joe McCabe, former Chairman; P. J. Daly, former Executive Director; Pat O'Brien, former Executive Director; Páid McMenamin, former Executive

Director; Jerry Kelly, former Manager, Electronics; John Kerrigan, former Manager, Engineering Division, Brendan Russell, former head of Financial Services; Frank Ryan, Manager, Software and Financial Services; John Lloyd, Manager, Healthcare and Engineering; Denis Molumby, Manager International Services; Dr David Hanna, Manager, Information and Communications Technologies; Tom Hyland, IDA-Ireland's Galway-based Area Director; Denis Fitzpatrick, head of IT and Marketing Services; Kathleen Fitzgerald, former Personal Assistant to Michael Killeen; Dan Flinter, Chief Executive, and Frank Murray of Enterprise Ireland. John Travers, Chief Executive of Forfás, facilitated the provision of its research findings. Forfás staff who assisted included David Lovegrove (Secretary), Dan Brennan and Clare Breen of its Planning Division.

Others who gave particular assistance included: Tomas Ó Cofaigh, former Governor of the Central Bank of Ireland; Dermot Desmond, Chairman, International Investment and Underwriting Ltd; John Fanning, former Managing Director, McConnell's Advertising Service Ltd; Willie Moloney, former Manager, USA, for Shannon Development; Neil Mulcahy, Secretary, Dublin Docklands Development Authority; Gus McAuley, former General Manager, Customs House Dock Development Authority; Michael Somers, Adrian Kearns, and Felix Larkin, formerly of the Department of Finance and now in the National Treasury Management Agency; Greg Sparks, Partner, Farrell Grant Sparks Accountants; Ken O'Brien, founder, *Finance* magazine; Brendan O'Donoghue, Director, National Library of Ireland; Liam Connellan, former Director, Confederation of Irish Industry; John Gallagher, Director General, Institute of Public Administration; Gerry Loughran, Permanent Secretary, Department of Enterprise, Trade and Investment, Northern Ireland.

We are grateful to the Oireachtas for the facilities provided at Leinster House by Librarian Maura Corcoran and Assistant Librarians Dr Patrick Melvin, Seamus Haughey and Maedhbh McNamara, and also to all the library staff at Independent Newspapers for their assistance in research, and for supplying most of the pictures for this book. We are also indebted to Peter Doyle, Director of the European Commission Representation in Dublin; Tim Kelly, and Mary O'Connor. They provided invaluable help with EU-related matters. We would like to thank officials at the Departments of Finance, Agriculture and Food, Enterprise Trade and Employment, and at the Central Statistics Office for their assistance in relation to statistical and other material.

This book is written in association with Joseph O'Malley, Political Correspondent of the *Sunday Independent* newspaper. He has been our constant companion in bringing this project to fruition, particularly by his coordination of our respective contributions so as to achieve the necessary continuity and consistency. Joseph's knowledge of the political and economic events of the times was invaluable in cross-checking our own recollections. Dr Kieran Kennedy, former Director of the Economic and Social Research Institute of Ireland, is our Consulting Editor. He has an unrivalled knowledge of the economic events we describe and is himself a distinguished author. We appreciate greatly his encouragement and assistance from the start of the project.

At our publishers, Marino Books/Mercier Press, Jo O'Donoghue and Rachel Sirr were always constructive in their suggestions and fully supportive in their role, while showing remarkable patience with our efforts.

CONTENTS

INTRODUCTION

Ray Mac Sharry and Padraic White

The Irish diaspora took different forms in the nineteenth and the twentienth centuries and, as the new century arrives, patterns of migration are changing again, this time for the better. In December 1990, when Mary Robinson delivered her inauguration address as President of Ireland and spoke of the 70 million people worldwide claiming Irish descent, she underlined the scale of the human exodus from this country over the previous century and a half. Now, with the dawning of the new millennium, Ireland's relationship with the great diaspora beyond these shores has altered unexpectedly. As the population increases once more, and living standards rise to reach average levels within the European Union, Ireland, so often a point of departure for emigrants leaving to find work abroad, has reversed a historical role and become more like a jobs haven for exiles wanting to return and work at home. The expatriates and others – economic migrants from the European Union and elsewhere – have been attracted both by the quality of life and the range of job opportunities Ireland can offer following the rapid rate of economic expansion, particularly since 1994.

In the past, the level of emigration was seen as a measure of national economic failure. However, over the last decade, the tide of emigration has turned. Ireland has reinvented herself successfully in economic terms, and the diaspora has acquired a new dimension. This global network of migrants provides a new source of labour supply for the economy, helping to fill job vacancies at home and raise the level of employment.

Today, the contrast with the bleak economic conditions of a century and a half ago could hardly be more striking. It shows how rapidly Ireland has advanced from 'famine to feast', and in a relatively short time. In 1963, President John F. Kennedy, in his address to the Joint Sitting of the Houses of the Oireachtas in Leinster House, spoke movingly in describing how, more than a century before, emigrants had left a country of 'hunger and famine' in 'a mixture of hope and agony'. In that memorable speech, he quoted some lines from an earlier Irish poet who said of their departure, 'They are going, going, going, and we cannot bid them stay.'

Now some of the descendants of those past generations who left because they had little choice are returning to a country which, by the close of the twentieth century, has managed a remarkable economic transformation. Sustained high growth has produced virtual full employment with low inflation, a sharply declining debt burden and large budget surpluses, all helping to complete this virtuous circle. Impressive economic indicators such as these have become the hallmarks of the Celtic Tiger economy. However, as the new millennium dawns, sustaining the momentum of growth that began in the late eighties, accelerated rapidly from the mid-nineties and shows little sign of faltering, is the immediate challenge.

*

The historic task of this generation is to ensure the economic foundation of independence.

Seán Lemass, 1959

Some 150 years ago, the situation in Ireland was all very different. After the failure of the potato crop, the Great Famine blighted the landscape. Many died from disease and starvation while more, to escape a similar fate, were driven into involuntary exile as emigrants. Within a decade – from 1845 to 1855 – some 2.5 million people had fled the country. Destitute, they secured their own survival as best they could and wherever they could, in Britain, America and further afield in Australia and New Zealand. Then, for a large part of the twentieth century came a second wave of involuntary emigration. The movement of people was mainly to Britain. And this time their reason for leaving was largely financial. They found themselves pushed by the depressed state of the domestic economy and pulled by the hope of employment, a better future and higher living standards, mainly in England or Scotland. For four decades after national independence, the pattern of heavy emigration continued. And so, by the fifties, as the outflow gathered pace, a crisis point was reached in our national economic development.

By then, the sheer size of the emigrant numbers raised major questions about Ireland's economic viability as an independent entity, namely, about whether the state could survive, given the rate at which people were voting with their feet and leaving the country. Increasingly, that sense of anxiety and doubt was reflected in government reports like the *Commission on Emigration* and in books such as *The Vanishing Irish* by John O' Brien, which questioned whether the Irish race itself was facing extinction. For by the late 1950s, the outlook was depressing. Nearly a million people had left the state since its foundation, while the population had dropped by some 5 per cent since 1922. Over the same period, living standards had barely risen at all, and a mood of pessimism gripped the country, lowering national self-esteem. As some wondered whether our economic problems were beyond solution, others worried that emigration had become self-perpetuating, and almost a natural way of life. An extract from a landmark report captured the sombre national mood when it noted that, 'After thirty-five years of native government people are asking whether we can achieve an acceptable degree of economic progress. The common talk among parents in the towns, as in rural Ireland, is of their children having to emigrate as soon as their education is completed, in order to be sure of a reasonable livelihood.'

The title of the report was *Economic Development*, and its author, T. K. Whitaker, as Secretary of the Department of Finance, presented it to the government in May 1958. In his 250-page analysis, the bleak scenario he outlined served only to emphasise the scale of the difficulties facing the economy. A radical change in economic policy was required. For if high emigration persisted, then a smaller domestic market, with fewer producers and consumers, would result, as the able and the enterprising took the emigrant boat or plane. And with their departure, society would lose the very people best equipped to reverse the country's declining economic fortunes; those with the necessary capital, initiative and human skills.

Native industry, sheltering behind high tariff walls, had become inefficient and uncompetitive. Secure from foreign competition and enjoying a guaranteed market, it faced little pressure to compete. A depressed business environment within a stagnant economy offered little incentive for any entrepreneur – whether Irish or foreign – to invest, at least so long as the protectionist approach and philosophy remained the cornerstone of government economic policy.

In that opening chapter of *Economic Development*, Whitaker had spelled out the message clearly that, 'Sooner or later, protection will have to go and the challenge of free trade be accepted. There is really no other choice for a country wishing to keep pace materially with the rest of Europe.' And, unless protection was dismantled and free trade adopted, he warned ' . . . We shall fail to provide the basis necessary for the economic independence and material progress of the community.'

A year later, the scale and nature of the problem was recognised publicly by Seán Lemass shortly before he became Taoiseach in 1959. Then, echoing the words of the Secretary of the Department of Finance, he accepted that 'the historic task of this generation is to ensure the economic foundation of independence.' Above all, that meant checking the slow and steady haemorrhaging of the population though emigration. For a new generation of pragmatic politicians – like Lemass himself – and the new breed of civil service technocrats – like Ken Whitaker – the challenge to secure the nation's economic survival became their most immediate priority.

Their simultaneous arrival to occupy the highest positions of political and administrative power in the state proved fortunate. For together, they acted to change the course of Ireland's economic history for the remainder of the twentieth century. They did so as the joint architects of a policy switch as far-reaching and dramatic as that instituted more than a quarter of a century earlier by Fianna Fáil. In the thirties, when protection-ism was first fully adopted, Seán Lemass was its strongest advocate. In the late fifties, when it was officially abandoned and the policy reversed in favour of free trade and foreign direct investment, Lemass, as Taoiseach, and an arch-pragmatist, was again spearheading the change.

By the time, in 1959, Seán Lemass finally succeeded Éamon de Valera as Taoiseach, T. K. Whitaker had served as Secretary of the Department of Finance in Merrion Street for three years. He was appointed to the top position as head of the civil service at an early age. At age 39, he had been promoted out of turn by the Fine Gael Minister for Finance, Gerry Sweetman, who had quickly spotted his outstanding abilities. It was to prove an inspired choice. Traditional Ireland, set in its conservative ways and personified in the ageing figure of de Valera, was to undergo a profound change. Old policy assumptions were challenged by the new ideas articulated by Whitaker and implemented by Lemass. A concern about economic performance took precedence over political nationalism and its preoccupation with issues like partition and the revival of the Irish language.

The role both men played in shaping the national response to the economic crisis of the mid to late fifties marked a major turning point in the country's economic development in the latter half of the twentieth century. The new policies adopted were to change a small closed economy looking in on itself into a small open economy looking outwards on the world, embracing free trade and abandoning protection. Up to that point economic nationalism had produced very limited returns, either in terms of jobs or rising living standards. Quite simply, it had failed to meet the expectations set after 1922, with the achievement of independence and the foundation of the new state.

At that time, the most urgent task awaiting the first government was that of nation-building: to establish the new state successfully and to reconstruct an economy damaged first by the War of Independence and later divided by a bitter civil war in 1922–3. For the Cumann na nGaedheal administration, circumstances allowed neither much time nor great financial scope for major initiatives to boost economic development. By temperament and character, the new leaders were conservative figures, more inclined to follow economic orthodoxy than to challenge the prevailing consensus that favoured free trade. Indeed, Kevin O'Higgins once described his colleagues as the most conservative revolutionaries in history.

One major government intervention in the economy was the setting up of the Electricity Supply Board (ESB) in 1927 and the construction of the hydroelectric scheme to harness the River Shannon at Ardnacrusha, outside Limerick. It was the first step in establishing the energy infrastructure that was to prove critical in the future development of the economy. The ESB was also the forerunner of a number of state-sponsored bodies set up from 1932 onwards, in different areas of the economy – transport, insurance, banking – where the private sector was unwilling to invest.

But from the outset, agriculture remained the Cumann na nGaedheal government's main priority. The agriculture sector, in which 53 per cent of the labour force was engaged in 1926, was also the country's largest exporter. And since the government viewed agriculture as the main means of generating economic growth, it was reluctant to adopt protectionist measures to assist 'infant industries', the policy favoured by the Sinn Féin leader, Arthur Griffith. The government feared that such a move could provoke retaliation and make agriculture less competitive by raising the sector's cost of production.

In 1932, an election saw Fianna Fáil's arrival in government for the first time and, with it, came a sharp reversal of industrial policy, both on political and economic grounds. Protectionism and the pursuit of self-sufficiency became key objectives in national economic development. The new administration favoured tariff protection for domestic industry, both as an expression of political independence and to facilitate the rapid growth of a viable industrial sector, sheltered behind high tariff walls. But soon, relations between Ireland and Britain became increasingly strained by a prolonged dispute over the repayment of land annuities. Better known as the 'Economic War', this Anglo-Irish row, which lasted six years, ended in 1938. By then, trade between the two countries had declined, while growth in the world economy had slowed with the onset of the global depression.

In the thirties, protectionism was dictated as much by political choice as by economic circumstance. For the Fianna Fáil government, committed to self-sufficiency and the need to create an industrial structure, it was a logical initiative to take. By the mid-thirties, Irish import tariffs, a third more than those in Britain, were amongst the highest in the world. Gradually, as the full international impact of the Great Depression of the 1930s was felt, free trade policies were readily abandoned by governments everywhere. And later, with the outbreak of the Second World War and the threat posed to industrial supplies this posed, self-sufficiency became not just a policy preference, but an unavoidable option.

After 1945, as the general post-war economic recovery got under way, it provided a temporary boost to the domestic economy. But, increasingly, the policy of protecting domestic industry was no longer proving either a sufficient or an appropriate response. The local firms were small and inefficient and unable to meet the country's employment needs. By 1950, manufactured goods still accounted only for some 6 per cent of all exports, with food and food products making up 73 per cent of the total. In the early fifties, Ireland's closed economy model impeded rather than facilitated the expansion of industry, with rising trade deficits reflecting increased import demand and contributing to balance of payments difficulties in 1951 and 1955. The high tariff walls, and the ban on majority foreign ownership of industry, secured by the Control of Manufactures Act of 1932, were both designed to help native firms develop and expand in a sheltered environment. But for more than a decade after the war, these restrictive measures continued to shield domestic industry from the spur of foreign competition.

The small size of the domestic market and the protection from foreign competition afforded by high tariffs and import quotas gave industry little reason to expand production and develop export outlets. Yet, the less equipped indigenous industry was to compete on export markets, the more it relied on protection simply to survive. Equally, the continuing legal ban on foreign ownership of domestic industry effectively ensured that in the fifties, the greatly increased international flows of foreign direct investment bypassed Ireland altogether. Foreign industry had no incentive to locate here. As a result, Ireland missed out on the full impact of the strong economic recovery in Europe, while the industrial sector became increasingly uncompetitive. In the 1950s, as the European economies achieved strong and sustained growth, the Irish economy marked time.

In agriculture, as the flight from the land accelerated and employment declined, industry was unable to absorb the numbers involved. This led to higher unemployment and increased emigration, with 409,000 leaving the country between 1951 and 1961. Between 1949 and 1956, while the Irish economy expanded at just 2 per cent annually, growth in Britain and the rest of Europe rose at a much faster rate. The early and mid-fifties in Ireland were years of stagnation, marked not just by budgetary and balance of payments setbacks, but also by a growing sense of hopelessness about finding a solution to the economy's woes. Political independence from Britain was not, as many had hoped, synonymous with economic independence. Self-government did not alter the laws of economics, or the way markets

operated. Even by the 1950s, almost 90 per cent of Irish exports
– mainly agricultural – still went to the United Kingdom. The
failure to diversify away from an exclusive dependence on the
British market was part of the price paid for keeping protectionist
policies in place too long, thereby delaying the opening up of
export markets for Irish industrial goods. This happened only
after the government changed policy direction, and encouraged
foreign industry – by grants and tax incentives – to locate here
and use the country as an export base for their manufactured
output. As Ken Whitaker was to write later, 'the years 1955 and
1956 had plumbed the depths of hopelessness', inducing 'a dark
night of the soul, shared by the principal politicians both in and
out of office and by concerned citizens and public servants'.

But out of that deep soul-searching, a new departure in
economic policy did emerge, finally. Foreign direct investment
was encouraged by tax relief – via a zero rate of tax on profits
derived from increased manufacturing exports, introduced in
1956 – and by substantial industrial grants. The Industrial
Development Authority (IDA) was given more extensive powers
and greater resources, while the restrictions on foreign investment
under the Control of Manufactures Act were phased out gradually
and economic planning was introduced.

The national plan produced in 1958 – the Programme for
Economic Expansion – was largely based on the proposals
outlined weeks earlier by Whitaker in *Economic Development*. It
favoured a shift away from social investment – schools, housing
and hospitals – and towards more productive investment.
Publication ensured that the new ideas enjoyed the status of
official policy, and also signalled that the government had
accepted the case for change. The government, through the
Programme, readily acknowledged that 'Production has not been
increasing fast enough to provide employment and acceptable living

standards for growing numbers of our people; large-scale emigration has been accompanied by a high level of unemployment. Emigration will not be checked nor will unemployment be permanently reduced until the rate of increase in national output is greatly accelerated.' In fact, between 1951 and 1958 the economy grew by less than 1 per cent annually.

So, Ireland had little choice but to accept free trade and seek foreign investment to try and create an industrial base that would employ surplus labour. Without such a move, the country risked falling further behind Britain and the Continental economies, as the tariff barriers to trade were dismantled. In Europe, with the establishment of the Common Market, which was agreed between the six founding member states in 1957, the move to international free trade was already well under way. Clearly, failure to move towards trade liberalisation would leave Ireland in a state of greater economic isolation, further depress the economy and encourage emigration. Almost certainly, it would mean defeat in the battle to secure the country's economic independence. In *Economic Development* the warning had been delivered in unequivocal terms that 'sooner or later, protection will have to go and the challenge of free trade be accepted.' In fact, it was sooner rather than later.

All in all, the economic progress achieved after the first thirty-five years of independence was disappointing. The population had fallen and emigration had soared while living standards had barely increased. And, particularly after the war, protection had failed to help establish a viable industrial base that would grow fast enough to absorb surplus labour and raise employment levels. Recognition, however belated, of the scale of that failure allowed for a complete reversal of policy to take place. Over time this has led – via EU membership and increased foreign direct investment – to a dramatic improvement in our economic fortunes.

Nothing better expressed the country's new-found self-confidence than the government's decision in 1961 to apply for membership of the European Economic Community (EEC), after Britain had first indicated her intention to do so. It took a further twelve years before, finally, this was achieved, with both Britain and Ireland joining in 1973. However, the boldness of the ambition to enter the Common Market put intense pressure on industry and agriculture to improve competitiveness and efficiency. The subsequent delay of more than a decade, while frustrating, proved valuable. It allowed more time for the necessary adjustments to be made, thus ensuring the economy was in a better condition to meet the challenge.

As Kieran Kennedy has noted in his essay 'Industrial Development', in the Thomas Davis series *From Famine to Feast*, the abandonment of protection in favour of free trade saw the emergence of a new outward-looking strategy that was concerned with export-led growth and had three main elements: 'First, capital grants and tax concessions were provided to encourage export-oriented manufacturing. Second, the IDA was given the task of attracting foreign firms to Ireland, again aimed at exports. And third, protection was dismantled in return for greater access to markets abroad, culminating in an Anglo-Irish Free Trade Area Agreement in 1965, and accession to the European Community in 1973.'

In addition, the government aimed to achieve a more rapid growth in the economy, through increased public spending in the context of its economic planning proposals. The Programme for Economic Expansion (1959–63) reflected an optimism about the future which, as events unfolded, proved to be well founded. Over the lifetime of the plan, the 4 per cent annual growth rate achieved was twice the level forecast.

But just how much of the economy's strong recovery from

1958 onwards was due to the Programme remains questionable. For the plan's publication coincided with, rather than caused, the sharp rebound by the economy out of a deep recession. However, the symbolism of the Programme, and the move towards economic planning that it signalled, mattered nearly as much as its content. On a psychological level, the plan helped raise public morale just when an uplift in national spirits was badly needed. It served as a powerful antidote in dispelling what Dr Whitaker later described as 'the palpable mood of despondency that prevailed at that time'. And undoubtedly, it acted as a catalyst for many of the policy changes that were made subsequently.

1
—

HIGHS AND LOWS: IRELAND'S ECONOMIC PERFORMANCE 1960–86

Ray Mac Sharry and Padraic White

All in all, the 1950s marked an important transition in Ireland's economic development, as the country moved from stagnation to rapid economic growth. The result was continuous economic expansion from the late 1950s to the early 1970s, and at a faster pace than previously achieved. In the sixties, living standards rose by some 40 per cent over the decade. The population, which in 1961 was the lowest since the foundation of the state, had reached its highest point by 1971. In that year, the census figures showed an increase of over 160,000 to just under 3 million people. But if the move away from protection to free trade marked the start of a change from a closed to an open economy, it also reflected a willingness to forge wider links with the outside world, particularly in the international economic arena. In 1957, Ireland finally joined the World Bank and the International Monetary Fund. Four years later, that transition to free trade was greatly accelerated by two developments: First, in 1961, came the application for EEC membership. And in 1965, was the signing of the Anglo-Irish Free Trade Agreement

(AIFTA). These were two important milestones in the reorientation of the economy towards greater trade liberalisation.

The AIFTA resulted in the phased lowering of tariff barriers between Ireland and Britain, with full free trade accomplished in 1975. This long transitional period gave industry time to adapt and caused less disruption to the economy. Studies conducted by the Committee on Industrial Organisation on different sectors and industries greatly facilitated the adjustment. Later, grants, loans and tax incentives were provided to help industry modernise and face up to the more competitive trading conditions that lay ahead. In effect, the AIFTA served as a stepping stone to EEC accession and also opened the way for membership of the General Agreement on Tariffs and Trade (GATT), which was finally achieved in 1967. In that year too came another highly significant development, this time in education, in a reform that over time helped accelerate the modernisation of the economy.

The 1916 Proclamation promised to cherish all the children of the nation equally. But by the early sixties, and after nearly half a century of self-government, the failure to live up to that ideal in the field of education was striking. Some twenty years after most other European countries had embarked on major investment in the reform of their educational systems, Ireland still lagged well behind. The OECD-sponsored *Investment in Education* report of 1965 highlighted some major shortcomings in this area – not least the limited access to secondary education. At a social level, the report revealed serious inequality of opportunity for children from poorer backgrounds. Fewer passed from primary to secondary education, and fewer still ever reached third level. The study showed that in 1961 half of the children (aged 15–19) of professionals and skilled workers were in full-time education, compared with just 10 per cent among those in the semi-skilled or unskilled categories. This huge social imbalance had to be rectified, both on grounds of equity and for the overall benefit of the economy.

So in the late sixties a long overdue reform in education began. In time, this resulted in greater participation at secondary level, and also the introduction of a much less academic syllabus. The change reflected a movement away from education for its own sake to a system more geared to the needs of a modern economy and the career opportunities of school leavers. At this time, the economy was in a transitional phase, both adapting to free trade and preparing for eventual EEC membership. In this adjustment process, the reform of education played an important role. Increased public spending on education became an investment in learning and the creation of human capital. In turn, this has raised the skills base of the labour force.

Over the past three decades the continuing investment in education made by successive governments has laid the long-term foundation for part of the economic success we now enjoy. Without such a policy change at that time, the Irish economy would look quite different today. The educated Irish workforce has become one of the primary reasons why the country has become such a favoured industrial location for foreign investment, particularly in the high-tech sectors – electronics and pharmaceuticals.

The catalyst for the education revolution was provided by then Minister of Education Donogh O'Malley in 1966: 'I propose from the coming school year, beginning in September of next year, to introduce a scheme whereby up to the completion of the Intermediate Certificate course, the opportunity for free post-primary education will be available to all schools.' In 1967 all secondary fees were abolished and free school transport was provided in rural areas. Enrolments increased by 18,000 in the first year, to 149,000. By 1997, some 370,000 students were in full-time education at second level, with 40 per cent of those of school leaving age moving on to third level. In 1964, just one in four of seventeen-year-olds were still in secondary education; by 1994 that figure had risen to 83 per cent. This was a remarkable transformation in just thirty years.

The growth and expansion at secondary level from the late sixties onwards created its own momentum. It led to major changes in third-level education – particularly in the technological sector, via the Dublin Colleges of Technology, the National Institute of Higher Education in Limerick and the series of Regional Technical Colleges (RTCs) that were set up in different industrial centres throughout the country. The key to the success of the regional colleges has been the close links established between these institutions and local business. In microcosm, Sligo, like many other towns, reflects that successful fusion of the academic and industrial worlds. There, the local RTC helped the town become the tool-making centre of Ireland. Today there are some 500 people involved in tool-making throughout the region, in Ballina, Tubbercurry and Sligo. Private jets fly in with large pieces of tooling equipment to be rejigged in Sligo or to have new parts added. The success of the regional technical colleges ensured the universities moved closer to the world of business, so now there is competition and people have greater choice.

The expansion in third-level education has helped redress the huge imbalance that existed within that sector some decades ago, when university education was a privilege of the few. At that time, Ireland was producing a surplus of doctors, dentists, lawyers and other professionals to her needs. As they emigrated to find employment, other countries benefited from the education provided, and partly paid for by taxpayers, in Ireland. Ireland's investment became Britain or America's gain. Yet, at the same time, the country was failing to produce enough people with the technical qualifications needed to support a developing modern economy. This greatly limited Ireland's potential as an industrial base for manufactured exports.

Free secondary education succeeded because it struck a chord, particularly with the numerous parents who themselves had missed out on educational opportunities but who wanted their own children to benefit from such opportunities and were prepared to make huge personal sacrifices to help them. Successive governments have recognised that determination. And so, even in times of economic retrenchment, spending on education has been spared, relative to the stringent cutbacks elsewhere.

Education provides opportunity and choice, broadens intellectual horizons and opens up a wider range of employment possibilities. In a knowledge-based economy, the standards achieved in education will determine how easily the workforce adapts to the rapid pace of technological change within industry. Increasingly, investment in human capital is seen as the key to increased employment, greater economic prosperity and social cohesion. Fortunately, all governments from the early sixties on were quick to recognise the potential of education and to invest in the future. And yet, without the motivation also of parents, teachers and students, that opportunity might never have been fully exploited. Today some four out of five school leavers apply for places in higher education. This helps explain the remarkable performance of the economy in recent years and remains one of the critical building blocks of the Celtic Tiger economy.

By 1972, the economic outlook certainly was a good deal brighter than in the late fifties. Ireland had benefited from the worldwide boom of the 1960s and early 1970s. Increased foreign investment helped raise the growth rate of the economy, which had averaged an annual rate of increase of more than 4 per cent since 1960. The government, in its White Paper (1972) on EEC membership, underscored that improved performance, noting that between 1958 and 1970, the economy had grown by 61 per cent, compared with a 42 per cent increase in Britain. The population, which, at 2.8 million in 1961, had touched its lowest point since the Famine, was rising again; emigration had been sharply reduced and the structure of the economy was undergoing a rapid transformation. In the process of adjustment and change, Ireland was becoming less and less an agricultural country, while industry, increasingly, became the driving force of future growth. Nevertheless, despite the better economic performance, overall employment showed no increase between 1961 and 1972, with the rise in industry and services being offset by the sharp decline in agricultural employment. But, at least, the decline in total employment was arrested.

Ireland's accession to EEC membership in January 1973 provided an opportunity to benefit from participation in one of the fastest-growing economic areas in the world. For industry, the benefit of open access to the British market under the AIFTA was further enhanced by the entry gained to the European market. It presented indigenous industry with the chance to reduce economic dependence on Britain and diversify its exports towards the more buoyant Continental economies. In addition, EEC entry made it easier to attract foreign direct investment to Ireland. Multinational firms locating here could use the country as a platform for exports to a European market of 250 million people. For farmers, the prize was the benefit from higher guaranteed agricultural prices in the Common Agricultural Policy (CAP) and the end of reliance on a single market – Britain – for the sale of their produce.

It was hoped that access to the faster-growing European

economies, both for agriculture and industrial exports, could transform the economy, not least by raising employment and absorbing surplus labour. And it did over time, particularly with the arrival of substantial US multinational investment, attracted by the combination of tax incentives and generous grant facilities. That acceleration of inward investment was to prove one of the most significant gains from Community membership.

However, on the negative side, indigenous industry contracted, with significant job losses as the economy adjusted to the restructuring of the manufacturing sector in the 1970s and 1980s. In the new environment, growth in manufacturing shifted from traditional indigenous industries to modern industries. These were largely foreign-owned and export-oriented. In 1973, foreign firms accounted for less than one-third of total industrial employment (68,511) and by 1988 this had increased to a 42 per cent share (85,851). Over that fifteen-year period, overall employment in industry had fallen 6.6 per cent to 204,184. Nevertheless, the employment gains in foreign firms – up by a quarter – had not outweighed the heavy job losses in the Irish-owned sector – which fell by more than one-fifth.

Ireland also benefited from a substantial level of receipts from the EU budget (see Chapter 6). The majority of financial transfers have been received under the FEOGA scheme, which provides funding for the agricultural sector. Payments were also received from the European Social Fund and Regional Development Fund throughout the 1970s. These grants increased significantly during the late 1980s as funding was raised to help, in particular, the EU's peripheral economies (Ireland, Spain, Portugal and Greece) adjust to the challenges of the single market and, later, the single currency. The less advanced regions of the EU were seen as potentially vulnerable unless they received development aid.

However, over the thirteen-year period 1973–86, the economy was buffeted by unexpected developments, both from outside and within. The external shocks were delivered by the steep increases in oil prices – both in 1973–74 and 1979–80. Internally, the shocks were more self-inflicted, as the public finances slipped out of control after 1979 and the economy was crippled by a rising debt burden.

Up to the early 1970s fiscal rectitude, in the form of balanced budgets, was the prevailing orthodoxy. Governments made little attempt to use fiscal policy either to stimulate economic activity or to try and lower the level of unemployment. However, in 1973, a fourfold increase in crude-oil prices led the government to raise spending to maintain demand within the economy. This was paid for by increased borrowing. The result was modest growth, but at the cost of higher inflation (21 per cent by 1975), increased borrowing and rising unemployment.

In 1977, the incoming Fianna Fáil government inherited a fiscal deficit of 3.6 per cent and made a dash for growth by implementing the manifesto commitments in its election programme. These called for a temporary increase in spending to lower unemployment, financed by increased borrowing. The economic stimulus was designed to be self-financing, through a combination of higher growth and increased tax buoyancy. However, the deflationary impact of the second oil-price rise in 1979 reduced growth, leaving the government with a large current budget deficit (6.8 per cent of GNP), a rising national debt and the prospect of a sharp deterioration in the current-account balance of payments. It meant there was little scope to use fiscal policy for any further offsetting expansionary measures.

By 1981, a sharply rising debt-to-GNP ratio (94 per cent) and a substantial current account balance of payments deficit of nearly 15 per cent forced a succession of different governments

– five between 1981 and 1987 – to confront the problem. The Fine Gael–Labour coalition, by relying on raising taxes to try and reduce government borrowing and stabilise the debt, had little success in rectifying the budgetary imbalances. In the early eighties, unemployment accelerated as growth contracted under the impact of deflationary measures, rising from 7.3 per cent in 1980, just above the EU average, to 17 per cent by 1986.

At the end of the period (1973–86), the overall economic position was disappointing. Despite the benefits flowing from EEC membership, the country was facing a crisis in the public finances and a crisis of confidence in the capacity of the political system to deal with it. In some respects, the situation was not unlike that of the mid-fifties. Unemployment was at an all-time high, emigration had resumed and growth was contracting. Even with substantial transfers from the European Community, the numbers employed in the economy had risen by just 43,000 – or 4 per cent – since 1973. However, between 1980 and 1985, employment fell by 76,000.

ASPECTS OF ECONOMIC PERFORMANCE 1960–86

Growth

Economic development was underpinned at home by increased public spending between 1958 and 1972. This saw total government expenditure rise from 29 per cent to 40 per cent of GNP over the period. Favourable external conditions prevailed, until the economy felt the negative effect of the two oil-price increases in 1973–4 and 1979–80. This had a major deflationary impact and, after 1979, created serious difficulties in the management of the public finances; these difficulties which lasted for much of the 1980s.

IRELAND'S ECONOMIC PERFORMANCE 1960–86

Between 1960 and 1986 the domestic economy grew by an annual average of 3 per cent in gross national product (GNP) terms. In Ireland's case, GNP is a more effective measure of economic performance than gross domestic product (GDP), as the former excludes both interest repayments to foreign holders of government debt and the repatriation of the profits of multinational companies. Since the late seventies, with substantial net outflows from the economy under both headings, the Irish GNP figure has been significantly lower.

Although the average 3 per cent growth figure over a quarter of a century was high, it also masked considerable variation in year-to-year performance. The economy grew by as much as 7.2 per cent in 1972, while GNP actually fell in 1982, 1983 and again in 1986. When comparisons are drawn between the growth of the OECD economies in GDP terms as against that of the Irish economy on a GNP basis, then for the most part, the OECD region has outperformed Ireland. This was particularly evident over the 1979 to 1986 period. The domestic downturn was both more severe and prolonged, as recessionary conditions were aggravated by a deterioration in the public finances, high inflation, rising unemployment and large balance of payments deficits.

Trade

In the sixties, the multinational companies that located here were attracted by high grants and low taxes. Their presence helped both to modernise the country's weak industrial base and to accelerate the pace of economic development. It was a vindication of the government strategy to pursue export-led growth. Increased foreign direct investment ensured the diversification of Irish exports into European markets, thereby reducing an almost exclusive dependence on Britain.

In 1955, some 89 per cent of exports went to the UK, but by 1973, the figure had dropped to 59 per cent. Then, following accession to the EEC, the figure fell sharply to 34 per cent by 1987. By this stage, a greater volume of exports (39 per cent) went to the European Community countries – excluding the UK – than to Britain. The lowering of tariff barriers and the reduction in import quotas began the process of liberalisation and made a small, and increasingly open, economy more dependent on international trade. Total trade – exports plus imports – accounted for 58 per cent of GNP in 1960 and rose to 105 per cent of GNP in 1987. But the gains in industrial employment that resulted were exceeded by the losses in the numbers employed in agriculture, as capital replaced labour. In 1960, agriculture accounted for 37 per cent of total employment; by 1973, it was down to 24 per cent and by 1987 had slumped to 15 per cent, with some 170,000 farmers working on the land.

As the rapid process of industrialisation got under way, the contribution of different sectors to GNP changed significantly over time. In 1960, agriculture, forestry and fishing accounted for nearly 23 per cent of GNP. By 1987 this had fallen to 10.5 per cent and, in that period, industry and services increased to a 36 per cent and 50 per cent share, respectively.

Fiscal policy
Prior to 1972, budgets were framed cautiously so that budget deficits were avoided. Current revenue matched current spending, and no borrowing was required to finance day-to-day expenditure. Borrowing for capital spending was justified on the grounds that the fixed assets financed by debt were capable of yielding an adequate, if not a commercial, rate of return. But from the early 1970s, the unwritten rule – no current deficit – was breached, and most seriously after the first oil-price shock of that decade.

The result was higher deficits, and an Exchequer Borrowing Requirement (EBR) that increased during the mid-1970s, before peaking in 1982, at 15.7 per cent of GNP. Although the EBR subsequently declined, it remained high and stood at 12.8 per cent in 1986.

As a result of high levels of government borrowing, the level of the national debt rose from £1,009 million (68 per cent of GNP) in March 1970 to £21,611 million (129 per cent of GNP) in 1986. As debt levels increased, so too did the cost of servicing it, requiring higher tax revenues. By 1985, service of the public debt had risen to 35.2 per cent of total tax revenue, or 93.5 per cent of income-tax revenue.

Balance of payments
The deficit on the balance of payments current account rose substantially during the late 1970s and early 1980s to reach £1,595 million in 1982, a record 14.6 per cent of GNP. The deterioration in the current balance reflected a number of factors. These included a rising trade deficit, and an accelerating national debt, where increased foreign borrowings were a feature. High interest rates pushed up the cost of servicing foreign borrowings, and this was reflected in a deteriorating 'invisibles' balance. The current account deficit fell during much of the 1980s and by 1987 had moved into a small surplus. This was due mainly to a decline in domestic demand, via reducing import volumes allied to strong export growth. Lower oil and other commodity prices resulted in more favourable terms of trade, and with reduced inflation, led to an improvement in Ireland's overall competitive position, with the economy recording a trade surplus by 1985.

Interest rates

Between 1960 and 1979, Irish and UK interest rates were broadly similar and moved in tandem whenever rate changes occurred. However, with the historic break between sterling and the Irish pound in 1979, which marked the end of a currency union that had lasted 153 years, a gap later developed. For much of the time between 1960 and 1982, Irish interest rates followed an upward trend. The very high levels of domestic inflation meant that in the periods 1971–8 and 1980–2, real interest rates – the nominal rate adjusted for inflation – were negative. Despite Ireland's membership of the Exchange Rate Mechanism (ERM) in 1979, Irish rates still continued to move in line with those in the UK, even though Britain had opted to remain outside the monetary system. Indeed, it was not until the late 1980s that Irish interest rates finally begin to track the lower rates in Germany as domestic inflation fell and fiscal stability began to be restored.

The government's decision to break the sterling link in favour of EMS entry in part reflected support for greater European integration, as well as a desire further to reduce dependence on the British market. For the first time, Ireland had an exchange rate based on the domestic economy. By joining a hard-currency regime, the aim was to benefit from the low German levels of inflation and interest rates within the EMS, since the Deutschmark was accepted as the anchor currency within the system. However, that goal of low inflation took some time to achieve, given the wide differential between Irish and German inflation rates that had to be bridged. In 1980, domestic inflation rose, boosted by the sharp rise in energy prices following the second oil shock, and by higher indirect taxes. However, from mid 1982, consumer prices eased progressively, and by 1990 inflation had finally fallen to the German level.

During the early years of the EMS, there were frequent realignments and, on most occasions, the central rate of the Irish pound was not changed. However, in March 1983 and again in August 1986 a realignment saw the devaluation of the central rate of the Irish pound. The currency had come under severe pressure within the EMS as sterling depreciated and speculation in the financial markets mounted that the Irish pound would be devalued. Large capital outflows occurred and, in both cases, the Irish pound was eventually devalued.

Inflation

Up to 1969, Ireland's inflation record was not very different from that of other OECD countries. But, from the late 1960s, Ireland, like many other countries, experienced an acceleration in inflation. However, the upsurge in prices began earlier in Ireland, and domestic inflation remained substantially higher than in the rest of the OECD. Between 1960 and 1969 the average annual inflation rate was 4 per cent, doubling to 8.3 per cent between 1968 and 1972 and increasing again, to average 12.8 per cent between 1970 and 1979.

The initial impetus came from external factors, beginning with the sterling devaluation in November 1967. Domestic inflationary pressures were fuelled by large pay increases in the 1969–70 wage round. Then, from 1973, higher import prices, which reflected the rise in commodity and oil prices, reinforced inflationary trends. By 1975, average inflation was running at just under 21 per cent, before decreasing over the next three years. However, by 1979 this trend had reversed itself, and despite Ireland's membership of the ERM, inflation again surged, to reach an annual average of nearly 20.5 per cent in 1981. After 1982, inflation fell sharply and by 1987 the annual average stood at 3.1 per cent. The decline was aided by ERM membership, but falling commodity prices and high domestic unemployment rates also contributed towards keeping inflation at bay.

Unemployment

A high unemployment rate became one of the most intractable problems facing the Irish economy during the 1970s and 1980s. Prior to this, emigration had acted as a 'safety valve' preventing a build-up of unemployment levels, which averaged about 5 per cent during the 1960s.

However, in the seventies, despite a rapid growth in employment – with 10 per cent more people at work over the decade – the numbers unemployed rose by 50 per cent. The extra jobs created were filled by those entering the labour force – immigrants, school leavers and women returning to work – rather than by the unemployed. Employment growth increased the labour force numbers, but without reducing the lengthening dole queues. Unemployment rose steadily from 1970 to 1976, where it peaked for the decade with 9 per cent – 105,000 persons – out of work. However, the subsequent decline to a 7.1 per cent rate of unemployment proved short-lived. And by 1986, a record 226,000 – some 17 per cent of the labour force – were jobless.

Industrial relations

The high numbers of strikes reflected the poor state of industrial relations within the country, an issue that was not satisfactorily resolved until 1987, when the number fell to eighty. This was the first time in twenty years there had been less than one hundred strikes in any one year. The number of industrial dispute increased in the late 1960s to over 125 per annum and peaked in 1974 at some 219.

Another measure of employer-union relations is the number

of days lost due to such disputes. This peaked in 1979 when 1.4 million man days were lost, attributable mainly to a postal strike. Between 1960 and 1969, the number of days lost averaged just over 420,000 per annum. Between 1970 and 1979, this rose to just under 584,000 before falling back to 387,000 between 1980 and 1986. After 1987, with the series of social partnership programmes, where strike action on pay is not allowed, the industrial-relations climate improved dramatically.

*

For most of the second half of the twentieth century, Ireland looked outwards as a closed economy was opened up to secure the benefits of expanding world trade and society was exposed to a range of liberalising international influences, both political and cultural. The end of the fifties marked the first of three turning points over the next four decades which, with hindsight, may be seen as defining moments in Ireland's economic development.

The first turning point was the sharp reversal in policy after 1958, as protection was abandoned in favour of free trade. There followed an increasing reliance on foreign direct investment to achieve export-led growth, both as the main means of job creation and also as the engine of growth in economic expansion.

The second was the decision to join the EEC. This not only gave Ireland a new-found self-confidence but also reduced our dependence on the sluggish British economy and secured access to the faster-growing Continental economies. Ireland gained as the net beneficiary of some £19 billion in Community transfers up to 1998. These grants have helped modernise agriculture and finance infrastructural investment, via the Structural Fund receipts from 1989, a factor that has underpinned the great economic leap forward achieved in the 1990s.

The third turning point came in the late eighties, when the battle to regain control of the public finances was won. After nearly a decade of struggle, debt was stabilised and reduced as a proportion of national income. Success there opened the way for the rapid acceleration in economic expansion, particularly since 1993: growth averaged an annual 8.3 per cent between 1994 and 1998.

Indeed, if Irish economic history had ended in 1986, the verdict on national economic performance since Independence would be damning indeed, as Kieran Kennedy and fellow economists Thomas Giblin and Deirdre McHugh noted in *The Economic Development of Ireland in the Twentieth Century*. There they examined the country's poor growth performance over that period. Between 1926 and 1985, Irish and British growth rates were broadly similar, averaging 2.1 per cent annually, while growth in income per head was only marginally higher (1.8 per cent), compared to Britain's 1.7 per cent, despite a slower rise in population here than in most other European countries. This meant that Ireland was simply keeping pace with Britain, a declining economic power, rather than catching up or passing it out, as might have been expected. However, since British growth rates were lower than those in Continental Europe, Ireland was also failing to narrow the gap in living standards with the latter. Of course, the rate of economic growth since 1987 has seen Ireland outpace both Britain and the other EU economies, with living standards here expected to match average EU levels early in the new millennium.

The same evidence prompted historian Joe Lee to remark that 'It is difficult to avoid the conclusion that Irish economic performance has been the least impressive in western Europe, perhaps in all Europe, in the twentieth century. It must count as one of the more striking records in modern European economic history.' And it was up to that point a case study in economic failure, just as it has now become a model of economic regeneration.

Nevertheless, from the vantage point of the end of the century, the recent golden years of economic success present a stark contrast with the country's undeveloped state after independence was achieved. The comparison is a measure of how much has been achieved and how much has changed. For within a couple of generations, a predominately agricultural economy has become industrialised and a once rural society has become one of largely urban dwellers. In 1922, over half the labour force was engaged in agriculture and two-thirds of the population lived in rural areas. Today, just one in ten work on the land, while two-thirds live in towns. And there are encouraging signs that the Irish diaspora, which had left Ireland with perhaps the highest rate of emigration of any European country in the past two centuries, is finally being reversed. Labour shortages in Ireland oblige the state agency FÁS to use employment roadshows in Germany and other EU member states to try and recruit workers for unfilled vacancies in financial-services and electronics firms at home. Just over a decade ago, that would have seemed an impossible dream, just like the Celtic Tiger economy.

2

THE CHALLENGE OF 1987

Ray Mac Sharry

When the Fine Gael–Labour government finally fell in January 1987, I had no intention of standing again for the Dáil in the subsequent general election. In my own mind, I was on my way out of domestic politics, no longer a front-bench member of the parliamentary party. Three years earlier I had been elected to the European parliament for Connacht–Ulster. At that point, I saw my political future in Europe, rather than in Leinster House. However, as the election approached, I faced strong pressure at both constituency and national levels of the party to change my mind. But I remained cautious, and for good reason.

In February 1982 Fianna Fáil had won three out of the four seats in my own Sligo–Leitrim constituency. Then, in the second general election in November, we failed to repeat that success. The vote-management exercise had backfired badly. Even though I was Tánaiste and Minister for Finance, I nearly lost my own Dáil seat, and was elected only on the final count. It was a chastening experience. In 1987, the party strategists once again felt that vote-splitting between our three candidates would work. Given the different and more favourable set of electoral circumstances, I was more confident of success. Fianna Fáil was in opposition, and the outgoing Fine Gael–Labour coalition government had collapsed in disarray. This time the gamble paid off, and we won. The seat proved to be a highly critical extra seat, as events showed some three weeks later in the Dáil. When Charles Haughey secured election by the Dáil as Taoiseach of a minority Fianna Fáil government, he did so only on the casting vote of the Ceann Comhairle. Without the third seat in Sligo–Leitrim, things might have been quite different.

After the election, I had quite happily returned to the European parliament in Strasbourg to resume the life of a Euro MEP – though still with a dual mandate. A few days later, I found myself as Charles Haughey's guest at a lunch with Ireland's European Commissioner Peter Sutherland in Brussels. After the meal, the Fianna Fáil leader took me to one side to offer me the post of Minister for Finance in the new government. I asked for some time to consider. Privately, I had two reservations about accepting there and then. First, I still saw my future career in Europe. Second, I was not happy with the fast-and-loose approach to economic policy the party had adopted in opposition. There had been too much opposition for its own sake, which I felt had damaged the party's credibility, particularly given our adoption of *The Way Forward* in 1982. In that economic plan, the Fianna Fáil government had set out very clear budgetary guidelines to be followed. And above all, that strategy implied an acceptance of fiscal restraint – even in opposition.

If the line of continuity with past policy was broken by Fianna Fáil in opposition, restoring it, I felt, was critical for the credibility of the new government. Already, the groundwork for that task was being laid in another quarter. Pádraig Ó hUiginn, as chairman of the National Economic and Social Council (NESC), was the common denominator. As the key figure behind *The Way Forward* in 1982, he was in 1986 once more one of the prime movers behind the NESC document, which was to prove one of the most important economic reports of the 1980s. Its significance lay not just in its stark analysis of the economic problems facing the country, but in the fact that the NESC members were also ready to support the report's tough recommendations in tackling them. So those central to the solution – employers, unions, farmers and others – not only had diagnosed the problem but had prescribed the remedy. That was exceptional. By comparison, both *The Way Forward* and the coalition's own plan, *Building on Reality,* were documents decided by governments but not agreed in consultation with the social partners. Nevertheless, I saw that NESC document – *Strategy for Development 1986–1990* – with its emphasis on the need for spending cuts, as restoring the broad approach that Fianna Fáil had outlined four years before.

Having fully considered the matter, I agreed to the Taoiseach's request to serve again as Finance Minister. I set no preconditions for my acceptance of the Cabinet post. However, I felt there was a clear, if implicit, understanding established between us: namely, that I would be able to do what was necessary either in terms of expenditure cuts or tax reforms, and that I could rely on Charles Haughey's full support as Taoiseach. On returning to Merrion Street and the Department of Finance for a second time, I recognised we were at a major turning point in our economic history. I knew the day of fiscal reckoning had arrived. It was time to call a stop – and mean it. For tough and unpopular decisions could no longer be avoided.

Most people, in managing their own day-to-day financial affairs, have to match spending to income, bridging any revenue gap with a loan or temporary overdraft facility from the bank. So why should governments not do the same? From 1972 until quite recently, a succession of governments had ignored the rules of basic housekeeping in managing the economy. In budgetary matters, tax revenue and current spending were never balanced. Governments lived beyond the means of taxpayers.

In fact, more than two decades elapsed before a revenue surplus was again achieved – in the 1994 budget. In the meantime, governments simply borrowed to finance the ever-greater shortfall between revenue and spending. This was the era of deficit financing. As a country, we paid a very heavy price for the series of unbalanced budgets over such a long period. By the late seventies and early eighties, the result was a deepening crisis in the public finances. The experience proved as damaging to the economy as it was shattering to our sense of national self-confidence. Over the years, those accumulated budget deficits mounted. As the national debt rose and the sum outstanding compounded annually, the interest-rate bill was paid by this and by the next generation – all from higher taxes. We were not just mortgaging our financial future. We were betraying future trust as well, by consuming today what others must pay for tomorrow. The choice was stark: either we reasserted control over our financial affairs or these would pass out of our control, and perhaps into the hands of the IMF. If that were to happen, Ireland would lose a large measure of her national economic sovereignty.

The outlook was indeed bleak. The domestic economy was caught in a debt trap from which it was proving more and more difficult to escape. Debt was exploding, since it was rising faster than the economy was growing. The Fine Gael–Labour government had been less and less able to finance the annual debt interest payments, despite ever-higher taxes. The situation looked increasingly desperate. Then, in the autumn of 1986, hopes were raised by the NESC report, which finally offered a way out of the crisis in the public finances. The debt burden was identified, clearly, as the central problem to be addressed. And stabilising the debt was the first step in restoring order to the public finances. Never before had such broad agreement on tough economic measures been achieved.

Usually, the social partners willed the end, but rarely the necessary means of achieving what invariably was an over-ambitious set of economic goals. This helps explain why the various forms of social partnership since the seventies had ended in different degrees of failure. But this time promised to be different. For, quite remarkably, the economic consensus extended from a shared analysis of the problem to a common prescription of the solution – with spending cuts accepted as a necessary part of the remedy.

It was clear that to rescue the economy, the country's growing addiction to debt must first be curbed, before it could be cured. And reducing public spending was the painful way of weaning all those hooked on borrowing – both politicians and voters – off a bad old habit. The social partners, having set the example, also gave an inspiring lead for the politicians to follow. Having recognised that sacrifices were required in the national interest, they at least were ready to make them.

At the time, the efforts of the outgoing coalition to stop the debt/GNP ratio rising had met with little success. The national debt had soared to £22 billion during Fine Gael and Labour's four-year term in office. When the coalition finally broke up in January 1987, it left the public finances in a far worse state than it had found them. The debt mountain I faced had nearly doubled in size since my earlier brief tenure as Minister for Finance in 1982. The budgetary arithmetic was chilling. By 1986, one in every four pounds of current spending represented the interest owing on past debt. But since those payments had to be financed from tax revenue, one-third of all taxes were required simply to pay those annual debt charges. In other words, some four out of every five pounds raised in income tax were needed to pay the interest on the outstanding national debt. Since servicing the debt had a prior claim on current spending, it meant higher interest payments also required higher taxes to finance them. The result was less money available to pay for day-to-day services in areas like health, education and welfare.

The response to the public-finance crisis was to prove a turning point in our recent economic history. It marked the beginning of the end of years of fiscal profligacy, which began in the early seventies and which ended by seriously threatening the financial viability of the state. The radical and painful correction in the national finances that got under way in 1987 paved the way for the benign economic conditions of high growth and low inflation that followed. And from these, the Celtic Tiger phenomenon was to emerge in the mid-nineties. However, the strong rate of economic recovery was also facilitated, and underpinned, by another important and visionary political development from the sixties – the introduction of free second-level education. Its economic impact, by enhancing and improving the skills base of the workforce, ensured Ireland in the late eighties was well placed to exploit the employment opportunities created by the new knowledge-based industries setting up here.

But before the fruits of the state's investment in education could be realised here by Irish people in domestic employment and not dissipated through emigration in a continuing human brain drain to Britain or America, the economy had to be brought back into balance. Regaining control of the public finances was an important step. Above all, this meant changing borrowing habits that had become deeply ingrained and were hard to change since deficit financing had first been introduced some fifteen years earlier.

The national political addiction to deficit financing may have started in a relatively innocent and rather experimental fashion in the early seventies, but over the next decade and a half, as the national debt mounted, government dependency on borrowing to pay for current spending grew until it brought us to the brink of national bankruptcy. The seeds of future difficulty in this regard were actually sown in 1972: George Colley, as Minister for Finance, broke with long-standing precedent when he chose not to balance the budget on current account. In doing so, the damage caused was less the result of the size – £28 million – of the planned deficit he proposed, than of the symbolic significance of the move. It set a headline, and a bad example, for others to follow and which they could not resist in more difficult budgetary times. An important principle of prudent economic management was abandoned. And so borrowing to finance day-to-day spending, which had started as a temporary innovation, quickly became the new conventional wisdom.

Unfortunately, this long-standing economic taboo against running a current budget deficit was broken at just the wrong moment. The National coalition government (1973–77), faced with the first oil-price shock in 1974, ran a succession of current deficits. The intention was to try and offset the impact of the inevitable fall in living standards, following the rapid rise in energy prices. All this served only to confer a degree of spurious legitimacy on deficit financing, and by 1977 some £747 million in borrowings had accumulated from current deficits in just four budgets. However, the debt habit, once formed, proved difficult to break. And with the arrival of the Fianna Fáil government to implement the 1977 Manifesto, the deficit total was set to rise even higher. Once again, borrowing was used to stimulate the economy, by financing tax cuts and raising spending at the same time.

One of the problems with the ill-fated 1977 Manifesto was that all the benefits were front-loaded, and the payback never came. Tax cuts were delivered in anticipation of pay moderation rather than in response to it. The Fianna Fáil government, which was returned with an historic winning margin – a twenty-seat majority in the Dáil – had to deliver on its promises first. It abolished domestic rates, scrapped car tax and raised housing grants. But two years later, without warning, the economic climate, once again, was transformed abruptly by the second oil crisis in less than a decade.

The initial strong fiscal stimulus was not expected to deliver growth, reduce unemployment and raise tax revenues on its own. It was meant to be self-financing. Revenue buoyancy and tighter spending controls would later restore stability to the public finances, as private-sector investment stepped in to sustain the economic momentum. The metaphor of the day to describe the whole exercise was that of the two-stage rocket. The booster rocket would propel the second rocket into orbit. But if the first was launched successfully, then the second failed to lift off. Fate – in the form of a second oil-price rise – had intervened. In politics, as in life, Murphy's Law – where the unexpected always happens – tends to prevail. And, unfortunately, the flaw in the 1977 Manifesto was that the economic blueprint erred on the side of optimism and allowed for no such economic contingencies.

In my first job in government, as Junior Minister for the Public Service in the Department of Finance, I played a central role in implementing one of the key Manifesto commitments – creating jobs in the public sector. In the eighteen months between mid-1977 and 1978, some 11,250 posts were authorised. Indeed, much of my time was spent on the phone beseeching other ministers to fill their job creation allocations. A civil-service joke then in circulation had an anguished official –

possibly from my old department – ringing a colleague elsewhere. Over the phone, he was delivering a very stern warning: failure to take up his department's quota of public-sector jobs would result in a sanction. Next year, he would get even more jobs.

But the real irony of my role as public service job creator only became fully apparent ten years later. In 1987, when I returned as Minister for Finance, one of the first decisions taken by the new government was to abolish Public Service as a separate department. Months later I introduced a voluntary redundancy scheme. This saw virtually the same number of people who had been taken on a decade earlier opt for early retirement.

Essentially, the 1977 Manifesto was a gamble on a benign world economic environment continuing. Others may claim it was reckless. I still believe, on balance, it was a risk worth taking. Certainly, a serious flaw in the plan lay in the unconditional nature of the tax concessions granted in return for pay restraint which was never reciprocated. It was all carrot and no stick.

With hindsight, one could criticise the government for underestimating the impact of the fiscal stimulus provided by the Manifesto commitments. In any small open economy, like that of Ireland, boosting demand may raise imports, push up inflation and produce a deterioration in the balance of payments faster than it will boost output and employment. And the failure to allow for contingencies also proved costly. So when – as happened – a systemic shock to the global economic system occurred, in the form of the second oil crisis, there was little protection available here. As the price of oil soared to more than $40 a barrel, the government found itself over-borrowed, and with too little room to manoeuvre. It was ill-prepared either to cushion the impact or to withstand the economic slowdown that followed.

Already in the US, the chairman of the Federal Reserve, Paul Volcker, had begun to raise interest rates to check inflation. It

was a profoundly significant move which had adverse consequences for the global economy. The result was the return of
real interest rates – where nominal rates are higher than inflation
– worldwide. In the seventies, negative real rates had meant that
debt was eroded by inflation. This was good for borrowers and
bad for lenders. It served to encourage imprudent borrowing by
sovereign governments, like Mexico, on the basis that countries
simply cannot go broke. The end of the days of easy international
credit ushered in the worst depression in the US since the
thirties. However, it also left sovereign borrowers, like Ireland,
caught in a debt trap that was set to tighten in the early eighties
– at great cost to our economic welfare.

*

In 1980, after Charles Haughey succeeded Jack Lynch as
Taoiseach, he set out his economic priorities in a major television
address: to reduce government overspending, and thereby the
borrowing needed to finance it. 'We have been borrowing
enormous amounts of money, borrowing at a rate which just
cannot continue,' he said. A restrictive budget stance was
adopted but eased later in the year, as the economy weakened.
Nevertheless, the current budget deficit came in at 6.1 per cent
of GNP – marginally lower than the 1979 outturn. However,
there were worrying signs that some of the key economic
indicators were starting to move in the wrong direction at the
same time. As growth was falling, inflation and unemployment
were rising, while the balance of payments position worsened.

The 1981 budget was set in an election year and against a
deteriorating economic background. Electoral needs had to be
reconciled and balanced with the growing fiscal constraints. In
any event, the government made an over-ambitious attempt to

contain the deficit, without pushing the economy towards recession. In doing so, it sought to switch the emphasis from current to capital spending in an effort to boost employment, rather than consumption.This proved unsuccessful.

By mid-year Fianna Fáil had lost office and serious slippages had emerged in the budgetary figures. This forced the newly elected Fine Gael–Labour government to introduce a supplementary budget in July. But perhaps the most worrying development was the sharply rising debt burden and its composition, with an increased reliance on foreign borrowing. By 1981, some 75 per cent of government borrowing was raised abroad, compared with only 16 per cent just four years earlier.

MINORITY GOVERNMENT BUDGET 1982

	CURRENT BUDGET DEFICIT		EXCHEQUER BORROWING REQUIREMENT	
	£m	%GNP	£m	%GNP
FINE GAEL / LABOUR – PROPOSED	715	5.8	1661	13.4
FIANNA FÁIL – ESTIMATE	679	5.5	1683	13.5
FIANNA FÁIL – OUT-TURN	988	7.9	1945	15.5

Source: *Budget Booklets*

In some respects Fianna Fáil's nine months in office in 1982 – from March to December – proved a dress rehearsal for what followed five years later in 1987, under even more difficult economic circumstances. The parallels were striking. On each occasion, Fianna Fáil was returned as a minority government, having won the same number of Dáil seats – eighty-one. Each time, the Fianna Fáil inheritance on taking office was an outgoing government budget that had been defeated in the Dáil and was later rejected by the voters. As a minority government in March 1982, Fianna Fáil relied in the main on the support of three Sinn Féin the Workers' Party (SFWP) deputies. Although no formal pact existed, as Minister for Finance I liaised regularly with them, explaining the background to some of the tough economic decisions we had to take.

The difficulty I faced was the lack of a real consensus, either inside the Dáil or outside, for the tough corrective action that was needed to restore order to the public finances. The hostility between Fianna Fáil and the opposition parties could hardly have been greater than at that period. In addition, little common ground then existed between the social partners. At that stage, economics was very much overshadowed by party politics, and political uncertainty and instability only increased as the year advanced. As a government, undoubtedly, Fianna Fáil had the political will to meet the economic challenge, but as a minority administration the party lacked the support in the Dáil to implement the radical changes that were really needed. The difficulty was well illustrated in the passage of the Finance Bill, implementing the budget-day measures. There, at committee stage, I found that four of some 116 amendments that were tabled passed only on the casting vote of the Ceann Comhairle. This was an unprecedented event, but a fair measure of the voting difficulties we faced in office.

Politically, the problem was that two general elections in less than a year had resulted in a change of government, but each time the vote had failed to produce a conclusive result. And that created uncertainty and tension.

The elections of 1981 and February 1982 were like battles in a long war, where a decisive victory had yet to be achieved. It meant that, almost from the day the minority Fianna Fáil government was formed in March 1982, the opposition had embarked on a permanent election campaign. It seemed they were waiting to pick a moment to bring the government down.

In addition, probably no nine-month period in the Dail's history was as dramatic and turbulent as that of the very short Twenty-Third Dáil. Even in August while I was on holidays with my family in the United States, there was no escape from the drama at home. I switched on CNN in my Florida hotel room only to find extensive coverage of the arrest of a double-murder suspect who was staying in, of all places, the flat of the Attorney General in Dublin. In the course of one year there were two challenges to Charles Haughey's leadership of Fianna Fáil, and two resignations from Cabinet – Des O'Malley and Martin O'Donoghue – while in Labour, Michael O'Leary dramatically quit as party leader to join Fine Gael.

Nevertheless, on coming into office in March, I was upbeat about our economic prospects. My optimism was reflected in the 'boom and bloom' remarks which were attributed to me – though incorrectly. Although I used the words, I did so in the reverse order; the actual phrase was 'bloom and boom'. To my mind, getting the words in the right order made all the difference in interpreting them. What I meant was that the economy would have to bloom before it could boom. The preparatory groundwork for this initial bloom phase of the economic cycle was to be laid via the national plan, and the government had already started work on it, through the Department of Finance. This involved discussion with outside bodies like the Central Bank, the Director of the Economic and Social Research Institute (ESRI) Dr Kieran Kennedy, and the NESC Chairman Pádraig Ó hUiginn. He was a key figure who later succeeded Dr Noel Whelan as chairman of the group drawing up the plan, midway through its work. Ó hUiginn enjoyed the confidence of both the Department of Finance and Charles Haughey, and a major part of his contribution lay in convincing the Taoiseach that the economic strategy proposed was the right one. In October, it was published as *The Way Forward* and had a central aim, phasing out the current budget deficit by 1986. But by then, it was too late. Instead, the plan became a major part of the Fianna Fáil manifesto in the November election.

In early July, the government had faced a vote of confidence in the Dáil and survived with the support of the Workers' Party. By October, when we faced another vote of confidence, their three deputies deserted us, and the government was defeated by a two-vote margin, thus precipitating the general election.

Officially, the reason for the Workers' Party's change of heart was the range of public-spending cuts the government had introduced in late July – via a public service pay freeze and some reductions in health expenditure. I remember preparing for a government meeting with Maurice Doyle, who was Secretary of the Department of Finance. The total cuts needed were over £100 million. 'We don't expect you to get the full amount, Minister, but if you get £50 million, it'll help,' Maurice remarked, as I left for the Cabinet session. I came out a few hours later with £120 million worth of savings – more than had been sought. Arguably, this was one of the few times a Minister for Finance had brought off such a real coup.

Personally, I think the SFWP really used the government's difficulty with its austerity measures as the excuse the party needed to precipitate an election. The primary aim, I felt, was to try and secure the election of party president Tomas MacGiolla to the Dáil. Indeed, from my own discussions with the party at that time, two of its three TDs seemed ready to back the government on the critical confidence vote, but the third – Proinsias De Rossa – was opposed. At the time, the SFWP was enjoying a consistently high level of support in the national opinion polls. However, the sudden leadership crisis that had developed in Labour, following Michael O'Leary's dramatic resignation, provided it with a whole range of reasons for withdrawing support from the government and causing a general election.

On fiscal policy, I had followed the broad outlines of the budget I inherited from John Bruton and adopted similar borrowing targets. But by mid-year, with expenditure running well ahead of estimates, I was forced to cut spending to bring it into line again. At year-end, even though total Exchequer borrowing (£1,945 million, or 15.5 per cent of GNP) exceeded my original target by some £262 million, I took some consolation from the performance in what were difficult circumstances. Expenditure was in line with the budget target, and the real problem arose from a significant revenue shortfall from income tax and indirect taxes. This reflected weak growth in incomes and a sharp decline in real consumer spending.

The 1982 minority government experience, while it seemed futile, proved valuable in a number of respects. For me it had demonstrated the importance of keeping expenditure under control and of basing budgetary policy on some clear medium-term perspective. This *The Way Forward* had provided. If given a chance, I believe that programme would have worked. It also meant, given the government's defeat, that relying on the unreliable – Sinn Féin the Workers' Party – was an unsatisfactory basis for holding power. It offered little basis for stability. At that time, the party had an ideological perspective that always placed its continuing support for the government in doubt. However, after 1989, with the collapse of the Berlin Wall and the death of communism, the split which resulted in the formation of Democratic Left saw the party move more towards the political centre and the mainstream of Irish politics.

FINE GAEL–LABOUR COALITION BUDGETS 1983–1986

	CURRENT BUDGET DEFICIT		EXCHEQUER BORROWING REQUIREMENT	
	£m	%GNP	£m	%GNP
FINE GAEL/ LABOUR (1983)	960	7.1	1756	12.9
FINE GAEL/ LABOUR (1986)	1395	7.9	2145	12.1

Source: *Budget Booklets*

Very often the success or failure of a government is defined by its actions in its first one hundred days in office. The so-called honeymoon period offers the scope and freedom for a new government to take tough or imaginative decisions. In this respect, the opening months for the Fine Gael–Labour coalition after its election in December 1982 were to prove critical. The new government enjoyed a comfortable majority, but the challenge remained the economy. In *The Way Forward*, Fianna Fáil had already set a £750 million figure as the current deficit target for 1983, as part of the phased elimination of borrowing over four years. The coalition proposed to eliminate the current deficit over five years. However, early in January, Alan Dukes, as the new Finance Minister, clearly was concerned to make a strong start in his first budget. But without consulting his Cabinet colleagues, he announced on RTÉ radio the same £750 million deficit figure that Fianna Fáil had proposed before leaving office. When he heard the news, Dick Spring, the new Labour leader, was recovering in hospital from a serious back injury. He was outraged. Spring saw it as a unilateral move, since the Cabinet had yet to discuss the matter, while Labour ministers also viewed it as a pre-emptive strike. It was seen as Fine Gael dictating terms to its smaller partner in government, and the row strained coalition cohesion.

The net outcome was a very public repudiation of Alan Dukes by his Cabinet colleagues, with Taoiseach Garret FitzGerald – as he explained in his autobiography *All in a Life* – later contacting Dr Henry Kissinger, the former US Secretary of state, for some confidential advice. Kissinger was running an independent consultancy, and was asked to inquire discreetly how the international financial markets would view either a £750 million or a £900 million deficit in the Irish government's first budget. The answer, within days, was that the markets were less concerned with the precise figure, and more concerned that the new government should adopt a programme it would follow, rather than opt for a more ambitious plan that would fall apart. And the general expectation, Dr Kissinger said, was that a £900 million deficit would be set.

That particular episode, and the form of the budget introduced in consequence, did irreparable damage to the new government. Alan Dukes was weakened when his own Taoiseach failed to back his Minister for Finance in what was a very public dispute. It also diminished Dukes's standing both in government and within his own department. Instead, the budget became a lost opportunity for the new government to make its mark. By merely matching general expectations with a £900 million deficit figure, it made little impact. And by raising taxes rather than cutting spending to reduce borrowing, the government caused the burden of adjustment to fall on revenue at a time of weak growth.

Perhaps, above all, it was a great missed opportunity by the new government to turn the tables on Fianna Fáil in opposition. This it could have done quite easily, by accepting the central thrust of the proposals in *The Way Forward* as the basis for the coalition's own plan. However, the document may well have been seen as a politically tainted, since, with the defeat of the government, it became a virtual economic manifesto for Fianna

Fáil in the subsequent election. Nevertheless, it also represented the consensus view of the independent members of the committee that had been set up to draft it – including the Central Bank, the ESRI and the Revenue Commissioners. At that stage, the trade unions – though sounded out informally – were reluctant to become involved. For the new government, it provided an immediate means of getting to grips with the main challenge presented by the public finances: the need to cut spending. Instead, the coalition favoured the establishment of a National Planning Board, under Dr Louden Ryan. It was set up in March 1983 and reported a year later with *Proposals for Plan 1984–1987*, which contained no fewer than 241 recommendations. This formed the basis for the coalition's own economic plan *Building on Reality*, published in the autumn of 1984. By that stage, some one and a half years had elapsed, and critical time had been lost.

What was evident in the first budget was apparent right through the remainder of the coalition's term in office. In 1983, the government raised taxes, with a 65 per cent top tax rate, added a 1 per cent income levy and failed to index the tax bands. It also introduced a residential property tax and increased standard and higher VAT rates by five percentage points. For the next four years the coalition tried and failed to break out of the vicious circle of high real interest rates, low growth, rising debt and ever lengthening dole queues. The Fine Gael–Labour government's problem was that it had relied too much on taxation and too little on spending cuts to redress the imbalance in the public finances. Debt interest payments were higher because, globally, real interest rates had risen sharply, while an unstable exchange rate – with two devaluations in four years – meant foreign borrowings now incurred a substantial interest-rate premium.

This combination of stagnant growth and tax rises deflated

the economy, so the revenue yield was disappointing. On the spending side, any reductions in overall expenditure were offset by increased debt service charges and higher transfer payments as the numbers unemployed soared. This approach failed to stabilise the debt, and the current deficit was higher in 1986 than in 1982.

To achieve debt stabilisation, the government had to try and secure a primary budget surplus – excluding debt interest payments – large enough to ensure the national debt no longer rose as a proportion of national income. However, this was never achieved. In 1982, the debt/GNP ratio stood at 94 percent and by 1986 it had finally peaked at 129 per cent.

Labour in government at a time of austerity was not prepared to accept serious spending cuts. And when these were proposed, belatedly, in late 1986, the cuts became the basis for disagreement between the coalition partners. This led directly to Labour's departure from government. In this respect, the contrast between Labour's performance in the mid-eighties, by comparison with nearly a decade later, is striking. Then, the party had the confidence to accept the Finance portfolio in the Rainbow coalition (1994–97), though admittedly in a much more benign economic environment. Ruairí Quinn as Finance Minister showed considerable resolution in keeping a relatively tight rein on spending. But in the eighties, Labour's reluctance to tackle spending forced the government into an over-reliance on taxation to try and achieve a fiscal balance. It never materialised, and the public finances deteriorated rapidly, in consequence.

In the 1987 general election, all the major parties were chastened by their lack of success: Fianna Fáil in failing to get an overall majority for the fourth successive time, Fine Gael in winning its lowest share of the vote since 1961 and Labour in achieving its worst result since 1933. Only the newly formed

Progressive Democrats had something to celebrate. The party took fourteen seats less than two years after its formation. At first glance, the result suggested a stalemate – and a return to the 1981–82 pattern, where three general elections took place in eighteen months and there was a change of government each time.

Then political instability had compounded the country's economic problems, where between 1979 and 1982, the national debt had doubled, and by 1986 had nearly doubled again. Clearly, the new government had to impose itself on the situation. Fianna Fáil with eighty-one seats – three short of an overall majority – was best placed to do so. And here it was helped by a fragmented opposition, following the break-up of the Fine Gael–Labour coalition, and by the tensions created by the arrival of the PDs in the Dáil.

From the bitter experience of 1982, I knew we could no longer depend either on independents or smaller parties. To govern effectively, we had to be prepared to live dangerously, and the inspiration was the minority governments led by Seán Lemass in the early sixties. Not only did the first Lemass administration run its full term, but it also achieved very far-reaching changes and reforms. These included the negotiation of the Anglo-Irish Free Trade Agreement in 1965, which paved the way for Irish entry into the European Community, and the introduction of turnover tax – the forerunner to VAT. Quite remarkably, the turnover tax passed the second and committee stages of the 1962 Finance Bill in the Dáil by a one-vote margin, thanks to the Mayo Independent Joe Leneghan. Subsequently, he was better known as 'Turnover Joe'.

However, the scale of our difficulty was well illustrated on 10 March, when the Dáil reassembled to elect a Taoiseach and government. Charles Haughey was elected as Taoiseach, but only after a tied vote, and then on the casting vote of the Ceann Comhairle. Nevertheless, already there were early grounds for encouragement, not least in the reaction of Fine Gael and its leader, Dr Garret FitzGerald. On the night of the election count, in an RTÉ interview, he pledged Fine Gael support to Fianna Fáil in the national interest, if the party in government pursued similar fiscal policies to those outlined in Fine Gael's draft budget in January. And that undertaking, subsequently, was reaffirmed by a statement from the party's front bench. It was the first indication of a move by Fine Gael towards consensus politics on the economy. Later, newly elected leader Alan Dukes formally set out this approach in a speech – the Tallaght Strategy – which is dealt with in the next chapter.

In 1987, for the first time, a political consensus on fiscal policy was beginning to emerge to underpin the economic consensus already outlined in the NESC report *Strategy for Development 1986–1990*, which had been published the previous November. The NESC analysis of what was wrong and the prescription of what needed to be done was agreed by all the social partners – including employers, trade unions, farmers and others – without dissent.

The NESC described the economic and social problems facing the country as 'extremely grave' and set debt stabilisation as a minimum objective of fiscal policy, while relying on public-spending cuts – not taxation – to achieve that adjustment. This was the most critical part of its overall strategy. The boldness of the NESC approach, the consensus of the social partners in backing it, and Fine Gael's generous promise of political support on fiscal policy all created a new opportunity to tackle, finally, the public finances.

In 1972, the national debt stood at £1.4 billion, and by 1986, it had risen to £22 billion. However, the annual interest bill was running at close to £2 billion. If years of borrowing had enabled us to live beyond our means, then by 1987 we were also living dangerously, and, increasingly, on borrowed time. By then, Ireland had one of the highest debt ratios in the industrialised world. Increasingly, the unspoken fear was that of financial default, unless the national finances were brought back into balance. But the political question was whether a minority government could survive the inevitable public backlash, once fiscal rectitude was introduced and austerity – in the form of spending cuts – was imposed.

The Fianna Fáil minority government had one important advantage in tackling the debt crisis. It inherited the consensus reached by the social partners within NESC and was well-placed to exploit the more positive mood it reflected. Its report set out in great detail the action that needed to be taken. On the election of the government, the Taoiseach and I quickly agreed a common approach. We recognised we had to seize the initiative from the spending departments, and do so from the outset. This was the only way to force individual departments to cut spending sufficiently to stabilise the debt, and so ensure it no longer rose as a share of national income. We also knew, and fully accepted, that major financial surgery would have to be performed. Except this time, the operation would have to be carried out on the patient without the benefit of an anaesthetic.

A very different approach was needed in order to succeed. Up to then, the traditional way of setting the spending estimates was for government departments to submit their annual pre-budget forecasts to the Minister for Finance. Invariably, the figures were grossly inflated for bargaining purposes. And all too often, the result was a predictable series of sham fights where, after some preliminary political jousting, token concessions were finally agreed by the spending ministers in a final showdown around the Cabinet table. Whatever savings were achieved merely slowed the rate of increase in spending. Clearly, this would no longer suffice.

THE 1987 BUDGET

	CURRENT BUDGET DEFICIT		EXCHEQUER BORROWING REQUIREMENT	
	£m	%GNP	£m	%GNP
FINE GAEL – DRAFT BUDGET *	1,293	6.9	2028	10.8
FIANNA FÁIL – TARGET	1200	6.4	1858	9.9
FIANNA FÁIL – OUTTURN	1180	6.2	1786	9.4

*20 January 1987

Source: *Budget Booklets*

When I returned to Merrion Street for the second time in four years, I knew the fiscal challenge the government then faced was far greater than in 1982, given the steady deterioration in the public finances. The draft budget Fine Gael proposed in January, which included spending cuts, was rejected by Labour. Nevertheless, those Fine Gael budget proposals set a benchmark the Fianna Fáil minority government knew it must match, if not surpass. As a new administration, we needed to show our commitment and resolution in tackling the public finances. So soon after the government was formed, one of the first decisions agreed between the Taoiseach and myself was to set a lower current deficit target in the budget than Fine Gael had managed.

Three weeks elapsed between the election of the new government and my presentation of the budget. In that limited time, the government began a searching examination of all spending programmes and managed substantial further cuts in departmental estimates, amounting to over £63 million gross. But having taken out some of the excess fat, I knew the real challenge was still ahead of us. It was to cut spending right down to the bone, in preparation for the 1988 spending estimates. In the examination of spending cuts no sum was too small to consider, and at no stage were budgetary matters far from one's mind − or allowed to be. At the time mobile phones were still in their infancy, and the signal started to break up near Kinnegad. Many times on the road to the west late on Friday evening, the ministerial car was flagged down by gardaí, and I went into the barracks to ring the department, invariably, it seemed, to settle some unresolved dispute about spending.

The economic success we were later to achieve reflected in no small measure the strength of the coordinated approach we adopted from the outset. Early on, an informal review group was established which exercised a critical influence both in shaping events and reacting to them.

The six were the Taoiseach, myself, Pádraig Ó hUiginn as Secretary of the Taoiseach's Department, Seán Cromien, Secretary of Finance, Maurice Doyle, Governor of the Central Bank, and Séamus Páircéir, the Chairman of the Revenue Commissioners. At these meetings, which lasted several hours, we reviewed overall economic performance under a variety of headings, which included whether tax revenues were on target, what taxes might be raised, the Central Bank view on interest rates and the progress of talks on the Programme for National Recovery. The effectiveness of the group lay in the fact that it operated as a team.

In my budget speech on 31 March 1987, I told the Dáil: 'The message I have to deliver is unpalatable but it is critical to the revival of our economic prospects. We cannot be content to announce our intention to curtail spending, while at the same time deferring action. We have to act now.' And I made it clear that the strategy and principles outlined in the NESC report would form the basis of the government's general approach.

The current budget deficit was set slightly lower than Fine Gael had proposed. Tax bands were not indexed for inflation, and a special 35 per cent withholding tax on professional fees paid by state agencies (medical, legal, financial, training and engineering services) was introduced. In addition, the government abolished the duty-free allowance for travellers who were outside the jurisdiction for less than forty-eight hours. Public-service pay was frozen from the end of June, and the embargo on recruitment was maintained.

The first one hundred days in power provide a new government with a temporary window of opportunity to take radical steps. In the budget I felt we had seized the moment; we had started as we hoped to continue – boldly and with a determination not to relent under pressure. In concluding my financial statement to the Dáil I underscored that point, by promising that 'people can plan in the certainty that there will be no change of direction. The public finances will be managed prudently, there will be a better distribution of the tax burden and the economy will become increasingly competitive.'

The opposition could not disagree. Fine Gael, as the main opposition party, had pledged its support, if Fianna Fáil pursued a broadly similar fiscal policy, and this had been done. The only question was how the minority government might fare later, when the second and further instalments of tougher austerity measures had to be delivered. Would Fine Gael continue to underwrite the government where it mattered most – in the division lobbies in the Dáil?

The government knew, and all the ministers readily accepted, that the only way to proceed was to turn our parliamentary weakness into a political strength. That meant refusing to do deals with any party, or with independents, in return for their voting support. In that sense the fate of the government rested in the hands of the opposition. For my part, I felt a bit like a high-wire artist performing without the reassurance of a safety net underneath. However, a number of factors ensured that the experience of 1987 was not going to be like that of 1982, when Fianna Fáil held power in similar circumstances.

This time, the degree of division among the opposition parties was far greater. The social partners had recognised the need to tackle the financial crisis head-on. They provided the critical lead. By doing so, all politicians were put under greater public pressure to join this consensus. Also, since all the parties in the Dáil this time had slightly different political agendas, a minority government might be more secure, despite the voting numbers. For the opposition seemed less likely to make common cause to defeat a new government at the earliest opportunity.

Labour had opted out of coalition, unwilling to accept spending cuts and specifically health cuts. It was badly bruised by its experience in government, and the heavy seat losses (down to eight seats from twelve) it had sustained. In reaction, the party talked about moving to the left. In Fine Gael, when Alan Dukes replaced Garret FitzGerald as leader, Dukes clearly needed time to consolidate his position and rebuild the party. By all accounts, he had just narrowly defeated John Bruton in the leadership vote. And the Progressive Democrats, having made windfall gains in seats, seemed unlikely to jeopardise their success. So, unlike 1982, there was no appetite for another election so quickly; for this time, there was no natural coalition alternative waiting in the wings to bring the government down.

The only question was how long this would last, particularly when the opposition was challenged by the tough spending cuts the government was planning. Would the opposition parties unite around a single issue in order to bring the government down?

Notwithstanding the significant cuts already realised in the 1987 budget, the government had committed itself to publishing the 1988 estimates in October 1987. It meant that from the first day we entered government, there was a relentless preoccupation with expenditure control. As a consequence, I found myself spending some Sundays in Merrion Street going through spending estimates and identifying savings as low as £1,000 on some expenditure items. The March budget represented simply the first phase of a sustained onslaught on spending. After its passage, we were ready to move up a gear. On this basis, the Taoiseach wrote to all the government Ministers on 13 May 1987. He gave them ten days' notice to come up with a preliminary paper outlining where the proposed cuts would take place within their department. Ominously, he warned them that 'no expenditure should be regarded as sacrosanct.'

The letter, which was leaked to the media some days later, was direct and specific:

Dear Minister,

It is imperative that we carry further the progress we have made so far this year in getting public expenditure under control. Unless we achieve further significant cuts in expendiure the growth in public sector debt will continue to be a burden on the economy, inhibiting economic growth and employment and making it impossible for us to get development underway.

We must begin to identify the specific programmes and expenditures for further cuts now if we want to get results for the remainder of 1987 and 1988.

I am anxious to get this process underway as soon as possible. I therefore ask you to submit to me, and to the Minister for Finance a paper by Friday, May 22, at the latest, identifying the proposed reductions to expenditure.

The proposals must have the effect of achieving a significant reduction on your Department's present level of spending. They may cover capital as well as current expenditure. Your paper should state whether legislation, or other important preparatory steps, would be required in order to bring them into effect, and the timetable you would envisage in taking these steps. It should also cost the proposals made, showing the possible long term as well as 1987 and 1988 savings.

In arriving at your proposals all options should be considered including the elimination or reduction of particular schemes and programmes, rooting out overlaps and duplications between organisations, the merger of organisations, the closure of institutions which may have outlived their usefulness, the scaling down of the operations of organisations and institutions and the disposal of physical assets which are no longer productively used. A radical approach should be adopted and no expenditure should be regarded as sacrosanct and immune to elimination or reduction. We do not want a series of justifications of the status quo or special pleadings.

I am depending on you to make it clear to officials that their full cooperation in and commitment to this exercise is required and that the government expect worthwhile results to emerge.

Following the 22 May, the Secretary, Department of Finance, will head a team of Finance officials to meet each Accounting Officer to review each group of votes to identify the savings that can be made.

The proposals identified will come before government for
decision. The timetable I want to hold to is that these decisions
be made on a weekly basis from end-May, and that we be in
a position to have the full programme of reductions agreed by
end August-early September.

In fact, the letter appeared in the newspapers on the day Ministers delivered their list of spending cuts and costs savings. Far from being an embarrassment, the leaked document was seen, publicly, as a measure of the government's determination to bring public expenditure under control. For once, this was a leak that worked to the government's advantage, even though I am quite certain it had not come from official sources.

However, to stiffen the resolve of ministers to achieve real spending cuts, an Expenditure Review Committee was established. It was more commonly known as An Bord Snip. But to secretaries of department under cross-examination by Finance officials, it may, at times, have seemed more like the Star Chamber. Every meeting of that Review Group was presided over by the Secretary of the Department of Finance, Seán Cromien, accompanied by the Second Secretary in charge of Public Expenditure Division, Bob Curran, and Kevin Murphy, Secretary, Personnel Management and Development. This group was strengthened by a blunt, outspoken Dubliner, Colm McCarthy of the economic consultancy DKM. If ever there was a successful quango – quasi non-government organisation – then this was it. Certainly, it must have paid for itself many times over in the expenditure savings it identified and realised.

Seán Cromien was concerned that meetings between this group and the Secretaries of the other departments should not be confrontational. He wanted from the outset to avoid any unnecessary stress from these sometimes painful encounters. I understand he even went to the trouble of ensuring that, for the seating arrangements at these meetings, the two sides were brought close so as to reduce the sense of confrontation, while tea and biscuits were served early on in order to put those involved at their ease and in good humour. This human psychology prompted some facetious remarks about the unexpected generosity and indeed self-indulgence of the Department of Finance at a time of national austerity.

The Taoiseach requested that Secretaries be invited to give their personal views to the Review Committee on how their budgets should be cut and on which schemes funded by their department might be dropped. For the most part, the meetings went as calmly as planned. However, there were exceptions. One irate departmental secretary almost came to blows with a senior Finance official, when neither was willing to give ground on a contentious issue.

At the time, Charles Haughey and I both felt that one major factor fuelling higher spending demands was pressure exercised by secretaries of departments on their own ministers. They were pushing them – particularly if they were young or inexperienced – to look for more resources. However, Seán Cromien did not agree. On the contrary, he claimed, it was the other way round. The pressure really came from ministers eager to make a name for themselves, and to impress their departments. And in many cases, he said, secretaries had told him, on an off-the-record basis, of schemes which had outlived their usefulness and should be terminated. But their minister wouldn't hear of it.

The Taoiseach's response was to authorise Cromien to send out the message to all departments that the game had changed. In parallel, he had backed this up with the letter he sent to all Ministers. Now departmental secretaries were expected to come up with their own personal proposals for abolishing schemes. If their minister had doubts, the proposals were still to be tabled, although ministers could of course voice their personal concerns at the Cabinet meeting. Against this background, the government set about taking, and publicly announcing, some significant public expenditure decisions. On 1 September 1987, it was decided to abolish An Foras Forbartha (the National Institute for Physical Planning and Construction Research), a move that sent tremors of apprehension through the whole public service. Closing down parts of the public service, even a state research institute, was unheard-of at that stage.

Critical to the success of the spending-cuts exercise, I felt, was the degree to which I as Minister for Finance had the full support of the Taoiseach. In this regard, Charles Haughey's backing proved to be unwavering. Around the Cabinet table, where issues came to be resolved and where a tough decision had finally to be taken on a proposal from Finance involving cuts, ministers would discuss the political implications, and then the Taoiseach – as Chairman – would turn to me and say, 'Well – what do you think, Ray.' My reply was to say simply, 'I think we have to stand behind the proposal.'

And invariably, that is what happened. But, more importantly, once that was seen to occur in 1987, it became easier the following year to secure the cuts required without too much resistance from the spending departments. The whole expenditure-control exercise worked well – and just how well was shown from the figures when they emerged. In October the estimates were published, as promised, and the government achieved a six per cent reduction in nominal spending – a new record.

Certainly, there was little to fear in the passage of the Finance Bill, where the government enjoyed huge majorities. It was a paradox that a government in a minority of three in the Dáil could be enjoying the biggest voting majorities in recent Dáil history. However, an analysis of voting performance in the initial three months in the Dáil – from April to June – showed this was happening. It also illustrated the acute problems Fine Gael faced in its opposition role. During that time, there were some fifty-three voting divisions, but on no fewer than forty occasions, Fine Gael had abstained. It meant a Fianna Fáil government enjoyed an average forty-seven-vote majority on each division. For a minority government, this was a remarkable achievement. And what a contrast it made with 1982, when the Ceann Comhairle's casting vote had been needed to pass four amendments to the Finance Bill, or indeed months earlier in 1987 when a similar vote had secured the Taoiseach's election.

What the voting figures failed to reveal was the tension developing within Fine Gael. The size of the Fianna Fáil majority reflected both the scale of Fine Gael's abstention and the degree to which the opposition parties were disunited, or were simply anxious to avoid a general election. The challenge facing the minority government was to survive until the June recess without compromising its authority. It was critical to do so since, with a three-and-a-half month summer adjournment of the Dáil, the government would avoid the embarrassment of parliamentary defeat. By October, the Cabinet proposed to complete and publish the 1988 spending estimates, and also to have secured a new national pay deal with the social partners, negotiated along the lines proposed in the NESC report.

However, before the Dáil rose, there was a important exchange on the health estimate, which had some significant implications. In Irish politics there is no more emotive issue than hospital closures or cutbacks in health spending. Proposed health economies had brought down two governments in 1982 and 1987. On coming into office, we found it necessary to add to the cuts in health spending proposed by Fine Gael in its draft budget in January. Up to that point, Alan Dukes had maintained a consistent but tough line in supporting the Fianna Fáil budget measures, which in many respects mirrored those inherited from Fine Gael. So much so, perhaps, that he faced internal party criticism that Fine Gael's opposition role was simply to prop up the government.

On the rebound from this criticism, he opted for an aggressive stance on the Health estimates vote, with the party threatening to oppose the measure in the Dáil division. This could have led to a general election. For here was just the issue on which the new government could not be seen to back down. It became a major test of political wills, and Alan Dukes blinked first.

He withdrew his threat to oppose, and instead Fine Gael abstained on the vote. The government's firmness was seen as a measure of its seriousness. This was a challenge it had to be seen to win. However, for Fine Gael, I feel, it forced an important tactical reassessment that had a major bearing on how politics developed over the remaining life of the Dáil.

3

THE TALLAGHT STRATEGY: AID TO RECOVERY

Ray Mac Sharry

Alan Dukes's address to the Tallaght Chamber of Commerce on 2 September 1987 proved to be the most significant economic speech made by an opposition leader in recent decades. I had no indication that his statement was coming. In fact, I was just as surprised by its content as many of his own parliamentary colleagues in Fine Gael. Having read the ten-page script, my immediate reaction was a mixture of bewilderment and delight. Of course I welcomed his promise of conditional support for the government on economic matters. Yet I was unsure whether the new Fine Gael leader felt he was grabbing a lifeline for his own party or throwing one to a minority government. However, one thing was clear: the government's ultimate fate lay with Fine Gael and how it voted in Dáil divisions.

The Tallaght Strategy was designed to serve the party and the country. It combined altruism with a degree of political self-interest, and, in fairness to Alan Dukes, perhaps more of the former than the latter. For Fine Gael it served two purposes: the strategy bought time for the party to reorganise itself, while it gave the government no excuse to call a snap general election. And by underwriting, conditionally, the government's economic approach, it also served the country. On balance, Fine Gael put the national interest in restoring financial stability ahead of any short-term party advantage. In doing so, no doubt there was an element of political calculation: that Fianna Fáil, in embracing fiscal rectitude and taking the tough measures needed to clear up the economic mess, would make itself highly unpopular. In that way, Fine Gael could hope to become the ultimate beneficiary from the electorate.

From the outset, the government had known that the 1987 budget was underwritten by Fine Gael. The party's own draft proposals in January had provided much of the groundwork for the budget I introduced in March. Nevertheless, after the passage of the 1987 Finance Act, the unanswered question was whether Fine Gael would continue to provide that support, or instead resume the old adversarial-style politics in the Dáil. For Fianna Fáil as a minority government, the answer would either shorten or lengthen the life expectancy of the Twenty-fifth Dáil. I recognised then that the budget was just the first in a series of tough measures required to restore order to the public finances

Alan Dukes provided the answer in unequivocal language when he set out the 'Tallaght Strategy' – defining Fine Gael's conditional support for the government on key economic issues. There, he recognised that 'the resolution of our public finance problems is the essential key to everything that we want to do in the economic and social fields.' He added, ' . . . What I want for the Irish people cannot happen until our debt burden is under control. It is the role of government to create the conditions in which all of these issues can be successfully addressed.' And he went on:

It is the role of the parliamentary opposition to ensure that the government does this, to re-direct government policy where it diverges from the right track, and to oppose government policy where it is wrong. That is the core of my role as Leader of the opposition. In specific terms, that means that when the government is moving in the right overall direction, I will not oppose the central thrust of its policy. If it is going in the right direction, I do not believe that it should be deviated from its course, or tripped up on macroeconomic issues. Specifically, it means that, if in 1988 the government produces a budget which opens the way to a reduction in taxes and particularly to a reduction in personal taxes, brings about a significant reduction in the current budget deficit below the figure targeted for this year, holds out a strategy for real employment expansion in future years, and does not add to debt service costs in future years, I will not oppose the general thrust of its policy. No other policy of opposition will conform to the real needs of Irish people: any other policy of opposition would amount simply to a cynical exploitation of short-term political opportunities for a political advantage which would inevitably prove to be equally short-lived. I will not play that game, because it would not produce any real or lasting advantage for the Irish people – least of all for those who currently have neither political nor economic advantage.

As events unfolded over the following months, the real significance of that speech became ever more apparent. Alan Dukes's statement of Fine Gael intentions came to be seen, and rightly, as a landmark political development. Over time, the Tallaght Strategy approach also served as a catalyst in redefining how politics was conducted in the Dáil, not just on economic policy, but in other areas as well. For it signalled the end of opposition for its own sake and ushered in a new era of greater cooperation and understanding between government and the opposition parties. On a range of issues, as consensus replaced confrontation, the political temperature in the Dáil dropped sharply.

Alan Dukes deserves more credit than he has received for his courage in adopting the Tallaght Strategy. But to many within his own party, it also seemed that he was embarking on a high-risk strategy. The party was sharing responsibility for tough economic decisions, though without sharing power, and Fine Gael was uncertain of how much credit it might, ultimately, be able to claim.

However, I believe that the Fine Gael leader's intention was based on a realistic analysis of the economic and political situation. Having spent four years in government, nearly all as Finance Minister, Alan Dukes knew there was no real alternative to what was being proposed. In opposition, and as a newly elected leader, he was prepared to put his leadership on the line, and did so with great courage. However, with the social partners likely to back the government approach, as negotiations under-way on the Programme for National Recovery neared completion, he also knew there was little to be gained from staying outside the developing consensus on the economy. Certainly the Dukes decision provided a spur for all those involved in the talks between the social partners to reach agreement.

The government, having won support from the social partners for the Programme for National Recovery (PNR), had to advance with some caution. In the three-year agreement, 1988–90, pay restraint was exchanged for the promise of income-tax reductions, increased social benefits and greater influence over aspects of economic policy. The government had to decide how best to implement the terms of the agreement without destabilising its own minority-government voting position in the Dáil. This had to be done in incremental steps, and the annual budget provided the opportunity to implement the main provisions on pay, taxation and debt stabilisation and reduction. The government had signalled its intention to publish the estimates early in the autumn, and so negotiations with the social partners on the PNR took place in parallel with Cabinet discussions to finalise the 1988 spending estimates.

The future credibility of the plan depended in large measure on how realistic the budgetary arithmetic in the January 1988 budget was. So to that extent, the level of spending cuts achieved was critical. These were seen as a measure of the government's overall seriousness. Nevertheless, it was a delicate political exercise. The risk was that a union leadership which had signed up to the terms of a draft national agreement could face a revolt from rank-and-file members, unimpressed by the pay terms on offer. Already, the opposition parties had given a hostile response to the PNR, and the government was concerned about how draconian spending cuts would be received. For if the public reaction was strongly negative, this could sway rank-and-file union members to vote against the PNR at the special delegate conference in November 1987.

However, once the trade union leaders had signed up to the plan, it was felt this would reduce their criticism of the severity of the spending cuts. Since the social partners had accepted in the PNR that tough measures were required to turn the economy around, then clearly they accepted the steps necessary to achieve that aim – namely reduced spending. Just a few days after the plan's publication, the spending estimates were published, with cuts of some £485 million proposed. The figures showed that the government had succeeded in one of its main objectives – to check the upward spiral in public expenditure. As I told the Dáil in a debate on the 1988 allocations: 'Expenditure has been reduced – in cash terms – for the first time in almost thirty years.'

The opposition's reaction proved surprisingly muted, and divided. Both Fine Gael and the Progressive Democrats refused to back a proposed Labour motion of no confidence in the government, while even within the Labour Party, opinion was split. Later, it became clear the opposition parties would base their criticism on the specific cuts, and reductions in services proposed. This line of parliamentary attack was set to present the government with its most critical time in the Dáil. For while there was a new political acceptance of the need for cuts in the abstract, the consensus did not extend to an agreement on the individual cuts to be made. However, it remained highly significant – and encouraging – that a minority government could still win Dáil support for overall cuts of £485 million.

Once Alan Dukes had announced the Tallaght Strategy in September 1987, the degree of informal cooperation between Fianna Fáil and Fine Gael in organising Dáil business expanded greatly. The liaison was designed to minimise political difficulty on economic issues. At one level, routine matters were settled between the government chief whip, Vincent Brady, and Fine Gael's Fergus O'Brien. This allowed for more consultation with the main opposition party on the ordering of Dáil business.

The unstated aim, of course, was to avoid a snap general election, caused more by accident than design. At other times I had contacts with Fine Gael's Finance spokesman, Michael Noonan, or with John Boland to smooth out difficulties that arose. In this regard the greatest problem lay with the weekly private-members business. This allowed the main Dáil parties parliamentary time – three hours weekly – to raise matters of public concern or to introduce a private members bill. Primarily, private-members time was used by the opposition as an opportunity to raise its political profile and launch a sustained assault on some aspect of government policy.

For Fine Gael, it meant the party had to devise the terms of the motions it proposed with particular care. Normally, an opposition party seeks every opportunity to inflict a voting defeat on the government, knowing the arithmetic is rarely in its favour. However, the operational terms of the Tallaght Strategy meant Fine Gael had to resist that temptation, while at the same time causing maximum political embarrassment to the government. On economic matters it could push disagreement to Dáil division, but without risking a voting defeat for the government. In practice it meant the party's front bench had to propose motions that were unlikely to unite all the other opposition parties (PDs, Labour, Democratic Left and Independents) behind the Fine Gael position. Equally, where a Labour or Democratic Left, seemed likely to command the full backing of the opposition parties, then a Fine Gael amendment would ensure the left-wing parties could not support it. So amendments adding support for privatisation or lower spending would be tabled.

The Fine Gael deputies, having adopted the Tallaght Strategy, found themselves in a vulnerable position. An Irish Marketing Surveys poll in the *Sunday Independent* newspaper in early October 1987, and conducted just after the adoption of that policy, illustrated the party's difficulty. It showed Fianna Fáil with 46 per cent support – some two percentage points higher than the general election result in February. So, despite the austerity policies and the promise of two further tough budgets, the government had gained rather than lost support after six months in office. Although the poll was taken before the terms of the PNR were finalised and the 1998 spending estimates were published, the public response offered more encouragement to Fianna Fáil in power than to Fine Gael in opposition.

Interestingly, the poll also showed Alan Dukes as the most popular party leader, with the highest satisfaction rating, even though his own party was deeply divided on the merits of Fine Gael offering conditional support to the government for its economic policy. Among Fine Gael supporters, opinion was split down the middle on the issue, with some 46 per cent in favour and 43 per cent against the Tallaght Strategy approach. The new Fine Gael leader's standing among party supporters was low: only 63 per cent were satisfied with his performance. It raised the question of whether Alan Dukes had gone too far in assuming some of the burdens of office by underwriting the government's economic policy where Fine Gael agreed and offering alternative spending cuts where it disagreed.

The Tallaght Strategy faced its first real test in November as the cutbacks in education spending, announced in the 1988 estimates, became apparent and INTO mobilised opposition to them. The cuts involved fewer primary teachers and therefore larger class sizes, and a higher pupil-teacher ratio. Already this had generated huge public controversy, resulting in some forty Fianna Fáil backbenchers holding a meeting with Mary O'Rourke as Minister for Education to press for changes. These, she resisted. Fine Gael used its private-members time to oppose the move, though the terms of its motion fell short of calling for the withdrawal of the department's circular on class sizes. However, because both the Progressive Democrats and Labour had already done so, pressure quickly mounted on Fine Gael to change its mind and adopt a more aggressive stance on the issue.

Before the party could decide, the government made what proved to be a tactical blunder. It tabled an amendment to the

Fine Gael motion, reaffirming its support for the proposed spending cuts. However, that created an unforeseen problem. Under the Dáil's standing orders, the government amendment took precedence, and therefore would be voted on first. But, with all the opposition parties in different degrees opposed, it meant the minority government faced defeat. This placed Alan Dukes in a very difficult position. Having pressed the government for a concession, he had been told, on apparent good authority, that one would be forthcoming at the end of the debate when the Minister was summing up. So Dukes again called on the Minister to withdraw the circular, with an understanding that a Quota Review Committee would be offered by the government in its place. This could determine class sizes and monitor and control the impact of the proposed cuts. It was something of a fudge. Except that there was one problem. Nobody had told either Mary O'Rourke or myself about the arrangement, if there ever was one.

In the Dáil, as the minutes ticked by before the division bells rang for the votes to be taken, suspense mounted. The political mini-drama was reaching a climax amid scenes of mounting confusion. Three times Alan Dukes rose from his seat. And each time with a greater sense of exasperation, he asked the Minister to confirm the assurance he had received, that the pupil-teacher ratio would be maintained. If that was done, he said, he would withdraw the Fine Gael motion. But Mary O'Rourke steadfastly refused to give way. Over her shoulder she received an urgent note from chief whip Vincent Brady urging her to say 'Yes'. As Finance Minister, I was sitting in the seat beside her, and with increasing vehemence telling her to say 'No'. Alan Dukes stared across from the opposition front bench with a look of angry amazement on his face. When the motion was put by the Ceann Comhairle, the amendment was lost by three votes, and the government had suffered its first Dáil defeat.

That night when Charles Haughey returned to the Dáil from a function at the RDS, he was furious. But for my part, although annoyed at the confusion, I also recognised that defeats on motions in private-members time were inevitable, given the government's minority status. In operating the Tallaght Strategy, the unwritten rule was that Fine Gael had to be seen to win sometimes; otherwise, its support for the government on economic issues would be impossible to sustain. The party would be seen to be exercising responsibility without power and, with little to show for it, a backbench revolt against a newly elected leader could not be ruled out. The only question was how that success would be achieved, whether formally, in a Dáil defeat of the government, or informally, by accepting a Fine Gael proposal or amendment that secured its support but did so without compromising the government.

In all, in the lifetime of the Twenty-fifth Dáil (1987–89) Fianna Fáil was defeated in Dáil divisions on six occasions, but never on legislation. Defeats on motions in private-members time, while embarrassing, had little practical effect. The government could note the terms of the motion but was not required to take any specific action to implement it.

To the government, the loss of face from such Dáil defeats was temporary. Certainly, it was preferable to making a major concession to the opposition to avoid defeat, particularly in the area of public spending cuts. If that happened, the government's credibility would vanish overnight. Lobby groups, scenting political weakness, would mobilise and increase pressure on opposition and government backbenchers alike in the future. A concession granted would set a precedent that, in turn, would be invoked by others to bolster their claim for similar treatment. No exceptions could be made and being seen not to make an exception also became critically important in showing the strength of the government's resolution.

Subsequently, on a few occasions, ministers came to me, concerned that Fine Gael was set to vote against the government and pressing for some concessions. But I refused to relent. As a result of my rigidity, stubbornness and indeed predictability, my job became much easier after the first year. Everyone then said, 'You're wasting your time going to Mac Sharry – he'll just say no.' The last thing that TDs in general want is an election, but as Minister for Finance at that time, I knew that every day it remained a strong possibility.

From the outset Ministers backed the need for spending cuts. However, as the cuts began to affect individual departments, that sense of shared resolution faltered somewhat among some of my Cabinet colleagues. Given the nature of current spending, where education and health count for the bulk of what could be described as politically sensitive spending, it meant a small number of ministers had to bear the brunt of public unpopularity. It placed those in the big spending departments – Mary O'Rourke in Education and Rory O'Hanlon in Health – right in the firing line. But they never wilted under the strain of what, at times, were very strong attacks. One abiding memory of that time was turning on RTÉ's *Morning Ireland* and hearing its presenter, David Hanly, say to an interviewee – perhaps to Rory O'Hanlon on the subject of hospital waiting lists – 'But people are dying, Minister, people are dying.'

Certainly, the Tallaght Strategy made parliamentary life easier for the government. Without such an arrangement then, as in 1982, an election was inevitable. That was avoided, and instead there was a recognition of the gravity of the economic situation by the opposition, and by the government of the role of the opposition. This was reflected in the extension of the committee system and the increased number of private-members bills accepted for discussion.

*

In March 1987, the economy was trapped in a vicious circle of high spending, high taxes, high interest rates and rising debt. All were contributing to weak growth and soaring unemployment. The task facing the new government was to turn the vicious circle into a virtuous one, where interest rates would decline, spending would fall, growth would accelerate, employment would rise and the debt burden would stabilise and fall. It was a formidable challenge.

However, within weeks of our taking office, the first encouraging signs emerged that the economy's downward spiral had been checked. Interest rates fell in response to the March budget measures. By April, the Central Bank's short-term facility rate dropped from 13.25 per cent to 11.75 per cent. A year later, it had fallen to 8.5 per cent. Declining interest rates provided just the stimulus the economy needed to offset the deflationary impact of spending cuts. Although interest rates were falling internationally, Irish rates were tumbling even faster. Foreign investors, who had retreated in 1986, worried about the apparent inability of politicians on both sides of the Dáil to address the crisis in the public finances, returned. They were impressed by the government's determined efforts to return to the straight-and-narrow path of fiscal rectitude.

Certainly the sharp fall in interest rates helped raise spending power all round. It gave a much-needed psychological boost both to consumer and business confidence. Lower rates, rather like tax cuts, left mortgage holders with higher disposable incomes. To the business sector, the decline in rates encouraged investment and expansion. For the government, the visible evidence to show that its austerity package was working proved critical. It helped underpin public support for its overall strategy.

Along with the efforts to curtail spending and secure a moderate pay agreement, the government was concerned to reform and lower taxes, as part of its commitment to the Programme for National Recovery. The bargain later struck was that in return for moderate pay increases, the government promised lower income tax to boost the real take-home pay of workers, thereby increasing competitiveness and raising employment levels.

From the outset this raised the question of what was the best approach to adopt in pursuing the goal of tax reform. On spending, the government had little choice but to opt for the 'big bang' strategy. By contrast, on tax reform, the approach was more cautious and reflected a much slower pace of change. Nevertheless, as changes in the tax code unfolded over a number of years, the cumulative impact was quite dramatic. In 1987 the standard rate of tax was 35 per cent and the top marginal rate 58 per cent. However, within ten years these rates were lowered to 24 per cent and 46 per cent, while the thresholds at which these rates applied were raised in real terms. The government's total taxation receipts, which in 1987 stood at 44.3 per cent of GNP, by 1998 had dropped to 40.2 per cent. But of the reform initiatives undertaken, none proved more controversial than the tax amnesty.

In fact no measure created more internal debate within my department than the government plan to introduce a tax amnesty as part of the 1988 budget. In the spending estimates, just £30 million was forecast for revenue. It actually yielded more than fifteen times that amount, some £500 million, when the deadline closed nine months later on September 30. Five years later, in

1993, another such scheme was introduced; this scheme raised some £260 million.

The whole amnesty idea was strongly opposed both by the Revenue Commissioners and Finance officials, and for understandable reasons. There was scepticism about its chance of success and a concern about the principle being conceded. It had been tried before and yielded little, while an amnesty for tax dodgers and defaulters seemed to be sending the wrong signal to the compliant PAYE tax payers. After all, here were people who, in some cases as employers, had collected their employees' PAYE tax receipts and failed to pass this money on to the state.

The inspiration for the amnesty arose from my own experience at constituency clinics and from what I had observed years earlier, as a member of the Dáil Committee on Public Accounts – the parliamentary watchdog on public spending. At clinics, an increasing number of people were coming to me and saying straight up, 'Look – I want to put my tax affairs in order. I have got a bill for £35,000 from the Revenue. But what I owe them is £15,000. The rest is penalties and interest charges. While I can pay the tax, I cannot pay the charges.' And in many such cases, the charges levied were double the tax owing. They claimed they were going to go out of business. But if they were, the Revenue were not putting them out of business. They themselves were doing so, through bad management of their own tax affairs.

In my nine years on Public Accounts, invariably, year after year the same issue won most media attention. This was the report from the Comptroller and Auditor General to the Committee, highlighting the hundreds of millions of pounds in uncollected taxes. Of course, much of this was a notional estimate, based on general assessments by the Revenue Commissioners of tax owing. However, it was not a strict liability which was actually collectible. But I had often thought if we could get just a fraction of that amount, it would make a dent in our debt burden. It would also broaden the tax base, by bringing these defaulters into the tax net for the first time.

When I chatted to my Fianna Fáil colleagues in the Dáil, over lunch or dinner, I found their experience was similar to my own. At their own clinics, they too had met with a similar response and come under the same pressure. Although many people felt, because of the failure of the previous amnesties, that this one would not work, I remained confident it would. For what we were offering this time was different. The government was waiving interest and penalty charges on tax outstanding. I knew that if the government could withstand the political criticism on that account, the revenue yield was likely to prove substantial. But just how big, I had never anticipated. In the final week, some £400 million came in, with some 40,000 personal callers to the offices of the Revenue Commissioners in Earlsfort Terrace.

I came under strong pressure from accountants and fellow ministers to extend the deadline. I refused to do so. For I knew that many accountants and solicitors were simply sitting on the money received from clients, with instructions to settle their tax affairs. I also recognised that any sign of political weakness could be fatal. The pressure to settle would be removed, and a backlash from the compliant PAYE taxpayer might develop. And rightly so, for the latter would see delay as yet another concession to defaulters.

Certainly the results of the tax amnesty highlighted just how inadequate our system of revenue collection was and revealed the scope for increased efficiency. Some years later in conversation with Finance officials I said that I thought the amnesty had brought many more people into the tax system. But they insisted that the revenue boost had come mainly from large tax defaulters. Instinctively, I felt, and still do, that many who wanted to become tax-compliant were deterred by the penalty and interest charges they would face in regularising their position. Partly for this reason the amnesty became known as the Tax Incentive Scheme. Certainly, the after-effect of the measure was to ensure much greater compliance from the self-employed, where tax avoidance and evasion had been significant. In broadening the tax base, the amnesty also helped to finance the tax cuts that were to follow in later years as economic recovery got under way.

As Minister for Finance, I was aware of the radical experiments in fiscal policy reform then under way in other countries, particularly New Zealand, which had an economy similar in wealth, structure and population size to our own. Moreover New Zealand too was struggling to overcome broadly similar problems, namely imbalances in the public finances. At that time, Roger Douglas, as his country's Finance Minister, favoured sweeping overnight changes, both in cutting expenditure and lowering tax rates, as the best way of achieving radical reform. To be effective, Douglas argued, tax changes must be made quickly. As he later wrote, his master plan was to 'Implement reform by quantum leaps. Moving step-by-step lets vested interests mobilise; big packages can neutralise them.'

The idea is that big tax packages help ensure there are more gainers than losers from the change. If achieved, this means a bigger political constituency can be mobilised in defence of the tax reform. As he saw it, the difficulty with small packages which offer piecemeal change is that the opposite applied. The tax winners may gain too little to offset the objections of the tax losers. But of course, if reform is faster, the benefits flow through much more quickly.

The government favoured the incremental route to tax

reform, something between piecemeal change and the big-bang approach. That response was largely dictated by our economic situation. We simply could not afford the unilateral big-bang tax strategy. Given the weak state of the public finances, dramatic tax reform, via a £500 million package, was impossible to deliver in a single budget. And yet if radical changes in taxation are to be achieved, such a major step has to be taken. But for such an initiative to win acceptance as 'tax reform' either politically or in the media, those deprived of tax reliefs and concessions must gain on balance from the overall reduction in taxation. Regrettably, this was not possible.

In addition, the government favoured a partnership approach, so reaching a consensus with the social partners became an important consideration. Tax reform was seen as a vital part both of the Programme for National Recovery and of all subsequent social-partnership agreements. In fact, the whole tax agenda became one of the most important features in securing trade union support both for this and the subsequent series of agreements.

It was evident to the government, and made clear to the public, that until a better balance in the national finances was achieved, there could be no significant lowering of personal taxes. Nevertheless, over the three-year life span of the PNR, the government had committed itself to some £225 million in tax cuts. In addition, it set a longer-term goal of ensuring that two-thirds of taxpayers paid at the standard rate. The immediate priority was to achieve a broader tax base. This would not just yield higher revenue but establish a greater degree of equity and fairness.

In March 1987, before talks on the PNR had got under way, the most pressing need was to cut spending and bring the public finances into balance as quickly as possible. This left little scope for overall reductions in the tax burden. In fact, the opposite was the case: since cutting public spending takes time to achieve its full impact, the government was forced to raise revenue where it could. For the overriding aim was to try to ensure that borrowing fell and the debt ratio began to stabilise.

So in the March budget, revenue was enhanced by a variety of measures. First, the tax bands were not indexed for inflation; second, a withholding tax for professional fees was introduced; third, there was a restriction on the duty-free allowances for cross-border travellers from the Republic, and fourth, the use of tax-clearance certificates was extended.

One important government decision taken at the outset was to make revenue collection more effective by better tax administration. So when the Department of the Public Service merged with the Department of Finance, some of the top personnel were redeployed to the Revenue Commissioners to tackle the problem of tax arrears.

A further innovation in 1988 was the introduction of self-assessment for the self-employed. This involved individual taxpayers computing their own final tax liability. In the first nine months, this brought in some £70 million more in income-tax receipts than expected and created an improved revenue flow for future years. Self-assessment also enabled the Revenue Commissioners to redeploy staff resources. In this way it was able to use the tougher enforcement measures on the statute books both to detect and deal with tax evasion. But above all, this new method of tax collection produced a remarkable change of attitude to tax compliance, particularly among the self-employed. It combined a carrot-and-stick approach, with Revenue given additional powers to deal with those who did not cooperate.

Some figures illustrate the point. In 1987–88, the year before self-assessment was introduced, only half of income-tax payers filed their returns on time. This figure has now increased to 77 per cent. When handling the Committee stage of the 1999 Finance Bill, Finance Minister Charlie McCreevy provided a professional insight into how the filing of tax returns was conducted before the change to self-assessment was made. At that stage tax compliance was taken far less seriously by many of the self-employed. The Minister, as a former accountant, was particularly well placed to judge the situation. Quite clearly, the whole tax-appeal mechanism was abused. It was used as a means to delay payment of outstanding taxes until the last possible moment. The result was administrative chaos and revenue loss for the Exchequer.

McCreevy told the Dáil Select Committee that each year, as a matter of course, accountants, on behalf of their clients, appealed whatever assessment was issued by the inspector of taxes. Later, adjournments were sought since, invariably, no accounts had been prepared at all by the client. But even after an exasperated Appeal Commissioner had finally reached a decision on a particular case, a further delaying tactic could be employed by the reluctant taxpayer; this time via an appeal to the Circuit Court.

The figures illustrate the scale of the problem. In 1986, there were no fewer than 59,888 cases on appeal before the Appeal Commissioners. By 1988 that had dropped to 9,779 and a year later to 1,181. The introduction of self-assessment largely brought about that change. Any appeals that are now made are either genuine appeals disputing the sums of tax owing or else are based on some points of law.

The success of measures like this went some way towards reassuring the hard-pressed PAYE taxpayer that serious attempts were now being made to broaden the tax base as the first step towards financing lower tax rates in the future. The successful implementation of self-assessment for the self-employed meant that in 1989 it could be extended to companies. Once again the results both in terms of compliance and collection have been dramatic. Then only 43 per cent of companies filed returns on time. Now the figure is 65 per cent and rising.

Generous tax concessions to business and industry had meant the tax contribution from the business sector was small by comparison with rates in other countries. But given the state of the public finances, there was need to address the issue with some urgency, both on that and other grounds – like employment and equity. In 1987, corporation tax totalled some £257 million – or about 1.5 per cent of GNP.

As Minister for Finance, I had inherited a continuing review of the corporation tax code, initiated by the Fine Gael–Labour government. On examination, it was clear the tax incentives on offer to the business sector were too generous, while the high reliefs available had produced a perverse effect. They simply encouraged investment in fixed assets at the expense of jobs. In an economy where the major problem was the high level of unemployment, a tax policy which resulted in capital replacing labour was counter-productive. Given the huge number of jobless in the economy then, substituting capital for labour, or machines for men, exacerbated, rather than addressed, an existing unemployment problem.

A year later, after the review was completed, the government agreed some significant changes. As I pointed out when introducing the 1988 budget: 'A broader-based tax with less generous reliefs and a lower standard rate will improve economic efficiency and will be fairer than the present system.' It was an approach already favoured by the Commission on Taxation in its report. The changes announced on budget day included a cut in Corporation Tax from 50 per cent to 43 per cent. In addition, accelerated capital allowances on new investment were reduced from 100 per cent to 50 per cent.

This represented a start on the major reform of corporate taxes that will not be completed until 2003. By then the standard rate of corporation tax will have been reduced to 12.5 per cent. A drop of some 37.5 percentage points in sixteen years makes it one of the most far-reaching policy changes ever attempted, and a critical step in helping to maintain Irish competitiveness. And for that, a succession of ministers for finance from different parties, all pursuing a common corporate tax policy, can claim the real credit.

On our coming into office and searching for ways to cut spending and raise revenue, nothing escaped our scrutiny. There was a tax clearance certificate procedure in place, requiring those seeking public contracts over £10,000 to have obtained Revenue clearance before tendering. The real value of the obligation was that it ensured only the tax-compliant could tender successfully for state business. In the course of becoming compliant, some £12.5 million was collected in back taxes. However, on closer examination, I found that this was not strictly true. A number of public bodies had failed to implement fully the necessary procedures. So in my budget speech, I made it clear that these must now comply, or else account for their failure to obey the law.

At the same time we set about introducing further refinements in the operation of the tax clearance system, with the stipulation that applicants for state and public-authority grants must give their tax number and confirm their tax affairs were in order before they could benefit. In subsequent years tax clearance was extended to pub licences. Once again the results were quite dramatic. In 1992, when the change first came into effect, only 20 per cent of applicants for tax clearance were eligible at first application. By 1998, some 85 per cent were eligible

The duty-free restriction that became known as the 'forty-eight-hour rule' was necessary because sterling's weakness had made cross-border shopping attractive to visitors from the Republic. The result was not just a loss of revenue to the Exchequer, but serious damage to the retail trade in the border areas. If the government announcement of the introduction of the rule annoyed Brussels, it infuriated some of the country's own private bus companies. They had developed a flourishing niche business, ferrying shoppers from the Republic over the border and back. It was estimated that cross-border shopping had cost the economy an estimated £300 million in 1986.

So to block it, the government required a traveller to spend at least forty-eight hours outside the state before he or she could qualify for the normal duty-free allowances – 300 cigarettes, one and a half litres of spirits, five litres of wine, etc. The government justified its unilateral action by claiming the European Community directive on travellers' allowances was defective since it made no distinction between genuine travellers and cross border traders who were keen to avoid paying higher rates of tax and duty.

Of course it was all a calculated gamble. From the outset, I knew the measure was almost certainly illegal under the Community rules. But I also recognised it could be some years before the European Commission and the European Court reached a final decision on the matter. In the meantime, the government was determined to sit tight, keep the duty-free curbs in place and await the final legal outcome. In fact Ireland was not alone in taking such unilateral action. Denmark had introduced similar restrictions because of a problem of cross-border shopping into West Germany.

It was the end of December 1987 before the European

Commission referred the matter to the Court. By then the fleets of buses had declined in number. Trade in the border towns had increased by an estimated 30 per cent as a result. Politically, it was an unpopular action, but equally, it was a measure of the government's concern for revenue and savings. Not until June 1990 did the European Court issue its definitive ruling. Not surprisingly, it held that the government measure introduced in the 1987 budget was illegal.

The challenge the government faced in bringing the public finances back into balance through spending cuts and tax reforms had to be combined with other policy initiatives if a full economic recovery was to be achieved. This required both innovation in economic management and a capacity for developmental thinking. Two such initiatives were attempted by the government, and both have proven successful. The first was the decision to change how the national debt was managed, by establishing an independent state agency: the National Treasury Management Agency (NTMA). This was to carry out the functions formerly handled by the Department of Finance. The second was the political act of faith that resulted in the setting up of the International Financial Services Centre on the old derelict Dublin docklands site (see Chapter 14).

Ray Mac Sharry

National Treasury Management Agency

NET PRESENT VALUE SAVINGS NTMA (£IR MILLION)							
1991	1992	1993	1994	1995	1996	1997	Total
69	78	141	9	105	57	31	490
OPERATING COSTS OF AGENCY (£IR MILLION)							
1991	1992	1993	1994	1995	1996	1997	Total
3.7	4.9	5.5	5.5	5.9	5.8	5.9	37.2

Source: National Treasury Management Agency

It was Winston Churchill who once remarked, 'There is no sphere of human thought in which it is easier to show superficial cleverness and the appearance of superior wisdom than in discussing currency and exchange.' But coming into government in 1987 and inheriting a £22 billion debt, the effective management of such a large portfolio was no longer a trifling matter. It became an issue of critical importance. The national debt had nearly doubled since I had left the Department of Finance more than four years earlier. The annual interest payments accounted for nearly £2 billion – or more than four-fifths of all income-tax receipts. And because some 40 per cent of our outstanding liabilities was in foreign currency loans, this carried a significant exchange-rate risk.

By international standards, Ireland now had a very high level of borrowings. Our ratio of debt to GNP – at some 120 per cent – was amongst the highest of our European partners. Stabilising the debt, so that it no longer outstripped the growth in national income, was the first priority and the immediate challenge facing the government. But this also called for effective professional management of the debt to produce savings in interest payments for the Exchequer.

At the time, debt management was handled by a division within the department. However, many of its highly qualified staff had left, attracted by the far higher salaries available in the private sector, particularly in the financial-services industry. And these highly skilled people were proving difficult to replace. These developments forced a radical rethink by the government. The Cabinet considered a range of options, which included handing over the whole national debt management operation to a bank or even hiring specialist staff on contract to do the job. But, ultimately, these were all rejected as impractical.

As secretary of the national debt management division, Michael Somers found the brain drain of talent to the private sector impossible to check. The main problem lay with the rigid pay structures applying in the public service. At a time of general wage restraint, public-pay guidelines could not be breached to stem the exodus of talented individuals. So Somers was the first to propose the radical idea of establishing a new agency, but independent of the Department of Finance. Subsequently, after consultations and advice taken from some international banks, this became the National Treasury Management Agency (NTMA).

As a separate agency outside the civil service, the NTMA could offer the pay terms to attract the skilled personnel needed to handle the specialised financial functions of borrowing and debt management. For the government, it solved a public sector pay problem. It meant the new Agency's pay arrangements could not serve as the basis for leap-frogging pay relativity claims from other public-service groups. However, it still meant the Agency operated under the minister's general control and supervision.

The NTMA was set up by statute under the terms of the National Treasury Management Act, 1990, by my successor,

Albert Reynolds. It has a mandate 'to borrow moneys for the Exchequer and to manage the national debt in a cost-efficient manner'. Each year the Agency has to gauge its performance against two criteria, designed to measure its success or failure. It must achieve a cash-savings target in servicing the debt and funding the government's borrowing requirement – where that arises. This figure is set annually by the Minister for Finance at budget time. In addition, J. P. Morgan, the US investment bank, sets a further measurement of performance, against an independent benchmark. Here the net present value (NPV) of both the actual debt portfolio and a shadow benchmark version is calculated, and the Agency's savings are measured by the extent of its outperformance against such a benchmark.

On this basis the results show an impressive record. Between 1991 and 1997 some £490 million have been saved. The Agency's operating costs over the same period were some £37 million. These represent significant savings for the taxpayer, more than justifying the NTMA's existence. The establishment of the Agency has attracted significant international interest, with frequent visitors from finance ministries throughout the world investigating a successful Irish experiment in national debt management. However, with Economic and Monetary Union, the national debt is now largely in domestic currency, since the euro is the state currency and the Irish pound merely a sub-division of it. In consequence, foreign-exchange risk to the Exchequer is greatly reduced. At the end of 1998, the national debt stood at £29.5 billion (58 per cent of GNP), some £4.4 billion higher than the £25.1 billion (99.4 per cent of GNP) total in late 1990, when the NTMA was set up. In 1998, the annual interest payment costs on the debt came to some £2.6 billion, or some 18 per cent of the government's net current spending, compared with 1990 figures of £2.3 billion and 27.3 per cent, respectively.

4

—

CONSISTENCY AND CONTINUITY
IN ECONOMIC POLICY

Ray Mac Sharry

The foundations for national economic recovery were first laid
with the decisions taken in the 1987 budget, and subsequently
in the development of the social-partnership model later that
year. It was underpinned by the cross-party political consensus
on the economy. The bipartisan approach on the economy
survived a series of changes of government over more than a
decade. However, without both a shared analysis and a common
policy prescription, the regeneration of the economy could not
have been achieved so quickly. Instead, the Celtic Tiger economy
would have been an unrealised dream.

For the first time in decades, successive Irish governments
had adopted and pursued a wholly consistent approach to
economic management. Whether in power or out of office, the
political parties maintained broadly similar policies. Each
acknowledged the gravity of the economic crisis facing the
country at the outset, and all recognised that a medium to long-
term strategy was required to overcome it. The result was greater
consistency between the different aspects of macroeconomic

policy. This continuity of approach became a critical factor in the rapid rate of recovery achieved.

The OECD report on the Irish economy in 1991 readily identified some of the elements of the early success. First was Ireland's commitment to narrow-band membership of the Exchange Rate Mechanism (ERM). This served as the anchor for an anti-inflationary monetary policy. Second was strict compliance with the moderate pay terms of the Programme for National Recovery (PNR). This helped keep wage inflation down, thereby increasing competitiveness. Third was the rapid decline in the Exchequer borrowing requirement (EBR). This reduced the debt-service burden and removed pressures on taxation. All of these factors had an impact by both lowering interest rates and raising business confidence.

Between 1987 and 1990, total employment grew on average by about 13,000 jobs a year. Nevertheless, emigration, which had resumed in the early 1980s, continued. Both combined in helping to ensure a reduction in the numbers out of work, down from 225,000 to 174,500 over the period, while an improved industrial-relations climate saw fewer strikes. But when the rapid rate of economic growth – averaging more than 4 per cent – was also accompanied by a very sharp fall in the fiscal deficit, the result caught nearly everyone by surprise.

For by 1990, and the end of the PNR, the current budget deficit had fallen to 0.7 per cent of GNP – down from 8.3 per cent in 1986. Such a rapid turnaround challenged the norms of fiscal policy and contradicted textbook economics. Normally when government expenditure is cut as drastically as this, severe deflation of the economy follows, resulting in widespread factory closures and rising unemployment. Yet to everyone's surprise, Ireland continued to achieve economic growth. An important, if not the principal, factor in this growth was the dramatic improvement in business confidence, based on an optimistic view of future developments in the economy and the steps the government was taking to bring the public finances back under control. This encouraged business investment. Among academic economists the Irish experience became known as an example of 'expansionary fiscal contraction'. This happens where a decline in government spending still produces a rapid rise in overall economic activity.

However, the real credit for the remarkable turnaround in the Irish economy after 1987 must go to a succession of ministers and governments – from different parties. Even a cursory examination of the record of the various Finance ministers shows a remarkable uniformity of approach on the major economic issues. And without just such a concerted and sustained effort, one thing seems assured: the economic miracle that finally emerged after 1993 would never have occurred.

Certainly, from my vantage point as Minister for Finance in 1987, I can say it would not have happened without the unqualified commitment shown by Charles Haughey as Taoiseach at that time. His contribution was to lead boldly from the front to sustain the momentum required for rapid economic change within a short time-frame, via lower spending, through agreement with the social partners on national pay policy and by pressing for the establishment of the International Financial Services Centre. In particular, the Taoiseach's support was critical whenever the ministers in the major spending departments showed signs of nervousness or weakness when faced with strong public or political resistance to the many unpopular decisions taken by the government. In seeking to turn the economy around so quickly, we faced a formidable challenge against daunting odds.

In government, the most critical relationship is that between the Taoiseach and his Minister for Finance in relation to general budgetary policy and ensuring that budget targets are met. My job, difficult as it was in the adverse set of economic circumstances that existed, was made easier by the unstinting support Charles Haughey gave me throughout. I enjoyed his unqualified backing, and he had my full confidence, and this provided a welcome degree of mutual reassurance. More importantly, I felt that evidence of a very close working partnership between the Taoiseach and his Finance Minister also helped steady the nerve both of the Cabinet and the Fianna Fáil parliamentary party whenever unpopular measures had to be defended publicly.

A minority government without a natural Dáil majority that hopes to push through unpopular but necessary measures faces a difficult challenge. To succeed, it must adopt a very single-minded and uncompromising approach right from the outset. If it does so with conviction, the threat of a serious challenge at a later stage diminishes. In this regard, within weeks of taking office, the first budget was used to signal the government's determination. There, the Taoiseach and I had agreed to aim for a lower current budget deficit than that set by the outgoing Fine Gael government after the break-up of the coalition. The strategy worked. The government's credibility was enhanced, and that was to help the later development of a political and social consensus, via both the Tallaght Strategy and the social-partnership terms of the Programme for National Recovery.

Each finance minister in his own way − myself, Albert Reynolds, Bertie Ahern, Ruairí Quinn and Charlie McCreevy − made a distinct contribution to that success. In my own case, I felt that building strong foundations for economic recovery was my particular contribution during my two-year period in Merrion Street. I prepared, presented and secured the Dáil's approval for the March 1987 and 1988 budgets and I also prepared the 1989 spending estimates which won parliamentary backing before I resigned as Minister to take up my appointment as EU Commissioner for Agriculture.

Albert Reynolds was my successor in Merrion Street. The challenge he faced was to deliver on the government's commitments in the Programme for National Recovery and to help negotiate its successor. Here, the critical element was to ensure the moderate pay terms of the accord were maximised by government tax cuts, thereby raising the real take-home pay of workers. Lower wage costs made Irish industry more competitive and, in turn, this helped stimulate investment and employment and fuel economic growth.

So in the 1989 budget, with the improvement in the public finances, there was finally some scope for tax cuts. The 35 per cent standard rate of tax was lowered by three percentage points, the first such change in some twenty years. The top tax rate was cut from 58 per cent to 56 per cent. Lower personal taxes raised the work incentive, which had been sapped by years of high rates of tax at relatively low rates of income.

A year later, as Albert Reynolds delivered his second budget, he could report substantial progress. On the Programme for National Recovery – which still had a year to run – the critical targets set for government borrowing and stabilisation of the national debt were surpassed. In 1985 interest payments on the public debt had peaked at 9.8 per cent of GDP; by 1990 the figure had dropped to 7.8 per cent of GDP as the success of the stabilisation policies helped reduce interest payments on domestic debt. By now the government's commitment on tax concessions under the social-partnership accord were more than fully honoured. And in return, the moderate pay provisions of the PNR were widely observed. A new medium-term target for the public finances was set, proposing both a debt/GNP target of 100 per cent and balance on the current budget in 1993.

By 1990, Fianna Fáil was in coalition with the Progressive Democrats, and the impetus for tax reform, if anything, was strengthened. The coalition programme – Programme for government – proposed a 25 per cent standard tax rate by 1993, and a single higher rate of tax to be achieved within the government's term in office. In the budget, as a further step towards that goal, the standard rate of tax was reduced by a further two points to 30 per cent, and the top rate was cut to 53 per cent.

However, a year later, the world economic outlook was no longer quite so benign. The Gulf War had begun, and the British and US economies were both in recession. And, in the aftermath of German reunification, the cost of reconstruction in East Germany put upward pressure on interest rates. These adverse external developments took their toll on the domestic economy and made slower growth inevitable. In 1991, a 2.2 per cent growth rate contrasted sharply with the 7.8 per cent achieved the year before. Unemployment began to rise again. Against an increasingly depressed economic background, the government found it harder to reduce borrowing and debt. Negotiating a new centralised pay agreement, the Programme for Economic and Social Progress (PESP), became more important than ever. Once again the social partners in their response proved highly sensitive to the deteriorating external economic environment. In agreeing the terms of a new accord, they broadly followed the lines laid down in the PNR.

But by this time, there was another consideration to be taken into account. Agreement on a single currency was looming on the political horizon, and this presented the government with an additional challenge in economic management. In Maastricht in December 1991, the EU heads of state and government agreed to create the new euro currency by 1997, or by 1999 at the latest. But to complicate matters, Britain obtained an 'opt out' during the Treaty negotiations, leaving Ireland to face a difficult choice. However, to qualify for membership, applicant countries had to meet a series of convergence criteria. Among the requirements for individual countries were:

- Low inflation – within 1.5 per cent of the average of the three lowest rates in the Community.
- A budget deficit no greater than 3 per cent of GDP.
- A public debt/GDP ratio of not more than 60 per cent, or falling rapidly to that level.
- No unilateral devaluation for at least two years before the start of the single currency.

When the new Minister for Finance, Bertie Ahern, came to present the 1992 budget, Charles Haughey had resigned as Taoiseach, to be succeeded by Albert Reynolds. The early nineties were to mark a shift in emphasis away from a singular preoccupation with restoring order to the public finances as the primary means of securing a strong economic recovery. The extra challenge was to ensure the Irish economy was both fit and ready to join the single currency later in the decade. This became a parallel and complementary goal. It meant accepting the discipline imposed by the Maastricht criteria. And so from the very outset, it was clear that Ireland intended to qualify as part of the first wave of countries joining monetary union later in the decade.

The fiscal-policy targets set out in the PESP reflected those parallel objectives: first, to ensure greater balance in the public finances, and to impose the necessary discipline to qualify for EMU. In this regard, reducing the size of the national debt became the greatest single challenge then facing the government. In 1990, the general government debt was some 95 per cent of

GDP, but with the economic slowdown in world markets, rapid progress became harder to achieve. By the autumn, turbulence in the international currency markets threatened to throw Ireland off course.

In some countries – like Britain – currency devaluations are viewed in much the same way military defeats were once regarded. They are seen as a loss of national honour, bordering on humiliation. Devaluation is seen as reflecting the failure of a key aspect of economic policy, therefore it represents a serious setback for the government that presides over such a dramatic reversal. Invariably, the party in power suffers later, when it may pay a heavy electoral price at the polls for misjudging the mood of the foreign-exchange markets. When a government loses the battle to defend the exchange-rate value of its own besieged currency, the financial speculators emerge as the only real winners.

Certainly that was true of the Conservative government in Britain in September 1992. However, when sterling was devalued, it also had serious knock-on consequences for the Irish economy. The result was a five-month-long currency crisis, ending in a devaluation of the Irish pound. But this was much less of a national humiliation for the Irish government, and turned out to be a blessing in disguise.

Britain's initial mistake was to enter the Exchange Rate Mechanism (ERM) in October 1990, at what was soon judged to be an uncompetitive exchange rate. Since Germany was forced to keep interest rates up because of the cost of financing German unification, British rates also remained high in response, since the deutschmark was the anchor currency within the ERM. This combination of high interest rates and an overvalued exchange rate meant that the British economy became less and less competitive.

Matters finally came to a head on Black Wednesday. Overwhelmed by massive speculation against sterling, British Prime Minister John Major was forced to take the currency out of the ERM. On the same day, the international financier George Soros won $1 billion by betting against the British pound. For Major's administration, this very public defeat proved a defining moment. After the currency debacle, his government's political fortunes – like his own – went into a steady but inexorable decline. The Conservative government lost its authority, bitter divisions on Europe were reopened inside the party and old leadership battles were revived.

With devaluation, the sharp fall in the pound's value meant the British government's reputation for economic management was devalued as well. But the real political price John Major had paid only became apparent in the election in 1997. There, the impact of devaluation, party divisions on Europe and leadership challenges all contributed to the Conservatives' worst defeat in 169 years. Labour returned to government with a 179-seat majority at Westminster.

By comparison, the Irish experience of devaluation has proved more benign, both in its political and economic impact. In August 1986, some seven months before the general election, the Fine Gael–Labour coalition was forced to devalue the pound by some 8 per cent against all the ERM currencies. This realignment was seen as an inevitable response to sterling's weakness. However, it took place too late in the coalition's term of office to have much impact either way on the government's fortunes. By then, relations between the parties in government had deteriorated, and within months the coalition partners had negotiated an amicable separation after failing to agree the terms of the 1987 budget.

In fact, the gains from devaluation accrued more to the

incoming minority Fianna Fáil government. The size of the exchange rate adjustment quickly dispelled any lingering currency uncertainty surrounding the value of the Irish pound. Evidence of exchange-rate stability facilitated the steady fall in interest rates in 1987. And just as the lower exchange rate made Irish goods more competitive, the Lawson boom in Britain, then gathering pace, greatly assisted Ireland's export-led economic recovery.

When we entered government in 1987, a stable exchange-rate was seen as a critical part of our overall economic programme, both to keep inflation down and to maintain overall competitive-ness. For the next five years, there were no major currency realignments, and this helped meet both those objectives. But in September 1992, after the exit of the British pound and the Italian lira from the ERM, the Irish economy again faced a serious challenge. The sharp fall in UK interest rates – down from 15 per cent to 8 per cent – meant a much weaker sterling. In turn, this left the Irish pound overvalued against the British currency. In the past, whenever this happened, the foreign-exchange markets assumed an Irish devaluation was only a matter of time. So, not surprisingly, in just a few days in September, over a billion pounds moved out of domestic financial markets, in anticipation of just such a reaction.

Although the defence of the Irish pound extended over many months, it was apparent quite early on that the government was fighting a difficult battle against long odds, and at increasing cost to the real economy. For the currency strategy to succeed, either German interest rates had to fall, or sterling and British interest rates had to rise. Neither happened, at least in the short term. In consequence, high domestic interest rates were needed to defend the Irish pound's value within the ERM. This produced an overvalued exchange rate against sterling, which was now floating outside the currency bloc. The result was a growing loss of competitiveness for firms either selling into the British market or competing against cheaper British imports at home.

Throughout the five months of the currency crisis the government faced major uncertainty in trying to second-guess the British government's intentions on both exchange and interest rates. Quite clearly, Britain was pursuing a competitive devaluation policy outside the ERM. The uncertainty lay with the balance it was trying to achieve between exchange and interest rates in the bid to regain competitiveness. How far would interest rates be allowed to fall and sterling to decline as Britain sought to accelerate economic recovery?

The Irish pound quickly rose from Stg £0.94 to breach parity and by early October had reached Stg £1.105 – its highest-ever level. But for the Irish government, the interest-rate weapon was a very blunt instrument when used as the main means of defending the currency. Over time, the continuation of high interest rates threatened to damage the economy and job prospects.

The government, in an effort to shelter industry from the impact of the loss of competitiveness, set up a 'Market Development Fund', which paid a weekly £50 job subsidy to firms. But clearly there was a limit to what could be endured. Throughout the currency crisis the government tried to show two things by its sustained and costly defence of the Irish pound: first, that the economy could survive sterling's weakness and second, that the refusal to devalue should be seen as the measure of Ireland's commitment to EMU participation as one of the hard-core currencies. The government's greatest fear was that a devaluation, caused yet again by a collapse in sterling, might seriously prejudice Ireland's claims to single currency membership. For if Britain stayed out of the currency union, and the Irish economy was seen as little more than a British satellite, this might be exploited by other member states and used as an excuse to question our suitability for single-currency membership.

However, in the end the defence of the currency proved unsustainable. If the government believed a devaluation was unjustified, given the economic fundamentals, the foreign-exchange market felt it was unavoidable for competitive reasons. The Bundesbank, as Germany's Central Bank, implicitly favoured an Irish devaluation and so was clearly unwilling to lend support to the currency. At home, after six months under siege, there were signs of a weakening in the 'no devaluation' consensus. To the speculators, the currency increasingly looked like a one-way bet. By the end of January 1993, overnight interest rates of 100 per cent had failed to stem the sale of Irish pounds, and there was a danger of a sharp rise in mortgage rates. So when, on January 26, the British government lowered interest rates to 6 per cent, it confirmed the Department of Finance's worst fears.

It meant that sterling had further to fall, and therefore the Irish pound could appreciate further. With the Bundesbank noncommittal in response to urgent requests to intervene in support of the currency, the government was left with little choice. It was forced on 30 January to request a 10 per cent devaluation of the currency within the ERM. However, since over the course of the crisis the Irish pound had appreciated by about a fifth in relation to sterling, the 10 per cent devaluation against the ERM currencies still left it higher against the British currency than it had been at the outset. Far from proving to be a disaster, as the conventional economic wisdom in some quarters had predicted, the devaluation restored a competitive edge to the economy. It laid the foundations for the years of rapid growth from 1993 onwards which became the hallmark of the Celtic Tiger economy.

Throughout the currency crisis, the options facing the government were never easy. If the government refused to devalue, it was putting the economy under strain, especially the small number of vulnerable firms and the mortgage holders faced with higher interest rates and larger monthly repayments. On the other band, the risk of an early devaluation was that it might prove premature. It could threaten to damage permanently Ireland's acceptability as a prospective member of EMU, and it would add considerably to the cost of the national debt.

Certainly, the government's determination to put up a strong defence of the currency made the pound less tempting to the financial speculators. Spain, in contrast, caved in to speculative pressures early on and devalued the peseta. As a direct result, the Spanish currency was devalued on two further occasions. The government's sustained defence of the currency over many months meant that when devaluation finally became unavoidable, it did not damage our chances of joining EMU. We had established our credentials as a serious candidate for future membership.

*

When Bertie Ahern introduced his second budget in February 1993, Fianna Fáil had returned to government, this time in coalition with Labour. However, in the aftermath of the devaluation of the Irish pound, continuing nervousness in financial markets led to a cautious response by the Minister for Finance on fiscal policy. The need to reassure the markets meant the budget measures were restrictive. They were designed to underscore the government's commitment to price and budgetary stability. However, the introduction of a 1 per cent income levy ran counter to the steady progress on tax reform. As a result, one of the tax targets in the PESP – a 25 per cent standard tax rate by 1993 – was not achieved.

Labour's arrival in government marked a shift in taxation policy; the emphasis switched to reducing the tax burden on the lower paid. By contrast, between 1988 and 1992, the middle- and high-income earners were the prime beneficiaries, when direct tax rates were substantially reduced, with the standard rate falling from 35 per cent to 27 per cent and the top rate cut from 58 per cent to 48 per cent.

A year later, against the background of the third centralised pay agreement – the Programme for Competitiveness and Work (PCW) – the emphasis in tax reform also switched from lowering tax rates to broadening tax bands and allowances, to help those on lower incomes. Once again the centrepiece of the new agreement was the trade-off between pay moderation and tax concessions, designed to increase after-tax incomes and raise employment. In gross figures, there was an 8.2 per cent increase in cumulative terms over the three years 1994 to 1996. This approach was designed to give relief where it was most needed, and to raise the incentive to work, by making work more rewarding than welfare for those on low incomes. So, those earning less than £9,000 no longer paid the health and the employment and training levies, while the 1 per cent income levy was abolished. In order to make it more attractive to hire low-paid workers, employers' payroll costs were reduced. A new, lower 9 per cent employer pay related social insurance (PRSI) levy on incomes below £9,000 was introduced.

In December 1994, for the first time in the history of the Dáil, a change of government occurred without a general election taking place. Nevertheless the transition was smooth, with Labour remaining in government, as Fianna Fáil exited. Fine Gael and Democratic Left joined what became known as the Rainbow coalition. With John Bruton as Taoiseach and Ruairí Quinn as Finance Minister, a remarkable continuity in economic policy was maintained.

Since this was Labour's first time holding the key Finance portfolio, it became a litmus test of the party's political maturity. Previously, Labour had always chosen the big spending departments – like health, social welfare and the environment – but as the coalition experience (1982–87) showed, the party had baulked at supporting spending cuts. This time it was Labour's chance to demonstrate it was now a serious party of government, able to manage the government finances while retaining the confidence of both the public and the business sector. However, it must be said the party was fortunate in its timing. Given the benign economic environment, it could not have secured the Finance portfolio at a more opportune moment. Nevertheless, Labour met the challenge.

As Finance Minister, it was Ruairí Quinn who embarked on the policy of cutting the standard rate of corporation tax to 12.5 per cent. Over the next two years, the numbers at work increased by some 120,000, with an average of more than 1,000 new jobs being created each week. Where previously it had taken eight years to achieve these dramatic employment gains, now this was done in just two years. The increased size of the labour force was reflected in the rapid growth in the economy, which expanded by nearly 9 per cent and 6 per cent in 1995 and 1996, respectively. At the same time, inflation remained stable while the debt ratio fell from 88 per cent of GDP in 1994 to 71 per cent two years later.

In the 1995 and subsequent budgets, the emphasis on broadening bands and allowances was maintained. For the third budget in succession, income-tax rates were left unchanged, and it was 1997 before the standard rate was cut to 26 per cent. The change in the focus of tax policy was also an attempt to remove some rigidities in the labour market, by increasing the incentive to employment, both for employer and worker. Employers' PRSI rate was further reduced to 9 per cent on the first £12,000 of the income of each employee, while for employees, the first £50 of weekly earnings was exempt from PRSI contributions.

However, for most of the nineties, different governments tried with less success to limit the increase in public spending to just two per cent in real terms. Invariably, the budget-day target was exceeded by year-end, but fortunately without adverse consequences for the public finances. Since the economy was growing even faster than the rate of increase in public expenditure, government spending was not rising as a proportion of national output. The rapid fall in interest rates since 1993 had cut the interest repayments on the national debt, while buoyant tax revenues from strong economic growth ensured that higher spending and tax reductions could both be readily afforded, without putting undue pressure on the public finances.

So governments over this period found themselves in an ideal position. They were able to pay for the tax cuts needed to underpin the series of centralised pay accords and thereby ensure wage moderation. They could do so without any need for extra borrowing, or without pushing up inflation. And also they had the benefit of Structural Fund transfers from the EU. At the same time, strong growth helped achieve rapid progress towards meeting the Maastricht convergence criteria to ensure Ireland could qualify to join the single currency. Generosity both in the level of spending and the size of the tax cuts was combined with some degree of fiscal rectitude. It was surely the best of times to be a Minister for Finance.

The change of government in June 1997, when Fianna Fáil and the Progressive Democrats were returned to office, was the fifth change of government in just ten years. At other times, as in 1981–82, when there were three elections in eighteen months, political instability and the lack of a clear consensus on the economy greatly hindered economic policy-making. Then, power was something of a poisoned chalice. But not any longer.

The Fianna Fáil–PD coalition was a minority government. It relied for its Dáil majority on support from three Independents, Jackie Healy-Rae, Mildred Fox and Harry Blaney, who were later joined by a fourth, Tom Gildea. Both parties had fought and won the election on a common platform of lower taxes. In office, they moved rapidly in the 1998 budget to fulfil that promise.

As Finance Minister, Charlie McCreevy met with some criticism for his reduction in capital-gains tax (CGT) – down from 40 per cent to 20 per cent. It was a bold move. However, if only to judge by the Department's own revenue estimates – where it projected a £19 million loss as a result of the change – it might have seemed somewhat ill-judged. In fact, McCreevy's decision showed a willingness to buck the conventional wisdom. He had calculated on a lower tax rate generating a far higher revenue take for the Exchequer. And he was fully vindicated. Far from representing a revenue loss, the 1998 yield was some £61 million greater than a year earlier.

Not alone did it release revenue for the Exchequer, the lower tax rate facilitated a greater sale of assets and raised business confidence. Nevertheless it was strongly criticised by both the opposition parties and the trade unions. They claimed it was unfair, and a disproportionate cut. However, previously, the 40 per cent rate meant only that assets – whether business, property or shares – were held until death to avoid any CGT liability. With the change, the lower tax rate both stimulated the more productive use of those assets and raised revenue for the

Exchequer. It showed yet again that 20 per cent of something is far better than 40 per cent of nothing.

When politicians keep faith with the electorate this only adds to their credibility. By doing so they are fulfilling their electoral mandates. Certainly in 1997, the general election, on the economic side, was won and lost on taxation, though public disenchantment with Labour's performance in office contributed to Fianna Fáil's success. Nevertheless, the government was criticised for favouring the better-off at the expense of the poor in the overall balance of the tax changes made. On income tax, there was a shift in emphasis back to reducing tax rates rather than increasing allowances and widening tax bands, as the Rainbow partners had favoured. Following the cut in capital gains to 20 per cent, this tax was lower than the 24 per cent standard rate tax, and less than half the higher 46 per cent rate – both of which were reduced by two points in the new government's first budget.

However, the 1999 budget saw a significant shift. It marked the first stage in the introduction of a tax credits system which made sound economic sense. It brought greater equity into taxation, by providing for the standard rating of personal allowances. This ensured that any increase in allowances was worth the same to all taxpayers, regardless of income. So a £1,000 increase in the basic allowance was worth £240 to those on £10,000 or on £100,000. Before that change, the same increase was worth far more – £460 – to the high earner. Above all, the move to tax credits made it easier – and less expensive for the Exchequer – to take those on low incomes out of the tax net, and therefore to widen the income gap between welfare and work.

For an economy that was enjoying rapid growth but experiencing labour shortages and therefore a risk of wage inflation, the move to tax credits was an appropriate response. Employment bottlenecks were appearing in some labour-intensive industries. Easing the tax burden on the low-paid helped boost the labour supply by making work more rewarding than welfare. The budget-day measure resulted in the single person on £100 a week no longer being liable for tax. Without it, the existing social partnership (Partnership 2000) accord could have been undermined, and hope of a new agreement jeopardised.

The strong state of the public finances allowed the Minister to finance a tax package of more than half a billion pounds while still projecting a budget surplus of nearly £1 billion in 1999. Certainly, the move towards tax credits represents the most fundamental reform in the tax system in years.

Thus, in twelve years, the Irish economy has been transformed in a way few would have thought possible in 1987. The public finances are not just back in balance, but in surplus; debt has been brought under control, while taxes have been reduced sharply, enabling Ireland to experience the fastest rate of employment growth in the EU, while unemployment has fallen dramatically. The figures speak for themselves:

- government debt as a proportion of GDP stood at 116 per cent in 1987 and had fallen to 55 per cent by 1998 but is expected to drop to 43 per cent by 2001.
- The current budget surplus reached some £2 billion in 1998, compared with a deficit of £1.4 billion in 1986.
- The 1990s have seen a decade of rapid economic growth, with GDP averaging 7 per cent annually, and some 9 per cent since 1993.
- Tax rates have fallen sharply: in 1987, the standard rate of income tax was 35 per cent and the higher rate

was 58 per cent. By 1999 these rates had fallen to 24 per cent and 46 per cent respectively.

- An average rate of inflation of some 3 per cent has been achieved since 1987, and Ireland's rate of inflation has been well below the EU rate over the period.
- The tide of emigration has been reversed: between 1996 and 1998, net inward immigration reached 38,000.

5

Social Partnership

Ray Mac Sharry

In the countries where national consensus and collaboration have been most successfully developed, the point of origin was usually some pressing emergency. In Sweden, the Basic Agreement arose out of a breakdown in industrial relations. In many other European countries, the impetus came from economic ruin following war and enemy occupation. If Ireland were to face a major economic crisis (for example, in servicing and refinancing foreign debts) a similar result might follow. The question is whether it is possible to force the pace of consensus and public understanding on long-term objectives and methods, in areas covered by the National Agreements and Understandings, so as to head off a major crisis, before the crash barriers are actually hit.

Pay Policy for the 80s (1982)

Recently, the Swedish Employers Federation turned to Ireland to study our model of social partnership in a bid to learn from that experience. In doing so they paid us a flattering compliment, for it seemed somewhat like the master taking lessons from the pupil. Sweden had pioneered the social-partnership model earlier this century and Ireland, for much of the past thirty years, has experimented with that basic template. Successive governments have adapted it to meet Irish conditions and our domestic pay-bargaining needs, and they have done so with different degrees of success. But if the Swedish model has faltered in recent times, the Irish version of social consensus has flourished, particularly since 1987. The series of four national agreements between government, employers, unions and farmers laid secure foundations for what has come to be regarded as the Irish economic miracle of the 1990s.

The parallels between the Irish and Swedish experience are interesting. In June 1981 the Federated Union of Employers (FUE) set up an expert group to examine pay policy for the decade ahead. At that stage, a succession of national wage agreements, followed by national understandings, had operated since 1970, but with mixed results. By then, both employers and unions, for different reasons, had begun to question their continuing utility. The FUE experts, who included Professor Michael Fogarty, Dr Louden Ryan and Dermot Egan, were asked to consider the alternatives. Having examined the experience of centralised bargaining over the nine different national agreements in that eleven-year period, one of the many conclusions the authors reached in their 'Pay Policy for the 1980s' report was that national agreements or understandings were still needed. However they entered a caveat: that some improvements and changes were also required to justify their continuation.

In particular, they felt the government, given its involvement in a dual capacity both as public-service employer and manager of the national economy, should, as one of the key social partners, play a much more assertive role in the negotiating process. Specifically, the authors argued that the government should use its strong bargaining position to try and build a realistic consensus on pay.

Drawing on their research, the authors noted that in the countries where a national consensus on pay bargaining had developed most successfully, it usually originated in some 'pressing emergency'. In Sweden, this followed a breakdown in industrial relations in the 1930s, while in countries like Germany, the impetus came from the ruinous economic conditions that followed war and military defeat. They conjectured that 'If Ireland were to face a major economic crisis (for example, in servicing and refinancing foreign debts) a similar result might follow.' And they went on to question 'whether it is possible to force the pace of consensus and public understanding on long-term objectives and methods, in areas covered by the National Agreements and Understandings, so as to head off a major crisis, before the crash barriers are actually hit'.

The question was posed in 1981. However, it was not to be answered for some time. At that stage, centralised bargaining had been temporarily abandoned, and it did not resume until 1987. By then just such a 'pressing emergency' had occurred, and it took the form of the crisis state of the public finances. The 'crash barriers' had been well and truly hit. However, like Sweden and Germany, a social consensus on how to handle it was emerging slowly in response. This was first established by the NESC document *A Strategy for Development 1986–1990*. There, in the autumn of 1986, all the social partners both recognised the scale of the problems in the public finances and supported the tough remedies that were needed to overcome these. Within a year, that critical NESC blueprint had been turned into a centralised pay and non-pay agreement involving government, unions, employers and farmers. As envisaged in 1982, the crisis had to happen. Yet when it did, the reaction from the social partners was better, and the pace of economic recovery faster, than anyone had dared expect – not least, perhaps, the authors themselves.

The Programme for National Recovery was finally agreed on 9 October 1987, but the seeds of success had been sown many years before. I viewed the Programme as essentially a continuation of the economic approach outlined in the 1982 national plan, *The Way Forward*, and further refined some four years later by the NESC report.

A common factor in the documents was Pádraig Ó hUiginn. He had been chiefly responsible for persuading the then government to adopt *The Way Forward*. And when he was appointed Chairman of the NESC in early 1985, he recognised the urgency of addressing the steady deterioration in the public finances. Traditionally, the Council produced an annual economic- and social-policy report, with a short-term perspective. However, Ó hUiginn knew the economic problems the country was then facing could not be dealt with adequately within such a limited time-frame. Instead, the NESC set its review in a medium-term context and provided a comprehensive analysis of the challenges ahead.

The NESC conclusions were far-reaching in their impli-cations. As the preface to the report noted, 'The fact that the various interests have been able to agree on the major elements of an integrated strategy and on the general policies for the major sectors of the economy should be a substantial help to government.' This was a very modest understatement of a highly significant achievement: the social partners had accepted the need for tough remedial measures as part of an integrated strategy, set in a medium-term context. Having looked into the economic abyss, it seemed that all those involved – employers, unions and farmers – had stepped back and had then acted in concert to check a national drift towards disaster. However, given the coalition government's state of political disarray at the time of publication of the NESC report, with Labour, as the minority partner, refusing to accept spending cuts and preparing an agreed exit from office, both government parties found themselves badly placed to exploit the report's potential. At that time, Fine Gael, ideologically, was ill at ease with social partnership and averse to conceding any outside influence over tax and social-welfare policy. Instead, the economic blueprint was to prove much more helpful to Fianna Fáil after the general election in February 1987.

The NESC report, which was sold out within three months of publication, boldly challenged politicians generally to follow the lead set by the social partners. They had accepted a balanced package of measures which, in the medium term, might ensure economic redemption. But, in the short term, implementing an austerity programme would involve considerable pain and sacrifice, not least for the trade unions and their members. Reducing the current budget deficit on the scale required involved sharp reductions in spending if debt stabilisation was to be achieved and debt reduction was to follow.

The compensating benefit on offer to the unions was tax reform, with the essential trade-off being pay restraint via moderate wage increases in return for tax cuts by the government to boost the real, after-tax income of workers. Yet what was most impressive was the unanimity of the social partners' support and their acceptance that tough measures were unavoidable.

Nevertheless, the question lurking in everyone's mind was how long such a consensus would last. Was it more than good intentions, and would it survive the attempt to translate word into deed? In other words, would it be possible to turn a commitment in principle and on paper into an agreement in practice that was binding on all those who accepted it?

During the interregnum, after the February 1987 election and before the formation of the new government, Charles Haughey as Fianna Fáil leader had been fully briefed by Ó hUiginn, as NESC Chairman. Ó hUiginn assured Haughey the trade union endorsement of NESC was a real commitment and not just empty rhetoric. And he told the Taoiseach he was confident he could deliver the essence of the NESC report, recast as a comprehensive new centralised agreement negotiated between the social partners. However, Pádraig Ó hUiginn set one condition. He wanted greater operational freedom in that role. He was willing to become involved in negotiations on the proposed new programme only if he could report directly to the Taoiseach and myself as Finance Minister and take instructions from us.

At the same time, Haughey had sounded out the top trade union leaders. He had made his determination clear to those, like the general secretary of the Federated Workers Union of Ireland, Billy Attley (later general secretary of SIPTU), that he was going to turn the economy around. As Attley later remarked, 'The subtext was that we could either be part of the solution or part of the problem.' By that stage the unions were clearly part of the solution. They had sensed, correctly, the government's clear will to succeed this time, either with or without them.

Negotiations on the new agreement continued throughout the summer and autumn of 1987. From the outset, the greatest obstacle was the scepticism of the employers, given their disillusion with aspects of centralised bargaining. Their suspicion was that the agreement would prove more apparent than real. In particular they were concerned that the pay terms would become a floor – from which unions would bargain for higher wages – rather than a ceiling that would limit pay demands to the strict terms of the agreement. In other words, they feared a return to past patterns of behaviour where, too often, national wage accords had been loosely interpreted and wage inflation had eroded competitiveness.

But this time, there were a number of important differences about the Programme for National Recovery. First, it was not just a pay agreement. Instead, it was an ambitious attempt to create real social partnership for the first time. In this respect, both the pay and non-pay elements would represent equally significant parts. The overriding challenge was to rescue the economy. And so the PNR was also seen by those negotiating its terms as a programme for national survival.

The employers knew that the consensus reached on the NESC report had helped establish a new realism on all sides. Even if the unions tried to break their commitment, as some employers had feared, they would pay a price. Pádraig Ó hUiginn had made this clear to the employers, by way of reassurance. For a start, he explained, if they failed to keep their side of the bargain they risked losing the tax relief that was spread over the three-year life of the Programme. Although that threat might prove hard for the government to implement, it nevertheless indicated our seriousness on the matter. We wanted to ensure that tax cuts – designed to boost small increases in gross pay – would follow pay restraint, and not precede it. In these circumstances, the downside risk for employers was minimal, and their continuing reservations were overcome. And so they signed up.

For the trade unions, in fact, there was little choice. Union membership was falling. Between 1980 and 1987, it had dropped steadily and was set to contract further and faster. So unless the rise in unemployment was checked, and the tide of emigration reversed, then the unions themselves had a bleak future. This meant rectifying the imbalance in public finances in the first instance. In addition, the unions also found themselves squeezed between recession and the arrival of the new market-led economics. In political terms this became the 'new right' phenomenon: in Britain under Margaret Thatcher, in the United States under Ronald Reagan, and latterly in Ireland with the electoral success achieved by the newly formed Progressive Democrats at the 1987 election.

Unless the unions adapted to these changed circumstances and found a new role for themselves, they risked being marginalised and becoming irrelevant. Their leaders recognised as much. For the unions, social partnership offered power with responsibility, and a way of adapting to those changed circumstances. Since 1980, and the ending of a series of national tripartite agreements, the unions exercised their power through decentralised pay bargaining but had no great influence over the direction of government policy.

As they looked across the Irish Sea to the British trade union experience under Mrs Thatcher, the union leadership were dismayed by unfolding developments there. They had seen how the Trade Union Council (TUC), which until 1979 had co-operated with government and business in formulating economic policy, had lost its access to government. The British Prime Minister had defeated the miners and introduced a series of legislative reforms to curb union rights, like banning secondary picketing. The Irish trade union leadership were quick to recognise that European-style social partnership promised far more for their members than the traditional confrontational approach on pay. As the Irish Congress of Trade Unions (ICTU) General Secretary, Peter Cassells, remarked at the time, 'We

Seán Lemass: 'The historic task of this generation is to secure the economic foundation of independence.'

Donogh O'Malley: His free secondary-education initiative in 1967 served as the catalyst for the education revolution that followed.

Taoiseach Charles Haughey with EU Commission President Jacques Delors, whose support for Ireland's case for Structural Funds receipts was significant.

Ray Mac Sharry with – from left – Secretary of the Department of Finance Seán Cromien and Governor of the Central Bank Maurice Doyle at the Currency Centre in Sandyford, County Dublin.

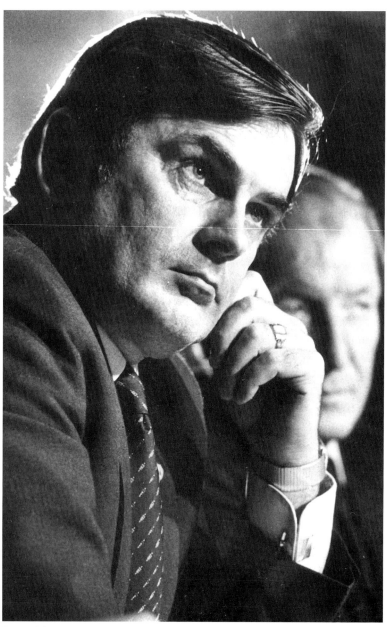

Launching the battle to regain control of the public finances: Finance Minister Ray Mac Sharry with Taoiseach Charles Haughey in 1987.

Pádraig Ó hUigínn played a vital role in securing social partnership, both as chairman of the NESC and, as Secretary of the Department of the Taoiseach, in subsequent negotiations.

SIPTU General Secretary Billy Attley with fellow trade-union leader Phil Flynn, General Secretary of IMPACT. Attley and Flynn were critical influences in favour of social partnership on the trade-union side.

Irish Congress of Trade Unions general secretary Peter Cassells epitomised the new style of trade-union leadership that emerged in the late 1980s.

Government ministers – from left to right, Minister for Energy and Communications Ray Burke, Minister for Labour Bertie Ahern, Taoiseach Charles Haughey, Minister for Finance Ray Mac Sharry, Minister for Industry and Commerce Albert Reynolds – and Pádraig Ó hUigínn, Secretary to Department of the Taoiseach, open discussions with representatives of the employers on the Programme for National Recovery in 1987.

The EU Commission in 1989 with Commission President Jacques Delors and Commissioner for Agriculture Ray Mac Sharry.

Ireland's EU Commissioner Peter Sutherland meets Minister for Finance Ray Mac Sharry at a social occasion in Dublin's Abbey Theatre in November 1988.

Bertie Ahern: As Minister for Labour and later Minister for Finance and Taoiseach, Ahern's contacts with trade-union leaders have proved critical in cementing social partnership.

took the view that the most acceptable models on which to build a Programme for National Recovery should be successful European countries such as Austria, Denmark, Finland, Norway and Sweden. These countries have rejected the confrontationist approach of the New Right and have lower levels of unemployment than the US or the UK.'

Cassells epitomised the new style of trade union leadership that emerged in the mid to late eighties. He preferred to look forward in confidence to what could be achieved through dialogue and cooperation between the social partners, rather than perpetuate outdated divisions between employers and unions. In 1987, he was one of the principal negotiators of the PNR, and served on the central review committee set up to monitor the implementation of the agreement. A year later, when he succeeded Donal Nevin as general secretary of the ICTU, he was in his late thirties, and well positioned to influence the development of social partnership over the next three national agreements.

His arrival at the top both coincided with, and increasingly shaped, the changing attitudes of trade unions to pay bargaining. Trade union militancy was less in evidence. The unions, as social partners, were concerned with a broader agenda than pay. They sought to exercise greater influence over the direction of economic policy in the non-pay areas. Equally, on the government side, Bertie Ahern, as a young Minister for Labour, was quick to see the significance of the shift in trade union thinking and its importance in securing the foundations for economic recovery. And he, too, was to play an important role in the evolution of social partnership over the next decade.

Negotiations on the PNR succeeded because all the parties, through their earlier involvement in NESC, were familiar with the scale of the problems facing the economy. They could not contemplate failure. To the government and employers, the value of the agreement was the certainty it provided on pay costs for a three-year period. If this was critical for maintaining competitiveness, it was also a vital first step in bringing the national finances into balance. With public-service pay accounting for half of all current spending, controlling that cost was a major part of the budgetary exercise.

For the trade unions, the social-partnership model, as it has developed over four agreements and more than ten years, also provided them with huge benefits. Union leaders have secured an access to government they had never previously enjoyed. Through the Central Review Committee, the social partners meet on a regular basis with government representatives to review and make recommendations on economic and social progress. This enables all the social partners to have a continuing input into government decision-making. It has allowed the union negotiators to make connections between pay and the provision of services in a way never previously attempted. Above all, this consultative role has provided a valuable political and economic education for those involved in making decisions on the best use of scarce of resources. In particular, the unions have learned that some of the more ambitious changes they sought – in areas like taxation and expenditure – could only be achieved over the lifetime of a series of national agreements. This gave them every incentive to pursue a medium-term strategy in negotiation, thereby helping ensure not only the evolution of the social-partnership model but also its survival for longer than most thought possible.

Indeed, there was a certain irony that the unions should have agreed such a comprehensive Programme with a new Fianna Fáil government in 1987. After all, just months earlier, in January, Labour – the political wing of the trade union movement – had walked out of government when it could not agree a budget with its Fine Gael partner, because of the proposed spending cuts. Throughout the coalition's tenure in office in the mid-eighties, the unions, despite the traditional Labour connection, were always kept at what they felt was an arm's length from power. Of course the political reality was that many trade union members were Fianna Fáil and not Labour supporters, and the attitude of the union leadership may have reflected that reality to some degree. But there were other factors as well. Indeed in trade unions circles it was often said that the union leadership preferred dealing with Fianna Fáil in government than with Labour. In that way they could do business with Fianna Fáil while also ensuring the Labour Party in opposition kept pressure on the government on their behalf. But with Labour in office, they felt they were somehow handicapped.

Historically, Fianna Fáil was more closely associated with centralised bargaining than any other party. In fact the first national wage agreement in 1970 arose directly from the threat by a Fianna Fáil administration to introduce a statutory incomes policy unless a moderate voluntary agreement between employers and unions was reached. But when Fine Gael and Labour entered government in mid-1981, and again in December 1982, the series of national agreements were slipping out of fashion. No longer were they strongly favoured by unions, employers or indeed by the incoming coalition itself.

After his retirement, Taoiseach Garret FitzGerald explained that his government would have liked to secure a PNR-style settlement but was deterred both by the hostility of the unions and the high level of inflation, which stood at 21 per cent in 1982. By 1986, that figure had been cut to over 3 per cent and represented one of the coalition's most singular economic achievements during its term in office. And that low inflation level also made it easier for the incoming Fianna Fáil government to press for moderate pay increases – some 2.5 per cent annually – for the three years of the lifetime of the PNR.

By contrast, Fianna Fáil had maintained steady contacts with the trade union movement. In 1984, Charles Haughey had discussions with the ICTU Executive on its own proposed national plan. This meant that when the NESC report was agreed with the social partners and formed the blueprint for the PNR negotiations, agreement was not that difficult to reach, given the degree of goodwill and trust that had already been established. For the unions, there was the desire to avoid marginalisation and exercise greater influence over economic decision-making. For the employers, the pay element of the PNR was unlikely to be lower in free collective bargaining. For the government, pay moderation was a critical first step in bringing the public finances back into balance. The terms of the Programme offered an attractive combination of pay restraint with a certainty about pay costs over a relatively long period – three years from 1988 to 1990 – all of which provided a boost to competitiveness at a critical time.

Unlike earlier national agreements and understandings, the Programme extended for three years to 1990. It included goals for fiscal adjustment, pay, sectoral development policies, tax reform and the pursuit of social equity. Stabilising the debt to GNP ratio over the lifetime of the PNR was a key objective, and this entailed a reduction in the Exchequer Borrowing Requirement to between 5 and 7 per cent of GNP, depending on economic growth and interest rates. The Programme provided for annual public-service pay increases up to 2.5 per cent over the three-year period, with the rises weighted in favour of the lower-paid, annually in each of the years 1988, 1989 and 1990.

In return for pay moderation, the government promised

income-tax concessions totalling some £225 million over the three years to ensure that two-thirds of tax-payers were on the standard rate. In addition the government pledged to maintain the overall value of social-welfare benefits and to extend social insurance to farmers and the self-employed from 1988. In fact in early 1990, when the Central Review Committee examined the progress made under the various headings of the PNR, perhaps the greatest success had been achieved in the tax area. The total value of income-tax reliefs at over £800 million in the three years was nearly four times the original government commitment.

When the PNR was announced in the Burlington Hotel on October 14, at a government press conference, the platform was shared with those who had made it possible – the social partners. Indeed, at the same venue five years earlier *The Way Forward* had been launched, with much less fanfare. But this time, the social partners, quite deservedly, stole the limelight, while government ministers sat demurely behind the trade union bosses. However, the agreement met with a mixed political response. All the opposition leaders, to a greater or lesser degree, were critical. Labour leader Dick Spring called on the ICTU to repudiate the Programme for National Recovery. He claimed it contained 'decisions which are hostile to the interests of working people'. He was particularly concerned by what he described as 'the most disturbing feature' of the document: that the national debt would be stabilised by 1990, but that no details had been given outlining the policy measures to achieve that goal. Yet ironically, the Irish Creamery Milk Suppliers Association (IMCSA), which represented mainly small farmers, had refused to sign up to the Programme. The ICMSA claimed the trade unions had exercised too great an influence over its content.

In contrast, the media reaction was much more encouraging.

An *Irish Times* editorial headed 'Haugheynomics' noted: 'Today may yet be Mr Haughey's finest hour. The headlines and the generalities may gain life in the unveiling of a new approach to the Irish economy, a strategy which will really manage to create jobs while reducing borrowing.' With hindsight, it probably was one of his most significant and far-reaching achievements in politics.

However, the real significance of the PNR was the social partnership model that was established. It was a return to centralised pay bargaining after a six-year gap. But this time the social partners showed a much greater degree of realism in the goals they pursued and in the time period − three years − in which they sought to achieve them.

*

The PNR was the first of four highly successful centralised agreements over more than a decade that have helped produce a remarkable transformation in the Irish economy, thanks to social partnership. Pay moderation has helped boost competitiveness and raise employment and growth. The industrial-relations climate has improved dramatically, with fewer days lost in industrial disputes. The fiscal correction achieved through controlling public spending and stabilising and reducing the size of the national debt has helped keep inflation low and underpin a stable exchange rate.

But the significance of the change since 1987 may best be gauged by taking a closer look at the slow evolution of pay bargaining over recent decades. The sixties saw the end of decentralised bargaining, amid industrial discontent and rapid wage inflation. The seventies became the decade of national wage agreements which − from 1979 − were called national understandings, with the framework extended to include government as a social partner. However, by 1981, this form of social partnership had ended in disappointment and some loss of credibility. So the early to mid-eighties saw a return to decentralised wage bargaining for the private sector, while the government negotiated a series of public-service pay agreements. By 1987, the crisis in the public finances had led to a revival of the social consensus approach, but this time in a more rigorous form. Throughout, these pendulum shifts between centralised and decentralised bargaining were responses to economic difficulties of varying proportions. They can also be seen as part of a long learning curve in the refinement and development of the social-partnership model.

The 'decade of upheaval' was how Charles McCarthy characterised the poor state of industrial relations in the 1960s, in a phrase which became the title of his book. It was a decade of strong economic growth and deteriorating industrial relations, with strikes by Dublin busmen and gravediggers and a six-month bank stoppage by the Associated Banks among the more dramatic events. However, the most damaging dispute came right at the end of the decade. In 1969, the strike by maintenance craftsmen was then regarded as the most serious work stoppage in the state's history. But it also proved to be a defining moment in the development of pay bargaining by employers, unions and government over the next three decades.

The nationwide dispute not only caused widespread disruption to industry, it weakened the authority of the trade union leadership; divisions opened, and then widened, between craft and general unions. On the picket line, striking craftsmen came face to face with their fellow workers, who staged counter-picketing demonstrations in protest at being laid off. The settlement terms to end the dispute were high – a 20 per cent increase over 18 months – and led to a series of escalating pay claims. In some instances, increases of 50 per cent and more were sought. The new wage round threatened to produce a damaging free-for-all, and, for the economy, a serious loss of competitiveness at a critical time. For Ireland was gearing up for membership of the EEC within a matter of years.

The gravity of the industrial-relations problem was reflected in the bleak strike statistics. In 1969, the number of man-days lost in industrial disputes was 936,000 and by the following year even that figure had been surpassed, reaching 1,008,000. By contrast, the average for the years 1961 to 1968 was less than half that, at 398,000. Against that background, the National Industrial and Economic Council (NIEC), the forerunner of the NESC, issued an important report, which triggered the first move towards more centralised pay bargaining and away from the series of more informal post-war pay rounds. These earlier settlements were either the product of a combination of local and national negotiations or reflected significant – headline – pay settlements in different sectors of industry that became national pay norms. These rounds had operated since 1946, when the wartime restrictions on pay movements were lifted.

The NIEC report on incomes and prices policy favoured a change of emphasis. The Council proposed to set down annual pay guidelines, but this was rejected by the ICTU in 1970 at its annual conference. Nevertheless, Congress was chastened by the experience of the maintenance dispute and by now favoured a more centralised approach to pay bargaining. In particular, the ICTU supported two of the key institutional recommendations in the NIEC document. These proposed the establishment of the National Prices Commission and a revitalised National Employer-Labour Conference (NELC). The government set up both, against the background of a deteriorating industrial-relations climate. The NELC provided the framework for centralised pay negotiations. As employers and unions tried, and initially failed, to finalise the terms of a national pay agreement, the government was forced to intervene. It introduced a Prices and Incomes Bill, which provided a legislative basis for the government to operate a statutory incomes and prices policy. Under the terms of the bill, Ministers proposed to restrict wage rises to 7 per cent and to keep prices under control. No sooner were employers and unions faced with the government threat to impose this legislation than they resumed negotiations and quickly reached agreement.

The result was the first of the series of national agreements and understandings that were reached over the next decade (1970–81). These initially bipartite (employers and unions) and later tripartite (government, employers and unions) accords changed their format over time. After a break in 1981, and a return to decentralised bargaining, the national-consensus approach was resumed in 1987, with a series of comprehensive multipartite social-partnership arrangements. But as centralised bargaining evolved over the decades, nothing changed more than the role of government in the whole process. Before the first National Wage Agreement in 1970, the government was a largely passive social partner, following rather than leading.

In general, it allowed private sector bargaining to set wage-round norms and, invariably, these were matched by the public sector. But from 1970 onwards, the role of government was forced to change. By the necessity of economic circumstance, it was compelled to become more interventionist and sought to influence more directly the outcome of national pay bargaining. The reasons were clear: first, its role as the state's largest employer, and second, its responsibility as an economic manager. In its employer role, the annual public-service pay bill was the largest single item of current spending and had to be financed from general taxation. And as an economic manager, the government also knew that private-sector competitiveness required non-inflationary wage settlements, with productivity rising faster than the rate of real pay increase.

In all there were some nine centralised pay agreements negotiated under the auspices of the Employer–Labour Conference, in three different phases over the 1970 to 1981 period. Each phase reflected an increasing involvement by government as an influence in the pay-bargaining process. In the first phase, from 1970 to 1974, the three national accords were solely between employers and unions. The only issue for discussion was pay, with the government attending in its role as employer. In phase two, between 1975 and 1978, the government became more involved in its role as manager of the national economy. In that capacity, it sought to secure pay moderation by offering some non-pay concessions on tax and social insurance in the budget. And in the third phase, where national agreements were broadened into the two national understandings in 1979 and 1980, the government played an even more central role, where a range of policies on employment, taxation, industrial relations and social welfare became matters for negotiation and agreement.

However, the economic background against which these national accords were negotiated in the seventies was far from favourable, given the inflationary impact of the oil-price rises in both 1973 and 1979. Initially, the impact of centralised bargaining saw a sharp reduction in the number of industrial disputes between 1971 and 1976, by comparison with the previous five-year period. But by 1979, with some 1.4 million days lost, Ireland was heading the international strike league table. At the same time, under the impact of the second oil crisis, which saw the oil price rise to more than $40 a barrel, both inflation and unemployment rose as economic growth contracted. By 1981, after more than ten years of centralised bargaining, an inevitable disillusionment with national agreements had set in among the social partners, as the economy turned down.

For workers, high inflation – again running at some 20 per cent – and high taxes eroded the value of pay rises. This led to huge street protests on tax by the PAYE sector in 1979 and 1980. Instinctively, many workers felt they might fare better with a return to local bargaining. The trade union leadership was critical of the government's failure to deliver on its job-creation targets. Employers were unhappy with the rising number of industrial disputes and the evidence of wage drift, with an increasing number of special pay claims negotiated above the standard terms of the pay agreement. But the government too found itself with less and less room to manoeuvre, given the rapid deterioration in the public finances as economic growth slowed under the impact of the oil-price rise. A rising budget deficit and an increasing national debt meant there was less scope for fiscal expansion to finance the employment measures.

So when negotiations for a new centralised agreement broke down in 1981, the newly elected Fine Gael–Labour government refused to intervene. Instead, there was a return to decentralised bargaining for the private sector for the next six years, while the government negotiated the first of a series of Public Service Pay Agreements (PSPAs) with the Public Services Committee of Congress. However, seven months later, in July 1982, within months of taking office as Minister for Finance, I was forced to take drastic action to keep public-service pay costs under greater control, with the government agreeing to a package of measures, including a freeze on special pay increases, a further extension of the existing embargo on recruitment in the public service and deferment of the third-phase payment of the PSPA.

Over the next four years (1983–86), the government sought to become the trend-setter in pay determination, both to keep pay costs – both public and private – down and to reduce inflation. By the end of the government's term, the annualised increase in public-service pay rates had dropped to 5 per cent, with the private sector following the lead set. But as Garret FitzGerald wrote in his autobiography, *All in a Life*, the achievement on public-sector pay was hard won, for the trade unions 'were clearly unhappy with our determined stand'. He found that throughout the coalition's term 'meetings between us and the ICTU were formal, often tense, and on the whole unproductive.' In part, he felt, this reflected an underlying sense of resentment at Labour's participation in the government. Certainly, the experience left the trade unions much better disposed to the return to centralised bargaining promised by Fianna Fáil.

Why have the latest four national partnership agreements in the decade since 1987 succeeded so well, by comparison with the disappointing performance of their predecessors in the seventies – the national agreements and understandings? There are many reasons, but an important one was that in redesigning the partnership model, past mistakes were recognised and not repeated. The social partners were more experienced and wiser, and the gravity of the crisis in the public finances was more apparent. So in the Programme for National Recovery, the trade-off between pay and non-pay issues became much more specific. The agreement on pay was negotiated within the framework of a broad national programme, as part of a wider policy agenda. And this time, it was underpinned by a strong and broad social consensus.

As the NESC report *Strategy into the 21st Century* pointed out, this linking of pay and non-pay matters was critical.

Agreement on wages was tied to agreement on a range of economic and social policy issues – ranging from macroeconomic stability to tax reform and employment. This was one of the most significant changes in the approach to centralised bargaining from the PNR onwards.

But among the social partners too, a greater air of economic realism was evident. They quickly recognised their own inter-dependence. The social partners knew their own individual goals – as employers and workers – would be best secured through a balanced accommodation of those interests. By trading pay restraint for tax concessions, everyone gained. However, import-antly, none gained at the expense either of the other or of the economy as a whole.

The worker welcomed the boost that tax cuts gave to after-tax earnings, and so pay restraint was mitigated by tax relief. The employer was reassured by the certainty a three-year agreement on wage costs provided, the boost it gave to competitiveness and the encouragement it offered both for planning and investment. The government was also a winner on two counts. As an employer, pay moderation ensured a smaller increase in the public-service pay bill; and as manager of the national economy, wage restraint was the cornerstone of the macroeconomic policies the government was pursuing as it sought to bring the public finances back into balance.

By contrast with the experience of the national agreements in the seventies, the social partners enjoyed a greater shared understanding on economic issues. All the social partners knew they must operate within tight fiscal constraints if debt stabilisation and reduction were to be secured. And they fully accepted that pursuit of higher real living standards – via a combination of pay moderation and tax cuts – must be consistent with the overriding imperatives of low inflation, national competitiveness, increased employment and prudent management of the public finances. Equally, the external discipline imposed by the Maastricht convergence criteria in order to qualify for membership of the single currency also helped.

The social consensus underpinning the four agreements since 1987 was, and remains, both stronger and broader than that established by the earlier series of national agreements and understandings. In the PNR, for the first time, farmers signed on as social partners, and in later programmes community and voluntary groups were also included. The Programme for Economic and Social Progress (PESP) saw a new approach to local development, by using area-based partnerships to tackle long-term unemployment. And later, in Partnership 2000, collaboration at the enterprise level was developed. Social partnership in Ireland has both widened and deepened, as it has evolved and developed.

Inflation too presented far fewer problems, unlike before. By the time of the 1987 PNR agreement, inflationary expectations had been wound down by the actions of the Fine Gael–Labour government. The inflation rate had fallen from 20 per cent in 1981 to under 4 per cent by 1986. Throughout the seventies, high inflation made pay moderation more difficult to secure, particularly since indexation was built into some of those national accords. As wages and prices chased each other higher, it became harder to check the inflationary wage-price spiral. But by 1987, the return to a low-inflation environment greatly facilitated pay moderation, while the government commitment to public-spending control, and to a strong exchange rate, also helped reduce any inflationary pressures building up in the economy.

On the industrial-relations front too, an equally significant transformation had taken place. The sharp deterioration in industrial relations at the end of the seventies eroded confidence – particularly among employers – in the effectiveness of national agreements. By 1987, the number of days lost in strikes had been scaled back dramatically. And indeed by 1994, this figure, at 25,550, was at its lowest level since 1922. Against a background of far fewer strikes, the social partners established a greater degree of mutual trust.

Since 1987, the four partnership agreements have averaged three years – similar to the life span of a government but more than twice as long as the previous national accords, where the duration varied between twelve and eighteen months. The change in length of the agreements has also meant the adoption of a medium- rather than a short-term perspective on the economy. And with it, as Paddy Teahon, Secretary of the Department of the Taoiseach and Chairman of the NESC, has observed, has come a 'switch from a technocratic, forecasting-based system to one that focuses clearly on strategic issues'. Instead of attempting to forecast employment and unemployment, which, he admits, they often got wrong, now the focus is on strategic issues – pay moderation, tax cuts and sound macro-economic policies – that have resulted in higher employment levels.

He has identified the three dimensions that help explain the success Ireland had achieved in operating national partnership as:

- strategy – the thinking on substance;
- structure – the institutional framework;
- and culture – the attitudes and behaviours of those involved in this case in the social-partnership process.

However, strategy itself is not sufficient to achieve a successful outcome, he argues, and must be set in an implementation framework of structure and culture. As a central figure in the development of the partnership process, Teahon is better placed to judge than anyone else.

Moreover, he has illustrated his arguments with concrete examples. On strategy, or longer-term thinking on content, he cites the series of agreements reached by the social partners that the public finances should be managed so that expenditure is kept under tight control and the debt burden is reduced, while still allowing the government some scope for tax reductions. In this way, moderate pay increases were enhanced by tax cuts.

For structure, or the institutional framework, the role of the NESC has proved critical. The Council has been involved from the outset in the preparation of the various national programmes. The social partners come together to agree on the issues to be dealt with by a new agreement, and to make recommendations. When the programme has been negotiated and agreed, the central review committee monitors its implementation.

The culture of social partnership is reflected in the participants' attitudes and behaviour, which have been developed over more than a decade. The participants, given their strong commitment to the partnership approach, are more prepared to communicate openly, and this greater informality helps ease any negotiating difficulties.

A measure of the success of national partnership has been its huge contribution to the remarkable economic progress achieved since 1987, over the lifetime of four such national accords. Though not the only factor in that success, it was undoubtedly one of the major ones. Indeed social partnership could well be regarded as the crowning achievement of the Celtic Tiger economy. A checklist indicates why:

- The series of four social-partnership deals has reversed the decline in real take-home pay prior to 1987. Since then average industrial earnings have increased by 58 per cent. But the rise in take-home pay – after tax reductions – has been some 80 per cent, while inflation over the period has been some 32 per cent.
- Unemployment fell from 16.9 per cent in 1987 to less than half that figure – 7.8 per cent – by 1998.
- Employment has risen by more than a third since 1987, with some 400,000 more people at work.
- Industrial disputes have decreased from more than a million days lost in 1979 to 37,374 in 1998.

THE SOCIAL PARTNERSHIP DEALS

YEAR	BASIC PAY INCREASE (%)	IN-FLATION	DEBT/ GNP RATIO	GENERAL GOVT. DEFICIT (% GDP)	UN-EMPLOY-MENT	INDUS-TRIAL DISPUTES DAYS LOST
PROGRAMME FOR NATIONAL RECOVERY (1988–1990)						
1987		3.1	112.4	(8.6)	16.9	264339
1988	2.5	2.1	108.3	(6.5)*	16.4	143393
1989	2.5	4.1	97.7	(1.8)	15.1	50000
1990	2.5	3.3	92.3	(2.3)	13	223000
PROGRAMME FOR ECONOMIC AND SOCIAL PROGRESS (1991–1993)						
1991	4	3.2	89.9	(2.3)	14.7	86000
1992	3	3.1	87.9	(2.5)	15.1	110000
1993	3.75	1.4	88	(2.7)	15.7	60986
PROGRAMME FOR COMPETITIVENESS AND WORK (1994–1996)						
1994	2	2.3	83.9	(1.7)	14.7	25550
1995	2.5	2.5	78.2	(1.9)	12.2	130300
1996 Jan–Jun	2.5					
Jul–Dec	1.5	1.7	72.3	(0.4)	11.9	114584
PARTNERSHIP 2000 (1997–1999)						
1997	2.5	1.5	68.9	1.1	10.3	74508
1998	2.25	2.4	57.8	2.1	7.8	37374
1999 Jan-Sep	1.5					
2000 Oct-Mar	1					

*exclusive of receipts under tax incentive amnesty

6

THE ROLE OF THE EU IN IRELAND'S ECONOMIC TRANSFORMATION

Ray Mac Sharry and Padraic White

We see a changed Republic of Ireland today: a modern, open economy; after the long years of emigration, people are beginning to come back for the quality of life you now offer; a country part of Europe's mainstream, having made the most of European Structural Funds but no longer reliant on them . . .

British Prime Minister Tony Blair, in an address to the joint sitting of the Oireachtas − Dáil and Senate − 26 November 1998

In 1974, a year after joining the European Economic Community (EEC), Ireland's receipts from the Social Fund were just £3.6 million. That was little over £1 for every man, woman and child in the country. It was scarcely the crock of gold at the end of the European rainbow many envisaged when they voted with such enthusiasm − by a four-to-one margin − in favour of membership. But of course this was just the beginning of a new and wider relationship between Ireland and Europe.

This association has proved both financially rewarding and deeply fulfilling on a number of levels, including the psychological one. The opening up of Continental European markets to Irish exports, both in industry and agriculture, has had a liberating effect, not least in reducing our economic dependence on Britain. For a small country with a weak economy and a peripheral location on the edge of Europe, that emphatic referendum decision to join the Common Market was virtually inevitable, once Britain had decided to join. Certainly, few could have envisaged that, by the turn of the century, Ireland would have almost caught up with average living standards in the rest of the Community. And fewer still that, by 2000, the country's unemployment rate would rank among the lowest of the fifteen member states that today constitute the European Union.

Ireland's accession to EEC membership strengthened the country's sense of identity, while the experience has raised national self-confidence immeasurably. It has set relations between Ireland and Britain within a broader multilateral European framework and placed the two states on a more equal footing. It has also taught us to look beyond Britain, and to other small-country models that were more relevant to our condition. Over time, more contact at European level between ministers and senior civil servants from the Irish and British governments has made it easier to tackle a common problem – that of achieving a lasting peace in Northern Ireland. The efforts of the Irish and British governments culminated in the Good Friday Agreement in April 1998.

Too often the gains from membership of the European Union are measured and assessed in terms of an economic balance sheet, highlighting the net benefit to the Irish economy. And since 1973, the cumulative net transfer has been substantial – more than £23 billion. However, this minimises and obscures the Community influence in other areas. Ireland has benefited greatly from participation in the experience of European integration. In matters of social policy, the pace of domestic reform accelerated with EEC membership, notably in regard to equal-pay legislation and the development of women's rights and industrial democracy through the provision for worker directors on the boards of state companies. In legal affairs, the European Court of Justice is the court of final appeal in deciding any conflict that arises between Community and Irish law.

But above all, joining the EEC, as it then was, allowed Ireland to step out of the shadow of British influence and to play a distinct role on a larger world stage. In giving up a form of national sovereignty that was always more apparent than real, Ireland gained far more than she lost from the new experience of shared sovereignty. Ireland's accession marked an important turning point in our national affairs. This was the first in a series of steps that saw the country move away from the exclusive economic dependence on Britain that had marked the first half-century since Independence:

- In 1973, Irish access to European markets for industry and agriculture led to a steady reduction in the proportion of our trade with the British market.
- Then, in 1979, came the decision to break the link with sterling and join the European Monetary System (EMS), while the UK remained outside.
- Finally, on 1 January 1999, Ireland joined the single currency. Here, yet again, while Britain stood aside from a historical development in European integration, Ireland never hesitated to sign up to economic and monetary union, despite the uncertainties created by that British decision.

Ireland clearly saw her future within Europe, and was ready to accept the challenges and opportunities presented by an expanding European Community, determined to achieve ultimate political union through greater economic integration. Britain's former Foreign Secretary, Douglas Hurd, speaking in Dublin at the Institute for European Affairs in 1994, summed it up well: 'For the Irish, membership in 1973 was about Ireland's place in history, confirming Ireland's position in Europe as a modern state . . . and its decisive shift away from the embrace of Britain.' If Britain's attitude to Europe has been marked by hesitation at every critical step along the road to greater integration, Ireland has always had a much clearer focus.

In agriculture, Ireland's accession ensured a bigger market, and a better price, for our agricultural exports, while for farmers it offered a welcome new deal – the Common Agricultural Policy (CAP). The CAP helped to increase output and raise farm incomes. For the first time in half a century, farmers could expand production, sell their produce into larger agricultural markets and do so at higher guaranteed prices. Previously, half the output of Irish agriculture was surplus to domestic needs and was exported to the only available market – Britain. That left farmers at the mercy of Britain's cheap-food policy. The British government kept food prices low, by deficiency payments or income subsidies to protect domestic farm income. Facing such difficult market conditions, Irish farmers struggled to raise their living standards and relied on substantial Exchequer subvention. This amounted to some £71 million, or 5 per cent of GNP in the years preceding membership of the Community.

For indigenous industry, the potential benefits of Community membership were highly significant, opening up a market of 250 million consumers. The initiatives that Seán Lemass as Taoiseach had taken after 1959 ensured that industry was well prepared for the trading opportunities the larger European market later offered. In 1961, the Committee on Industrial Organisation was set up to report on industry's readiness for trade liberalisation. Adaptation Councils encouraged adjustment and restructuring, through adaptation and re-equipment grants. And in 1965, with the signing of the Anglo-Irish Free Trade Agreement, Lemass stepped up the pace further, by imposing the discipline of free trade on industry. Tariff barriers on British imports were reduced over a ten-year period, with completely free trade established by 1975. This meant that by 1973, when Ireland finally joined the Community, there was virtual tariff-free trade with our main market, Britain. A further five years elapsed before, in 1978, the same unrestricted trade access between Ireland and the economies of the Continental EEC countries was achieved.

However, for overseas industry locating here, Ireland being within Europe held out even more attractions. Foreign firms were first attracted to the Republic by the low tax regime. Increasingly, after EEC membership, the multinationals were eager to use the country as a manufacturing base and a platform for their exports to Europe. Later, the scale of American investment, particularly in the high-tech sector of industry – electronics and pharmaceuticals – offered the most dramatic illustration of this trend.

So Community membership opened a very different chapter in our economic and political history. On the one hand, Ireland was ending a reliance on the slow growing British economy, which had been in a state of steady decline for a century or more. At the same time, by joining the more dynamic Continental economies that were expanding much more rapidly, Ireland was diversifying export-market outlets. The result is that, today, Britain buys about one quarter of Ireland's exports, compared with more than half in 1973.

As a small, peripheral economy on the edge of Europe, Ireland was well placed to benefit from the substantial financial transfers from Brussels, both under the CAP and via the Regional and Social Funds. These inward financial flows from the Community budget helped raise living standards and modernise the economy through the investment in infrastructure and education that resulted, particularly after 1989 through the two rounds of Structural Funds. Over the quarter-century or so since accession, the scale of those transfers underpinned the transformation of the Irish economy as it became one of Europe's industrial pace-setters.

From the outset, farmers were the prime beneficiaries of Ireland's Community membership. The phased five-year transition to full EEC prices by the end of the decade ushered in a brief golden period of affluence for the farming community. Between 1972 and 1978 farm incomes rose over 40 per cent in real terms, while the price of agricultural land soared. In 1975, the Regional Fund was introduced. However, its budget was too small to make any serious impact on regional disparities within the Community. And since the Fund was divided on a national quota basis, all member states applied for funding up to the quota limit. In consequence, the poorest regions of even the richest countries managed to qualify for support. The Regional Fund was designed to complement the Social Fund and to help Ireland – along with Italy – as one of the Community's weaker economies, to overcome the many disadvantages of size, location and underdevelopment.

However, it was quite some time before the Regional Fund managed to fulfil that role of securing greater economic convergence between the richer and poorer regions adequately. This only happened after the enlargement of the European Community to include Spain and Portugal in 1985, and later with the introduction of the Single European Act in 1987.

These events served as the catalyst for the change of attitude that took place. The reform of the Structural Funds – defined in the Single Act as the European Regional Development Fund, the European Social Fund and the Guidance Section of the European Agricultural Guidance and Guarantee Fund – was specifically required by that Act. The rules were amended and made more flexible and the fund allocations were increased. This time the focus was on the poorer regions, and the aim was to help prepare them for the challenges ahead, first of the single market and later of the single currency.

The result was that the Structural Funds were twice doubled in size, first in 1988 and again in 1993. These transfers assumed great significance for the subsequent development of the Irish economy. The funds helped finance a major investment in infrastructure that, in turn, has facilitated rapid economic expansion over the last decade. The EU moneys were one among many factors that helped to set the country on a sustained growth path in the 1990s, stimulating the economy to expand more rapidly than other member states. As a result, within a decade, the gap in living standards between Ireland and the other Community members had narrowed greatly.

The past is, indeed, a foreign country. The Ireland of the early seventies was a very different place and in some aspects, when viewed from the perspective of the end of the century, almost unrecognisable. Then one in four workers were employed in agriculture, now it is just one in twelve. And that figure is likely to decline further. It was Alan Dukes who captured well that sense of the rapid pace of economic change throughout the country, a change that took place within less than a generation. He remarked how back in 1972, the country had just one stretch of dual carriageway. This ran from Newlands Cross to Naas.

Today, the contrast between Ireland's underdeveloped pre-EEC past and its affluent present has become both more striking and more stark. In 1998, when Jacques Santer, President of the European Commission, addressed the Seanad, he noted how 'It is rare to find any period of such profound transformation which has been as successfully managed as here in Ireland.'

When Ireland joined the European Community, living standards here were less than two-thirds of the Community average. But since the late eighties, Ireland's income and output growth have increased more rapidly than those of the other euro economies. Today, living standards are close to the average EU level. And by 2007, almost certainly, our long-standing relationship of financial dependency on Brussels will have altered dramatically. For by then, Ireland, the greatest net beneficiary of Europe's largesse on a per capita basis, will be a net contributor to the Community budget. It would be a landmark development in our economic history, particularly as Ireland approaches a century of independence since the establishment of the Irish Free State in 1992.

Few would have dared predict such an economic scenario in 1972, before Ireland joined the Community; fewer still in 1982, when successive governments struggled to stabilise the public finances and check the drift towards national bankruptcy. This great economic leap forward has come only within the last decade or so, particularly since 1994. In the words of the OECD report on Ireland (1999), there then followed 'five straight years of stunning economic performance', reflected in an average 9 per cent growth in GDP. This was underpinned by the £17 billion received in total EU support since 1989 – more than half of which came from the Structural and Cohesion Funds.

The Economic and Social Research Institute (ESRI) calculate that the cumulative impact of the two rounds of Structural funding over the 1989 to 1999 period raised GNP by between 3 and 4 per cent above the level it would have reached without EU transfers. A proportional breakdown of the most recent Community Support Framework (1994–9) shows how the CSF was funded by four financial instruments amounting to some £4.65 billion, and further separate transfers from the Cohesion Fund:

- European Regional Development Fund (ERDF) – 45 per cent
- European Social Fund (ESF) – 35 per cent
- The Guidance Section of the European Agriculture and Guarantee Fund (EAGGF) – 19 per cent
- Financial Instrument for Fisheries Guidance (FIFG)

The Cohesion Fund was established to complement the Structural Funds. It was designed to assist preparations for Economic and Monetary Union (EMU) in four countries – Ireland, Greece, Portugal and Spain – with a GDP per capita less than 90 per cent of the EU average in 1992. Ireland was set to receive between 7 and 10 per cent of the total Cohesion Fund budget, or over £1.2 billion. The Cohesion Fund focuses on supporting large infrastructure projects, where it can provide up to 85 per cent of the total eligible cost of projects. The Fund operates on a project-by-project basis.

The benefits provided by both these European Union funds have been felt throughout the country. In transport, their impact is readily apparent: from the road, rail-port and airport projects undertaken. The environment has been improved by the water supply projects and waste water treatment schemes that have been established. The transfers have helped fund the construction of the Dublin ring road and major bypasses in Kildare, Portlaoise and Nenagh. And in rail, the European moneys have financed extensions to Dublin's DART network and an upgrade of the Dublin–Galway railway.

STRUCTURAL FUND RECEIPTS

First tranche (1989-93)
Assistance from the EU totalled £3.1 billion under the Community Support Framework. Four main areas of activity were identified for support: agriculture, fisheries, tourism and rural development. Some 8,600 farms were supported, with 120,000 farmers receiving compensatory allowances. In the food-processing sector, 102 projects helped create 3,363 jobs, while a total of 2,030 young trained farmers received installation aid.

The industry programme contributed to the development of the manufacturing and international-services sector. Industrial output expanded by almost 7 per cent annually over the period, with similar rates of increase in the manufacturing and building sectors.

Between 1989 and 1993, some 307 km of national primary roads were improved or upgraded, along with 170 km of roads supporting industrial and tourism development. Facilities at Dublin, Shannon and Cork airports were upgraded, and the Dublin–Belfast rail link was improved. In addition, investment has been concentrated on ports. Over the first programming period, some 250 km of sewers and 166 km of trunk water mains were installed, and 52 sewage pumping schemes were constructed.

Ireland has a higher proportion – more than a quarter – of young people under twenty-five years of age, by comparison with the EU average. In the five-year period of the programme, some 500,000 people benefited from courses at different levels.

Overall, economic growth averaged 5 per cent over the period, while inflation, at 2.5 per cent, was almost half the EU average. Manufacturing employment grew by about 1 per cent annually from 1989 to 1992, compared to an average decline in the Community of 2 per cent. By 1993, total employment was 66,000 higher than five years earlier. However, despite that increase, the unemployment rate in 1993 was 18.4 per cent – and the second-highest in the European Community. But the gap between Irish and average EU living standards narrowed from 64 per cent of GDP in 1988 to 78 per cent in 1993.

Delors 2 (1994–9)

By the end of the six-year funding period, Ireland will have received £4.6 billion and secured the highest per capita allocation of all Community Support Framework Programmes within the EU. Some 45 per cent of the total aid has come from the Regional Fund, with 35 per cent from the Social Fund, 19 per cent from the European Agricultural Guidance and Guarantee Fund, and 1 per cent from the Financial Instrument of Fisheries Guidance.

The overall development strategy – underlying the ten operational programmes that make up the CSF – was designed to capitalise on the strengths of the Irish economy, while remedying some of its structural weaknesses. The government identified four priority investment areas (the productive sector, human resources, economic infrastructure and local and urban development sectors) in the national plan to secure European aid and investment under the CSF agreed with the Commission in 1993.

For the productive sector (44.6 per cent of funds), four operational programmes, designed to improve the climate for enterprise, develop competitiveness and raise productivity and employment, were put in place. Agriculture, forestry and rural development received 16.79 per cent of total funding, with the aim of supporting diversification of agriculture and raising the quality of food products. Industry received 18.3 per cent, tourism received 8.09 per cent and fisheries received 1.37 per cent.

The main aim of the investment in human resources (30.8 per cent) was to raise the skills base of the workforce, by boosting human capital through investment in education, for those in employment, those out of work and those wishing to join the labour market. The investment was also intended to improve the job prospects of the unemployed – particularly the longer-term unemployed. Overall, some 39 per cent of European Social Fund support was invested in second- and third-level education, with support for training and apprenticeships benefiting some 255,000 young people. The other areas of focus were the reintegration of the socially excluded and adaptation to industrial changes.

Under the economic infrastructure priority investment area (19.8 per cent), transport (15.8 per cent) – mainly roads and public transport – received the bulk of receipts. Water and the environment (1.4 per cent), energy (1.2 per cent), communications (0.7 per cent) and health (0.7 per cent) account for the remainder.

Local urban and rural development (4.6 per cent) concentrated on local area partnerships in disadvantaged areas and enterprise development support through County Enterprise Boards. It also enabled local communities to develop their own areas, from either an economic, environmental or social perspective, and included funding for urban-renewal plans in Dublin, Cork, Galway, Limerick and Waterford.

*

In March 1999, at the European Council in Berlin, Ireland's negotiating position for the Agenda 2000 discussions on future financing of the EU budget and Structural Fund allocations (2000–06) contrasted sharply with that adopted seven years before. At the Edinburgh summit in 1992, Irish unemployment – at some 17 per cent – had been amongst the highest in the EU. By 1999 it was amongst the lowest, at less than half that figure. Over the period of the Delors 2 package, Ireland's rate of economic growth easily surpassed that achieved by the fourteen other member states.

Such rapid growth meant increased prosperity, ensuring that the country as a whole no longer qualified for Objective 1 funding status. The threshold set for qualification required per capita income in the selected region to be less than 75 per cent of the EU average income, as measured by GDP. And since, by 1998, Ireland's GDP per head had reached more than 100 per cent, the government was forced to adopt a different approach to regional development for the new round of structural funding.

The government decision to divide the country into two regions was accepted by the Commission and has resulted in the gradual phasing out of Objective 1 status for the more affluent eastern and southern counties, while the thirteen border, midland and western counties (Galway, Mayo, Sligo, Donegal, Roscommon, Leitrim, Longford, Cavan, Monaghan, Louth, Westmeath, Laois and Offaly) retained Objective 1 status. The agreement reached at Berlin meant that Ireland secured structural and cohesion fund transfers of some £3 billion, or about half the level of the Delors 2 package. So, by the end of the seven-year period, the national contribution to the EU budget could be running at more than £1 billion annually. On this basis, Ireland, by 2006, could find herself a net contributor to the Community budget, and no longer a net beneficiary. Nevertheless, it would represent a remarkable achievement to have moved from a position in 1973 where Irish living standards were less than two-thirds of the EU average to one where, within less than half a century, Ireland has managed to close that gap.

However, rapid economic success creates its own problems. The acceleration in growth in the nineties has left Ireland with an infrastructural deficit. The rate of expansion has outpaced the capacity of the economy to cope with such a high level of economic activity. With EU funding set to decline, the investment in infrastructure required to overcome these capacity constraints will have to be financed, increasingly, from domestic resources. Thankfully, given the healthy state of the public finances, Ireland has never been better placed to make that investment than it is now.

The implementation of the two CSF programmes has been very satisfactory. To date, the benefits from the financial transfers under the Structural Funds have certainly matched, if not exceeded, expectations. For the first three years of the Delors 1 package, close to 99 per cent of planned expenditure was achieved. In fact, Ireland was the most successful of the Objective 1 areas in reaching the spending targets set in the CSF. And certainly, this stood to the country's credit when the second round of Structural Fund allocations were under negotiation in 1992 and 1993.

The ESRI, reviewing the mid-term progress of Delors 2 (1994–9), was highly impressed with Ireland's performance. It described the implementation of the CSF as 'a notable success story'. And it added: 'Funds have been deployed effectively to support and enhance what has been a remarkable economic recovery . . . Capacity and capability has been increased in the productive sectors; there has been a quantum leap in the provision of public infrastructure; education and training attainment forges ahead; and experimental institutional arrangements have galvanised local initiatives.'

However, the sizeable financial transfers – nearly £10 billion over the eleven-year period – were just one of a number of factors that contributed to Ireland's stellar growth performance. Although the Structural Funds flow made a significant contribution to that performance, it would be wrong to exaggerate their impact. As Dr Garret FitzGerald pointed out in a paper entitled 'Twenty-five Years of EU Membership', delivered in Kenmare in October 1998, 'the Structural Funds account for one-tenth of our growth during the past decade.' In fact the ESRI has estimated that the single market was responsible for three times more growth than the Structural Funds.

But perhaps Ireland too was fortunate. At a time when the size of the Structural Funds was increased significantly, Ireland's EU Commissioners, by securing key portfolios in the Commission – Agriculture and Social Affairs – were well placed. Commissioners, though appointed by national governments, do not take their instructions from these governments. The Treaty requires them to be individuals whose 'independence is beyond doubt'. Nevertheless, their background invariably lies in domestic politics or public affairs, and this provides them with a sensitivity to national concerns and an ability to interpret such matters – not least to their fellow Commissioners – without compromising that independence. And dare we say it ourselves, we think they managed to do so.

7
—

ACHIEVING CONVERGENCE AND COHESION WITHIN THE EU

Ray Mac Sharry

The passage of the 1987 Single European Act opened the way for the creation of the single market in goods, services, capital and people by 1993. As a balancing measure, the European Community revised its whole approach to assisting the less well-off countries and regions. Under the terms of the act, the achievement of economic and social cohesion became a formal policy objective of the Community. In this regard, Structural Funds were seen as the best way to reduce the income and other disparities between regions and to compensate the poorer member states for the competitive gains the larger economies – Germany and France – would make once the single market began to operate. By improving Ireland's infrastructural base, via large-scale investment in both physical and human capital, the first tranche of Structural Funds (1989–93) helped ensure the economy was fit enough to compete successfully. And later, the second round of funding (1994–9) made it easier to join the single currency.

Following proposals from the President of the European

Commission, Jacques Delors, a new approach to aid for the poorer regions was adopted. Subsequently known as the Delors 1 package, this resulted in the doubling of the Community's three existing funds – the Regional, Social, and Guidance sections of FEOGA. Collectively, these were called the Structural Funds. The main emphasis was on areas classified as Objective 1 regions, where average GDP per head was less than 75 per cent of the Community average. On this basis Ireland qualified as a single region for the first two tranches of the Structural Funds between 1989 and 1999.

In 1988, as Minister for Finance, I helped prepare the government's application for Structural Fund support. But, as we did so, ministers faced a difficult dilemma. The most immediate challenge was to bring the public finances back into balance and stabilise the national debt. Containing public expenditure was the primary means employed to do so. But the medium-term opportunity presented by the Structural Funds also beckoned. And here, the Community was offering generous financial support, on very favourable terms, to finance major – and much-needed – investment in public infrastructure. But since this required co-financing to be availed of, it meant more spending by the government. However, the terms were generous. Given Ireland's Objective 1 status – where the whole country was regarded as a single region – then, in return for every pound invested by the state, typically the EU would match it with three pounds from European taxpayers. The government finally managed to combine fiscal rectitude with prudent long-term capital spending. The combination produced a good return on investment in the years that followed.

A year later in Brussels, following my appointment as Commissioner for Agriculture, I was sitting around the table in the Berlaymont with my sixteen fellow Commissioners. There, we examined the detailed national plan from the Irish government, seeking support for their Structural Fund application. It certainly gave me a unique perspective on the application. I found myself scrutinising in Brussels the proposals which, months earlier, I had helped prepare in Dublin as Minister for Finance. After negotiations on the plan, the Commission agreed a Community Support Framework (CSF) for Ireland by October of that year. This set out the development strategy to be followed and defined how the member states would implement the Framework over a five year period (1989–93) via a series of operational programmes.

However, while the government was intent on maximising the returns from the new funds for infrastructural investment, at the same time, given the imbalance in the public finances, overall expenditure had to be tightly controlled. Spending restraint had ensured there was a large backlog of capital investment projects, postponed from earlier years. In that respect, the new Structural Funds could hardly have come at a more opportune time. The financial transfers, by facilitating rapid investment in infrastructure, eliminated bottlenecks that otherwise could have occurred. And if they had, the slow pace of economic recovery then under way might well have been imperilled.

For the government, investment priorities were easy to identify but somewhat harder to match with available European funds. Although governments were not allowed to displace their own public spending with Community money, much depended on how proposals by applicant governments were presented in the national plan, and later, how the detail of the case was argued in Brussels.

Ireland's plan for the use of funds was submitted to the European Commission in March 1989. It was called 'Ireland – National Development Plan 1989–93' and was approved within six months. The Community Support Framework set out in great detail the country's main development priorities for the five-year period. There the plan identified two underlying objectives: 'to address the economy's structural weaknesses and deficiencies, especially those associated with peripherality and late development, which place Ireland at a competitive disadvantage in the completed Internal Market; and to support the government's efforts to create an environment conducive to increased productive investment, especially in the internationally competing sectors, and to support domestic policies which are designed to develop and exploit the potential of certain key economic sectors.'

The CSF was implemented through twelve operational programmes. It meant Ireland received £3.5 billion over five years. This provided the country with much-needed infrastructural development, particularly in roads and telecommunications. But, as well as the direct gains to the economy, the government benefited greatly from the discipline imposed by the multi-annual budgeting exercise. This involved the planning and operation of the Structural Funds on a medium-term basis and marked the end of the 'stop go' approach to capital spending. The government knew not only what it had to provide in capital spending over five years but also for certain, the amount of matching EU funding that was available. Such certainty gave the government every incentive to maximise the benefits of the Structural Funds. And it did, as is evident in the clear strategy for economic development outlined in the national plan.

Under Delors 1, the funding approach adopted was more focused than before. It reflected a switch from project-based to multi-annual programme operations. This time, there was more concentration on a small number of key objectives. And, to a greater extent than previously, a real sense of partnership was created in the administration of the fund by linking the Commission, the member states, and the regional or local authorities. So the social partnership that had just been established in the Programme for National Recovery was further underpinned and extended. The social partners, including government departments, state agencies and the European Commission, were represented on the monitoring committee managing each of the twelve Operational Programmes (OPs) that made up the CSF.

The financial transfers from Brussels under the Structural Funds were designed to help the weaker countries – like Ireland – invest heavily in infrastructure, and so cope more easily with the competitive challenge that arose, initially from the introduction of the single market and later from the single currency. The single market, by integrating the economies of the member states, made business easier to transact across national frontiers and facilitated the restructuring of industry. The worry was that in such a highly competitive environment, the core economies might gain at the expense of peripheral regions – like Ireland.

And so the claims of economic efficiency and social equity had to be balanced with care. For without Structural Fund support, a two-tier Europe could easily have emerged, leaving the weaker economies to struggle with higher unemployment. In that situation, only the core economies would benefit. Income disparities would widen as economies diverged and divisions opened up between richer and poorer regions and states. The generous scale of the transfers via the Structural Funds prevented such an outcome. Instead the funds facilitated faster growth in the poorer states and produced greater economic convergence with the Community's wealthier economies. Ireland's rapid rate of expansion over the past eleven year, since 1989, has ensured the economy has managed to catch up with average EU living standards. And she has done so more quickly than most people – including the economists – had predicted.

Ireland not only used all the money allocated but also used it wisely and well. Accordingly, within the EU, the state quickly won a good reputation and served as something of a role model in relation to the effective use of Structural Funds. In other instances, member states that had won significant funding sometimes were either unable or unwilling to provide the matching finance from their own domestic resources. Consequently, they failed to exploit fully the available transfers. Northern Ireland, though it too was an Objective 1 region, fell into the latter category. It failed to capitalise on the fund and take up the money on offer.

In the course of discussions on Structural Funds matters with my colleagues, quite often I would suggest to Leon Brittan, one of Britain's two EU Commissioners, that Northern Ireland be included in a particular programme or project. Although he would never object, clearly there was some resistance on the British government's part. For it seems the Treasury felt the UK was already paying heavily through its national contribution to the Community budget, while also funding the sizeable annual subvention to Northern Ireland. In addition for the British government, most parts of England, Scotland and Wales were classified under Objective 2 headings. And there, the EU offered just 25 per cent support, and this made the Structural Funds a less attractive investment proposition.

Overall, Structural Fund support has played a significant role in helping to achieve convergence and cohesion within the EU, by reducing regional disparities. The former Regional Affairs Commissioner, Wolf Mathias, speaking in Cork in 1998, identified the fund as one of the three central pillars of the European economic and social construction, alongside the single currency and the single market. And, quite correctly, she recognised that for 'the European integration process to remain politically acceptable to all and therefore durable, greater efficiency (the single market) and stability (EMU) should go hand in hand with stronger solidarity (the structural and cohesion funds).' Without such a balance, the Community would be unlikely to survive the social tensions generated by the introduction of the single market and single currency in such quick succession.

*

As Commissioner for Agriculture, part of my brief was handling the FEOGA guidance aspect of the Fund. This provides funding for structural policies designed to increase the efficiency of agriculture and improve the rural infrastructure. It supports improvements in farm structures and investment in the food sector and makes compensatory payments to farmers in less favoured regions. By virtue of my office, this also meant that I was a member of an important subcommittee dealing with the detailed operation of the Structural Funds. The other members included Commission President Jacques Delors; Bruce Millan the British Commissioner in charge of Regional Affairs; the Social Affairs Commissioner, Vasso Papandreou; and Henning Christopherson, who was a vice president of the Commission and responsible for the overall coordination of the Structural Funds.

This subcommittee exercised a decisive influence, since any policy or proposal it was supporting was less likely to be changed by the Commission itself. But if a Commissioner was dissatisfied with the outcome, he or she could revisit the matter again at plenary session. It meant that, if necessary, there was still scope to influence or change a decision at a later stage. Subsequently, when Padraig Flynn succeeded me in Brussels, his appointment as Commissioner for Social Affairs meant he exercised a similar dual role in decisions on Structural Funding.

Remarkably, in 1992, when the Commission first proposed the introduction of a Cohesion Fund, the proposal did not include Ireland. The new fund was introduced to complement the other Structural Funds. However, Ireland's success from the Delors 1 package meant there was resistance to the country securing further financial transfers from a new Community source. I objected strongly to this development and argued that Ireland's success in spending EU funding served to demonstrate the impact the Structural Funds could make on a peripheral economy. Why stop now, I said, and risk putting the whole EU policy on achieving cohesion into question?

The Danish Commissioner, Henning Christopherson, accepted the validity of my argument. With his support, the point was accepted. On that basis Ireland was included among the four Cohesion countries, together with Spain, Portugal and Greece. The Fund amounted to some £12.1 billion, with Ireland receiving between 7 and 10 per cent of the total. By the middle of 1998, some 107 projects, amounting to £1.03 billion, had been approved for assistance from the fund.

The Cohesion Fund provides Community financial contributions to projects in the fields of environment and trans-European networks in member states with a per capita GNP of less than 90 per cent of the Community average. As a Community initiative, it meets not just national requirements, but also European needs – as in the case of transport and environment infrastructure. The focus of the fund is on large infrastructural projects in these two areas. However, the high level of aid available – from 80 to 85 per cent of the total eligible cost of a project – has made it a highly attractive source of financing for governments.

When I took over the Agriculture portfolio in January 1989, the need for reform of the Common Agricultural Policy (CAP) had become quite apparent. A year earlier, the European Council of Ministers had introduced some measures, including an 'agricultural guideline', limiting the growth in farm spending to 74 per cent of the overall Community budget. It was clear that radical action was required. The existing financial support system guaranteed high prices for farmers, but the budgetary costs had become unsustainable. The CAP, or the European Agricultural Guidance and Guarantee Fund – better known as FEOGA – was designed for the 1960s and had operated well for some two decades, but by the early 1980s, as food surpluses mounted and intervention costs soared, the defects of this form of agricultural support became obvious to everyone. In 1984, some remedial action was taken. The milk superlevy, which placed quotas on milk production, was introduced in an attempt to check overproduction. However, since farmers could expand output in other areas, the problem of surpluses continued and budgetary pressures intensified.

As Farm Commissioner, it became my responsibility to change the guidelines governing the Common Market in agriculture and to produce a more cost-effective alternative. Quite simply, a new CAP was required. The Commission needed to take steps to bring demand and supply of agricultural products into better balance, and at lower cost to the Community taxpayer. Hopefully, such a reform would also stem growing international criticism, with other countries accusing the Community of unfair competition in agricultural trade. The United States, in particular, had become increasingly vocal on this issue. The American concern lay with Community subsidised exports and their impact in depressing agricultural prices in international markets. It meant agriculture was destined to become a major issue in the upcoming world trade talks.

Since 1962, the CAP had served as the cornerstone of the European Economic Community. The agreement on agriculture was seen as a trade-off between France and Germany that reconciled the mutual interests of both countries. The quid pro quo between Paris and Bonn was guaranteed markets for French agricultural products in return for access to larger markets for Germany's manufactured goods. But over time, as agricultural production steadily exceeded consumption, the cost to the Community of supporting guaranteed prices rose. And as it did, agriculture accounted for a higher proportion of the EU budget. In 1973, when Ireland joined the Community, agriculture absorbed more than four-fifths of the budget. By 1988, although this figure had dropped to 65 per cent, it was still far too high.

The financial burden of the CAP was crowding out new spending in other areas. Over time, the high guaranteed prices paid to farmers for their produce meant Community prices were some two to four times higher than the world market level. Public concern, at the cost, the wastefulness and the environmental aspects of an unreformed CAP, began to mount in different quarters. Consumers became more resistant to high food prices and also were dismayed at the sight of European plenty – the agricultural surpluses – in a world where famine still blighted parts of the Third World. Member states – like Britain and Prime Minister Mrs Thatcher, who was concerned about a budget rebate – resented agriculture's dominance of Community spending. Internationally, the European Community was under pressure to liberalise world farm trade and to dismantle its protectionist policies in the context of the Uruguay Round of the General Agreement on Tariffs and Trade (GATT) negotiations. It meant that agricultural expenditure had to be contained, and reduced.

In the initial years of its operation, the CAP was well suited to the Community's requirements. Europe was in deficit for most agricultural products. The need then was to guarantee food supplies, at reasonable prices, both for producers and consumers. But by the eighties, the clear imperative was to cut production and reduce the 'butter mountains' and 'wine lakes'. For these had to be financed, either when stored as intervention stocks, or later when sold at subsidised prices on world markets. The huge surpluses arose from the guaranteed minimum prices the Community paid to farmers for their output. In turn, those price guarantees only gave farmers a major incentive to intensify production. So between 1973 and 1988, while food production rose by 2 per cent a year, food consumption increased by just 0.5 per cent.

In the reforms I introduced, I proposed to cut guaranteed prices and bring them closer to world market levels. I also wanted to change the direction of the Community's agricultural policy from price support to income support: in other words to support people rather than products. Farmers were compensated for their income loss by direct income payments, and in return they agreed to 'set aside' some 15 per cent of their productive land. And so, after a fifty-hour meeting of the Council of Ministers in May 1992, these reforms were finally accepted.

The measures involved a 30 per cent cut in cereals-support prices and a 15 per cent cut in beef-support prices. Farmers were compensated for their loss by direct payments, and limits were set on production that was eligible for price support. In addition, I introduced a set of accompanying measures. They consisted of three different schemes designed to promote forestry, to encourage early retirement of farmers and to improve the rural environment via a Rural Environment Protection Scheme (REPS). Under REPS, payments were made for the improvements undertaken.

The reforms were strongly opposed by the European farming organisations, including those in Ireland. They all produced gloomy forecasts about the adverse impact the new CAP would have on the farming sector. But as Professor Seamus Sheehy and Dr D. O'Connor observed in a recent review (1999) of the future of Irish farming, that anxiety proved to be misplaced. As they noted in their report on the future of Irish agriculture: 'Beef market prices, instead of falling by 15 per between 1992 and 1995, actually rose by some 10 per cent. At the same time, the premia and area aid payments agreed in 1992 were being introduced, so that farmers experienced a very substantial windfall gain in those years. However, beef prices did begin to fall after 1995 and by 1998 had finally fallen in line with the earlier reduction in support prices. The story for cereals was along the same lines. Cereal prices were again higher in 1995 instead of being 30 per cent lower. Only by 1997 had they fallen in line with support prices.'

However, the authors also pointed out that farmers' aggregate Family Farm Income (FFI) actually rose by 19 per cent between 1992 and 1995. After allowing for the continuing fall in the farm labour force, the average income rose by some 28 per cent over the same period. So even with a fall in incomes in 1997 and 1998, on a per worker basis incomes were still some 21 per cent up on the 1992 base year. Indeed, at the time I remember pointing out at a CAP reform conference in Dublin in 1992 that one of the authors of the report – Seamus Sheehy – was 'among the unfashionable minority who were prepared to look at the reform proposals'.

The package of measures was described in some quarters as the most radical reform of the CAP since its creation some three decades earlier. Certainly, the reforms ensured EU farming became more competitive and that agricultural production was brought back under control, thus helping to close the gap between EC and world prices. But the reforms also helped agreement to be reached in the Uruguay round of the GATT negotiations on agriculture. And by 1998, agriculture's share of the EU budget had fallen below 50 per cent.

My intention in introducing the new compensatory payments was to provide full compensation for all but the largest farmers. However, the Council of Ministers amended my proposal in order to ensure that larger farmers also secured full compensation. A regrettable consequence has been that within the EU some 80 per cent of the direct payments go to the top 20 per cent of farmers. However, in Ireland a better balance has been achieved. Data from Teagasc's 1997 *National Farm Survey* showed that 80 per cent of payments in that year went to the top 60 per cent of Irish farmers. As the Department of Agriculture pointed out in its 1998 *Annual Review and Outlook*, this may be explained by the fact that 'there are relatively few very large farms, particularly those under arable crops.' Nevertheless, Ireland's typical farm size remains above the EU average and is the seventh largest in the Community.

In addition, the 'accompanying measures', which I brought in as part of the package of CAP reforms, were designed to help farmers adjust to the cutbacks in traditional agricultural production, by offering them some alternative sources of income. These initiatives opened up opportunities for farmers by offering them growth areas for the future. The additional measures also enjoyed a substantial (75 per cent) rate of co-financing from the Community, with expenditure financed from the guarantee section of the agricultural budget.

In presenting my reforms, I had made it clear that farmers had a dual responsibility, both as food producers and, in their new role as guardians of the countryside, as protectors of the environment. Under the Rural Environment Protection Scheme, farmers agree an environmental farm plan. In return, they receive annual payments on the first 40 hectares of their land. At the end of 1998, more than 39,000 farmers were benefiting, with a quarter of all agricultural land being farmed in accordance with the REPS standard. And a year later close on 50,000 farmers were participating, with total expenditure reaching some £450 million on what is Ireland's most important agri-environmental programme.

The early-retirement scheme helped facilitate structural adjustment. It provided older farmers – those between 55 and 65 – with a strong financial incentive to leave farming in favour of qualified entrants in return for a pension. This gave neighbouring farms a chance to achieve economic viability or offered opportunities for new land utilisation, in accordance with environmental land use and conservation requirements. And given that Ireland has the lowest proportion of the land area of the state given over to forestry in the Community – just 7 per cent compared with an EU average of 25 per cent – the afforestation measures provided a wide range of incentives; with the Forestry Development Programme subsidising both the planting and management of trees and paying annual premia for some twenty years after planting.

The Structural Fund receipts since 1989 have helped raise the productive capacity of the economy, through the investments in infrastructure, industry, education and agriculture. However, the transfers under the Common Agricultural Policy since 1973 have greatly overshadowed these in size. The CAP has accounted for more than 70 per cent of the £29 billion in total gross receipts that Ireland received from the EU up to 1998. This breaks down into £19.2 billion in payment for price supports under the farm guarantee scheme and £1.8 billion from the guidance section to pay for farm modernisation and improvement. By comparison, some £3.6 billion has come in transfers under the European Social Fund and £3.9 billion from the European Regional Fund – or just a quarter of total gross receipts.

Despite this huge level of financial support, employment in agriculture, in Ireland as everywhere else in the EU, has fallen. When Ireland joined the EEC, nearly one in four people was employed in the sector, but today that figure is less than one in twelve. Agriculture's share of economic activity has witnessed a parallel decline. It has dropped from 16 per cent of GDP to some 5 per cent of GDP today, as the flight from the land accelerated and workers chose better-paid job opportunities that were opening up in industry.

The operation of the CAP has provided a double benefit to the Irish economy at a time of rapid change. To farmers, it supplied generous financial support, while to the Exchequer it lifted a huge burden from taxpayers. The cost of national farm price subsidy payments was transferred to Brussels. But it has also helped farmers adjust to the impact of change, as agriculture becomes a more competitive and less protected sector, as the differential between EU and world prices for agricultural products narrows, and as Community subsidies for farming are reduced. For as agriculture has declined, the CAP reforms have facilitated greater mobility and have done so with minimal hardship for those affected.

But if for farmers the gains from the CAP are obvious and have been quantified, then the savings for the Exchequer, by no longer having to subsidise agriculture, have been considerable. Colin Hunt, chief economist with Goodbody Stockbrokers, in an analysis of the impact of EU membership on the Irish economy – 'Eurovision 2006' – addressed that issue. He pointed out that if successive governments had to provide the same level of subsidy to farmers as the Community has provided since 1973, the consequences for our public finances would have been very serious indeed. On one measure, he estimated the national debt to GDP ratio would have peaked at 147 per cent in 1987, rather than the 115 per cent figure achieved. Such a high level of debt would not only have required higher interest rates to finance the extra borrowing. It also would have made social partnership – underpinned by tax cuts – harder to deliver. And in that event, the defiant roar of the Celtic Tiger might never have been heard in recent years.

8

EEC Membership: A Boon
to Foreign Investment

Padraic White

Once the results of the May 1972 Referendum confirmed that Ireland would join the European Community the following January, the IDA focused on promoting the country as a base for international investment, highlighting it as a profitable and strategic location within the Community. In the advertising and marketing campaigns, and in presentations to business, Ireland was portrayed as an integral part of a large and wealthy market, which could be served most effectively from this country. And, in discussions with business, the IDA stressed Ireland's place as a full and equal member of the Community, with a direct input into political decisions affecting business. Over time, as the EC removed the residual barriers to genuine free trade, particularly through the single-market initiatives completed in 1992, Ireland's credibility as an export platform for the European market was greatly enhanced.

The IDA's prime target was to persuade companies to locate their strategic European manufacturing or software facilities here. The experience of the established multinational firms already demonstrated that Ireland could produce goods and services very profitably and efficiently, with reliable and speedy delivery to any part of Europe within forty-eight hours. As companies sought to consolidate their operations, the range of business functions attracted to this country was extended, whether for warehousing, customer orders and support services, currency and treasury management or reservation centres.

Full membership of the Community helped Ireland to overcome the limitation of being a small and peripheral island economy, with a domestic market of 3.6 million, situated on the western edge of Europe and separated by two strips of sea from the main European markets. The foreign-investment benefits to Ireland of EU membership are incalculable and enduring. Capital investment and annual expenditure by overseas companies dwarf the strictly financial gains from EU sources.

Since 1973, foreign investment in Ireland has benefited from almost every item of spending under transfers from what in the late eighties became the EU Structural and Cohesion Funds. However, at the outset there was one weakness in Ireland's case for foreign investment: the lack of a skilled industrial workforce. Ireland was perceived to lack an industrial tradition. And here, direct funding of IDA training grants by the European Community became a matter of critical importance. For as the old protected industries declined, the redundant workers lacked the skills needed by the new foreign industries locating here. In addition, the IDA was committed to encouraging foreign companies to set up in the less developed regions, where there were few large exporting firms operating. As a result, potential investors worried about getting suitable workers and feared that the cost of raising labour productivity in the early years would mean reduced profitability or losses.

To plug this hole in the Irish case, and to turn a weakness

into a competitive advantage, the IDA, from 1970, provided generous training grants for staff recruited to foreign companies either investing, or expanding, in Ireland. If Irish staff had to receive training abroad, the grants were also paid towards the cost of wages, travel and subsistence related to training at the parent plant. These grants were often the deciding factor for a company weighing up an investment decision and greatly eased its concern about setting up here. They proved a potent weapon in the IDA's armoury and were not well understood by its competitors. The training supports were included with capital grants and reported under the single heading of new industry grants.

The spirit in which the IDA deployed the grants is well captured by the succinct statement in the 1973 Annual Report that 'training grants are tailored to the needs of each project and are administered in a flexible manner.' Over time, as the industrial base in Ireland became more developed and sophisticated, greatly enhancing the country's credibility as an investment location, the scope of the training grants was restricted and reduced. However, they remain an essential part of the incentive package for new greenfield investments. The national manpower organisation (originally ANCO and latterly FÁS) acted as the IDA's trusted agents in drawing up formal training plans in consultation with the company and in verifying that the grants were used properly.

In March 1973, the IDA set up a special EEC staff unit to prepare applications to the Commission for 50 per cent reimbursement from the European Social Fund for training grants for new or expanded foreign industry. By the end of 1974, the IDA had been approved in principle for £5 million reimbursement. This was half the total value of training grants awarded by the IDA for 21,000 workers. From 1978, the reimbursement rate was increased to 55 per cent. As foreign direct investment increased, so did the recoupment of funds from the Social Fund. And so, by 1983, ten years after EEC entry, the IDA had recovered £33 million from Europe, and £8 million in that year alone.

From 1989 onwards, national funding from Brussels came within the more comprehensive Structural Funds programmes, which include the Social Fund. And since then the IDA has received payments annually from these sources. In addition to training, the employment grants paid by the IDA for actual jobs created in the new international services, such as call centres and reservation centres, became eligible for European funding. The reimbursement rate for training and employment grants for new companies went up to 65 per cent, and to 75 per cent from 1994. In 1998, the IDA received £8.4 million from the Structural Funds, of which £6.2 million went towards encouraging research and development in industry, with the European Social Fund receipts being £2.2 million. And in the five years ending in 1998, the average annual cash refund to the IDA for training and employment in foreign companies was £5 million.

There is no doubt in my mind that the availability of European Social Funds for training of staff in new foreign companies, coupled with the positive training programmes they funded, were among a small number of crucial determinants that influenced companies to choose to locate in Ireland. Since the IDA was confident of recouping at least half the cost, it was organisationally attractive. And it had the extra bonus of raising the cash offer which the IDA had on the table, in competition with other countries. The government too was able to secure substantial recoupment for various elements of the foreign-investment programme, such as new industry grants and advance factories.

Directly after Ireland became a member of the EU, the IDA and staff did heroic work in qualifying Irish agri-industry for grants of up to 50 per cent under FEOGA, the Agricultural Guarantee and Guidance Fund. But to get access to these funds, a company's investment project first needed to secure financial support from an official agency in the member state. The IDA, in consultation with the Department of Agriculture, agreed to act as the qualifying agency in Ireland. I recall many long hours at board meetings, assessing and approving projects for IDA backing, even if nominal, in order to meet the periodic EU deadlines for receipt of the agri-industry applications. As a result, the Irish dairy cooperatives, beef, poultry, dairy and animal-feed companies benefited to the tune of £200 million from the EU agri-fund grants.

9

—

THE EVOLUTION OF THE IDA

Padraic White

After a decade and a half as Minister for Industry and Commerce, Seán Lemass had left a defining mark on that department, when Fianna Fáil was finally voted out of office in 1948. The Inter-Party government, the country's first coalition, was returned, but Lemass was quite unfazed by defeat. Instead, he saw the loss of office as 'nothing except a post-election interval'. His ministerial successor, Dan Morrissey of Fine Gael, presented a major contrast, both in terms of style and experience. A former Labour TD who later joined Cumann na nGaedheal, Morissey had never before served in government. By contrast, Lemass had spent fourteen of his previous sixteen years as minister in the same department. From the early thirties, he had made his political reputation as the main architect of industrial policy. He had masterminded the switch from free trade to protectionism, built up an industrial sector from behind high tariff walls and developed new state companies like Bord Na Móna, Irish Sugar and Irish Shipping.

In 1949, when the new coalition government announced the establishment of the Industrial Development Authority (IDA), the new agency was born in controversy. Predictably – and publicly – the proposal met with strong resistance from two quarters: from the opposition, but more unexpectedly – and privately – from inside the civil service itself. Lemass vigorously attacked the proposal and claimed it hindered, rather than helped, the country's industrial effort. At the same time civil servants passionately disagreed about the IDA's role and function as a promotional agency.

The Department of Finance was hostile to the IDA's formation. Its worst nightmare was that the new board might prove to be 'a gang of crackpot socialist planners', as an internal memorandum from that department had suggested. Specifically, it feared the new state agency would supplant the efforts of private enterprise. Within Industry and Commerce, other civil servants worried about a loss of administrative control, since the new Authority occupied a slightly ambiguous position, being neither fully within nor wholly outside departmental structures.

However, neither the worst fears of Finance nor Lemass's own strong reservations about the IDA was realised. The IDA proposals were modest and general, and were set against an economic background where protectionism was still the corner-stone of industrial development policy, and remained so, at least until the late fifties. Two years later, in 1951, when Seán Lemass returned as Industry Minister, he accepted fully the IDA's responsibility, after defining it more precisely. But if that role seemed minimal at the outset, it assumed far greater significance within a few years.

Under statute, the IDA had a dual function: to advise the Minister on industrial development and to promote greater investment in Irish industry from whatever quarter. Its terms of reference gave the Authority a specific mandate to attract new industrial investment to Ireland. That remit evolved continuously over the next twenty years, as the IDA expanded and focused increasingly on securing foreign direct investment. From the outset, although the new Authority had a separate board, its civil servant staff was subject to all the normal tight administrative controls, with formal departmental approval required for every item of expenditure.

By 1951, the Inter-Party government was faced with a depressing economic outlook. The post-war economic recovery had gathered pace in Europe, but left Ireland largely untouched. Some 41 per cent of the labour force was still employed in agriculture, with just 15 per cent in manufacturing industry. Emigration had resumed, economic growth was minimal and the economy was in the throes of the first of a recurring series of balance of payments crises.

The government, seeking an outside perspective on the country's economic problems, commissioned IBEC Technical Services Corporation, a US consultancy, to do a detailed analysis of the Irish economy. In its report a year later to the IDA, the IBEC analysis offered little consolation. Having outlined the range of difficulties the government faced, and identified its dilemma in tackling them, one of the headings to its final chapter concluded baldly, 'Not sufficient government initiative for socialism – not sufficient incentive for private enterprise.' The IBEC analysis was highly critical of government policies, not least in the area of industrial development. There, it noted:

The heavy hand of government controls has extended widely over all business operations in a manner that tended to stifle private initiative. Price controls, exercised not as an emergency measure but as a continuing instrument, have tended to become profit controls, justified not as a means of controlling inflation, but on the ground that profits beyond a certain minimum are an evil that should be penalised, regardless of whether they result from monopoly or from superior efficiency of operation in a fully competitive situation.'

The advice from the US consultants to the government was plain and to the point. First, the government should clearly define its economic goals. Second, it should decide whether private enterprise or state socialism was the means of achieving them:

Again, Ireland must make up its mind as to the direction it wants to take. If it elects to place major dependence upon socialist procedures, that is certainly within its proper prerogative. But if it means to depend importantly upon individual initiative in the accomplishment of its development aims, it cannot hope to be successful unless it is willing to allow sufficient differential returns to elicit extra effort, imagination and operating effectiveness. Without such incentives, the system of private competition won't work.

The government was in little doubt about the answer. The passing of the Undeveloped Areas Act, 1952, which introduced financial grants for industries locating in the less developed western and midland regions, was the first small step towards an industrial-development programme based on private enterprise. At the same time, the government decided to separate the Authority's promotion of new industry from any grant-giving function. So from 1952 onwards there were two sister organis-ations – the IDA to promote new investment and Foras Tionscal (the Industry Board) to vet and pay applications for financial grants.

In 1956, the IDA's mandate was extended to the promotion of new industry throughout the country. Also in that year came the first of two highly significant industrial-development measures that gave foreign companies the incentives they needed to locate in Ireland. The introduction of Export Profits Tax Relief in the Finance Act, 1956, initially gave 50 per cent tax remission on export sales – increased to 100 per cent two years later. The measure provided full relief for fifteen years and tapering relief for a further five years. It became the IDA's most distinctive investment incentive, and over time its most powerful single weapon in the international industrial promotion battle.

Two years later, the government, keen to encourage foreign industrialists anxious to locate in Ireland, went a step further. The Control of Manufactures Acts, passed in 1932, had sought to keep the ownership of Irish industry in native hands. The government decision to ease those restrictions and phase them out completely six years later helped transform the climate for foreign direct investment in Ireland

In parallel with those changes, the publication of *Economic Development* in 1958 marked a turning point in national economic strategy. With government approval, this official report, written by T. K. Whitaker as Secretary of the Department of Finance, signalled a decisive shift in economic policy away from protectionism and towards free trade. Manufacturing exports were finally seen as the key to economic development. The change stemmed from a belated recognition by the government that the small protected Irish market, sheltering behind high tariff walls and weakened by stagnant growth and high emigration, could never hope to meet the future employment needs of the country.

Too many firms found themselves caught between a domestic market that was too small and where profits were low, and an export market that was too challenging and where they were unable to compete. For if success in the domestic market was secured by high tariff walls that minimised competition, ultimately, it was achieved at a price. Since exported goods relied on imported raw materials that were subject to tariffs, the finished goods as exports were too expensive, and industry was uncompetitive.

With the publication of *Economic Development* followed by the First Programme for Economic Expansion covering the years 1959-63, the government clearly favoured export-focused industrial development based on free trade as the way forward. The policy changes were critical in underpinning the IDA's own efforts to promote the claims of Ireland as a location for foreign investment. The outward orientation of economic policy received a setback in 1962, when Ireland's appliation to join the nascent European Economic Community failed to progress following the firm '*non*' from French President Charles de Gaulle to the British application. Despite this disappointment, Ireland tried to maintain the free-trade momentum by unilateral tariff cuts in following years and by negotiating the Anglo-Irish Free Trade Agreement in 1965. A full decade was to pass before the ambition of membership of hte EEC was relaised – a status which was to prove central to Ireland's drive for foreign investment.

*

Traditionally, the main source of foreign investment in Ireland was Britain, and British firms responded to the era of high tariffs by setting up subsidiaries behind the tariffs largely to serve the Irish market. They also responded to the post-war era of the promotion of export-oriented industry by Ireland, principally in engineering and consumer industries, and Britain remained the single largest source of additional foreign investment and related jobs until overtaken by the United States in 1970. In the fifties, West Germany initially provided the main new source of foreign interest in industrial development in this country. Marshall Aid helped revive Germany's post-war economy and, once again, Germany's traditional family companies had begun to look abroad to international markets for expansion. The new German companies that set up in Ireland were, according to the IDA's Ted O'Neill, the wonder of the times. These were the first foreign-owned industries to build new factories where the output was produced for export and not sold in the protected Irish market. Such 'new wave' German companies included Liebherr cranes in Killarney, Crown Controls in Galway, Chipboard Ltd in Scariff, Krups kitchen appliances in Limerick and Faber Castell pencils in Fermoy. With the exception of Krups in Limerick and the Fermoy pencil plant, they are still operating.

In the 1960s, United States investment came in response to government and IDA promotion, aided occasionally by Irish-American connections. One of the major coups was the decision by Pfizer Corporation to set up a chemical plant in Ringaskiddy in Cork in 1969. The man pushing for the Irish location was Jack Mulcahy. He had emigrated to America, after being embroiled in the Civil War in 1922–3. There, he founded a successful engineering company, which he later sold to the US pharmaceutical company Pfizer in exchange for shares in that company. Mulcahy sat in on the negotiations between the Pfizer executives and Ted O'Neill for the IDA. But it was clear to O'Neill that Mulcahy was the dominant influence on the decision in favour of Ireland since he owned about one-third of the company shares.

Another influential arrival was the powerful General Electric Company of America, which put two electronic-type industries into Ireland, EI to Shannon (1963) and Ecco to Dundalk (1966).

Both Pfizer and General Electric acted as credible references in the United States for Ireland as the IDA fought to establish the country's süitability for incoming industry. In hindsight, both companies were also founding members of two sectors that were subsequently to prove outstanding successes in Ireland – chemicals/pharmaceuticals and electronics.

The enhanced industrial promtion of the 1960s did yield considerable fruits. Some 450 foreign companies negotiated new projects or major expansions with the IDA in this decade and were employing 34,000 people by 1972, the three dominant countries of origin being the USA, Britian and Germany, accounting for one-third, one-quarter, and one-fifth of the new jobs, respectively. But, increasingly, the heads of the twin development agencies – John Walsh, then Chairman of the 'old' IDA, and Ted O'Neill, Chairman of Foras Tionscal (the grant-payment body) and also an Executive Director of the IDA – found themselves frustrated by the constraints imposed by the civil service employment structure. To hire a typist, they needed the approval of the Department of Finance; to go on a European investment mission, they needed permission from the Department of Industry and Commerce. Both men felt the IDA's growth and development was being impeded. Nevertheless, the Authority had opened six foreign offices to promote inward investment – in London, Paris, Cologne, New York, San Francisco and Chicago. But rather than rely on the Embassy network to work there, the IDA appointed its own directors in each case.

At that stage, Walsh and O'Neill were also acutely conscious that Ireland no longer had the investment-promotion field all to herself. Countries like Britain had started to compete for mobile foreign investment. So the Authority responded by commissioning the American consulting company A. D. Little to review the way Ireland organised its industrial promotion effort. Its report in 1967 was clear and unequivocal and recommended that the twin agencies should be merged into a single Industrial Development Authority and be taken out of the civil service and established as a separate state agency.

The American consultants highlighted an endemic problem for the IDA, so long as its staff were civil servants. Those wanting early promotion applied for promotion posts throughout the parent department. However, if successful, they were then lost to its two industrial-development subsidiaries. The report's recommendations were accepted by the Minister of Industry, George Colley (1966–70), and the legislation, largely drafted by Walsh and O'Neill, was designed to give the new IDA all the powers it needed to do a professional job in promoting Ireland's industrial development attractions.

The new Industrial Development Act, 1969, which Colley piloted through the Oireachtas and which became law on Christmas Eve, gave the Authority a powerful statutory mandate to act under the Minister 'as a Body having national responsibility for the furtherance of industrial development'. It was a legislative masterpiece and covered IDA promotion, capital grants, the development of industrial estates and advance factories. The legislation also allowed for the provision of houses for key workers and training grants for staff development; it even enabled the agency to take equity stakes in companies. But, in addition to its role in promoting foreign investment, the IDA now had responsibility for modernising and developing indigenous industry, and encouraging small Irish start-up companies. Also included was the right to finance company research and development. In 1969, that was still a visionary concept.

As the necessary legislation passed through the Oireachtas, John Walsh, the Chairman of the outgoing agency since 1965, was replaced in November 1969. An architect of the industrial development approach up to that time, he was a scholarly and thoughtful man, retiring by nature, not a 'front of house' man.

This change over – from civil service to state-sponsored body – marked a major transition in the IDA's development from limited to full autonomy. The Authority could look back with satisfaction over the previous two decades, where some distinguished public servants – like its first chairman, J. P. Beddy (1950–65) had shaped the early years of industrial promotion. But others, like Pádraig Ó Slatarra and Ted O'Neill, spanned two very different stages of the IDA's development. In particular, O'Neill became one of the key figures to bridge the old and the new IDA. He was also one of the most remarkable of those unsung pioneers of the early years. In that critical twenty-year period, 1950–70, he was involved in every milestone of industrial promotion. He joined the new IDA at its inception in 1970, and for a further ten years, until his retirement in 1980, Ted O'Neill remained a most influential figure.

BRENDAN O'REGAN

Seán Lemass once quoted with approval President Roosevelt's description of the Tennessee Valley Authority (TVA) as 'a corporation clothed with the power of government, but possessed of the flexibility and initiative of private enterprise'. For Brendan O'Regan, who was asked by the government in 1943 to take over catering at Shannon and open a restaurant for sea planes in Foynes, the TVA initiative was the inspiration both for that and later developments in the region. He went on to create a series of world firsts at Shannon, most notably the first duty-free shop in an airport in 1947. In the immediate post-war years, nearly half the passengers flying the North Atlantic route stopped at Shannon. Later came the first Industrial

Export Processing Zone, with companies exempt from all import duties and tariffs and from tax on export profits. This was set up alongside the airport in 1959. O'Regan succeeded in having a new company, the Shannon Free Airport Development Company, established outside the civil service to develop and manage all his development initiatives.

The first 'advance factories' in Ireland were built at Shannon Free Zone in 1960 to encourage foreign investment to locate there. The new Free Zone area at Shannon proved successful, attracting in those early years industries like SPS Engineering from the USA and De Beers Diamond from South Africa. By 1970, some forty-five companies had located at the industrial estate, employing some 3,500 people.

Other regions looked enviously at Shannon's special tax status. In 1964, the continuing success of the Shannon experiment prompted the government to set up a Committee on Development Centres and Industrial Estates. It recommended that other regional centres should also have industrial estates. A year later, the government decided that the first two should be built in Galway and Waterford.

So it was that John Gannon, then with the IDA, went out and acquired an initial 60 acres in both cities in the autumn of 1966. The well-designed and well-maintained industrial estates first developed in Shannon, Galway and Waterford under state ownership and control proved highly successful in attracting foreign industry. These provided the models for the industrial estates, business parks and individual advance factories that were to follow later throughout the country in the quest for balanced regional development.

MICHAEL KILLEEN

When Michael Killeen became managing director of the IDA in 1970, he was seen as one of the state sector's new young high-flyers. Just forty-two when appointed, Killeen had been general manager of

Córas Tráchtála (the Export Board) for the previous three years. Tall, dark and exceptionally good-looking, with a pipe invariably at his lips, he had a commanding presence. A good listener and shrewd observer, he combined charm with a certain ruthlessness. Colleagues and subordinates from those early days variously described him as 'charismatic', 'engaging' and 'a great persuader'. They also remarked on his air of maturity at a relatively young age and his clarity when briefing staff.

In business, Killeen was a driven man – and also a born leader. He never seemed to suffer from fear of failure. Yet he was sensitive to the different talents and abilities in those around him. Long before management gurus like Tom Peters and 'The Pursuit of Excellence' movement of the eighties had developed this theme, Killeen exemplified that perfectionist quality. In doing so, he imbued the IDA with his own high standards. Everything had to be perfect: documentation, presentations. An immaculate dresser himself, he set an automatic standard for IDA staff. The new organisation needed neither dress codes nor value statements. All were personified in one highly regarded individual whose accomplishments and sense of style were emulated at all levels of the organisation.

Killeen's pursuit-of-excellence philosophy also reflected a strong sense of public service. He viewed the IDA's industrial development role as a form of practical patriotism. Certainly, his dedication left an enduring imprint on the whole organisation that survives to this day. From the start he set specific targets for the achievement of jobs and industry strategies. This highly quantified approach was new to state agencies. But he insisted on this management-by-objectives approach, both as a way of making the executives in the organisation accountable and as a means of measuring internally the progress in different countries and sectors. Michael Killeen took the risk of declaring the IDA targets in public and of reporting on their attainment. In this way, he believed, IDA achievements could be related easily to the country's overall job needs, both at the national and regional levels.

*

When, in November 1969, George Colley, Minister for Industry and Commerce, picked Michael Killeen to replace John Walsh as chairman of the 'old' and managing director designate of the 'new' entity, it was a sudden and sensational move. Killeen was then head of Córas Tráchtála (the Export Board), and the legislation for the new IDA was in its final stages in the Oireachtas. In January 1970, Killeen moved in. One of his first actions was to call all the staff to a meeting in the canteen on the fourth floor of Lansdowne House, the IDA's new headquarters. He told them bluntly that the government had asked him to do a job. As he spoke, his determination to succeed was obvious and his message unmistakable. From all those who wished to remain with the IDA, he expected full cooperation. And while some senior staff did leave, some 80 per cent of the 132 civil servants from the merged agencies (IDA and Foras Tionscal) elected to stay on. For them, this decision represented something of a career risk. They were swapping the security of civil-service tenure for an untried state agency, and under the leadership of the reportedly ruthless Michael Killeen. They took that risk.

Straight away, Killeen set about recruiting a remarkable range of talent from right across the private sector to add to the hundred-plus civil servants he had inherited. First, he took on Joe Dunne from Bord Bainne as Head of Administration. Together, they sought out the best talent in the private sector, hand-picking them by multiple tough interviews. The new recruits included Ray McLoughlin, then best known as an Irish rugby international prop forward; Brendan Swan, a swashbuckling marketing man with a background in the Canadian textile industry; Brendan Cassidy, former Commandant of the Army Cadet School; others like Joe O'Sullivan, John Lyons and Joe Beirne came from indigenous Irish industry.

Inside eight months, the IDA, which retained its six overseas offices, had assembled 230 staff. It was a remarkable cocktail of talent from two different business cultures – the public and private sector. Just over half came from the civil service, with years of experience in promoting industrial investment from within a government department. The remaining hundred or so had come straight from the marketplace. And while the latter group knew a good deal about how private industry operated, they knew nothing about promoting a country to foreign investors. However, they learned fast under Michael Killeen, the master blender of talent. Over time, the IDA pioneered and perfected the industrial development strategy to win direct foreign investment to Ireland. Not only is much the same strategy used by the agency today, but the IDA itself has become a role model for other countries seeking to emulate the Irish success.

My entry to the new IDA was through one of the twenty-one job slots that were filled by open competition among civil servants from all departments. In 1970, I was an administrative officer in the Department of Health and guaranteed promotion within two years. One day, when strolling through the corridors of the Custom House, I came across a formal notice pinned to the message board. It sought applications for the post of Planning Officer in the Industrial Development Authority. I was curious, applied for the post, and was invited to an interview at IDA headquarters in Lansdowne Road in October 1970. The reception area on the fifth floor of Lansdowne House in autumn 1970 had all the outward and visible signs of a corporate culture that I had not seen in Ireland before. There was an elegant reception area, a breezy receptionist and a bank of electronic pagers. These were collected or deposited by young men in a hurry and beeped periodically as they passed by. I thought to myself: 'This is it, this place is really buzzing.'

I was called to a second interview and by then I was hooked on the challenge this new organisation presented, if I were given the chance. When I was offered the job, I consulted many people about the merits of leaving the civil service. Most counselled me against moving, saying there was no security in this new organisation. However, the die was cast one evening in Maynooth College. I was sharing a platform on the theme of western development with Willie Moloney, a young economist with Shannon Development who was familiar with the emerging IDA. His advice was succinct: 'Go for it – Killeen will make it work.' So that night in November 1970, I decided to join the new organisation .

I later found out that they gave me a job in the new Regional Planning Team even though it wasn't the job I had applied for. Why? Because, it seems, I was so carried away, at that first interview, with my opposition to the *Buchanan Report* published in 1968, which favoured concentration of industry in growth centres. As a Leitrim man, I felt strongly about the need to bring industry to the smaller towns and communities as well.

10

THE IDA PHILOSOPHY
THROUGH THE DECADES

Padraic White

From the beginning the IDA took great care to ensure it met the needs of every new company locating in Ireland, either by doing so itself or by mediating to resolve any problems that arose. This latter role included interceding with government departments or local authorities where necessary. The IDA sought to provide a 'one-stop shop' service. Once new foreign firms began production, the Authority kept in contact at two levels – both with the Irish plant and its foreign parent. Such a hands-on, company-friendly approach yielded rich investment dividends, particularly in later years. Multinational companies, which might easily have diversified elsewhere in Europe, instead expanded their production in Ireland. In stressing this aspect of the IDA's after-sales service to such companies, Albert Reynolds, as Industry Minister, used to tell his investor audiences: 'Ireland believes that a satisfied customer is the country's best salesman.'

In the global battle for foreign direct investment, the proven success of the IDA's industrial-development techniques gave the staff both a resilience to adversity and a determination to succeed, no matter what difficulties they met. Over the next three decades there were many obstacles to be overcome. Some were domestic – like the Northern Ireland troubles and the mismanagement of the public finances. Others were generated externally: like the two oil-induced recessions in the seventies and the Gulf War slowdown in 1991. For most of that period, the IDA had three chief executives – Michael Killeen in the 1970s, myself in the 1980s and Kieran McGowan in the 1990s. Sean Dorgan succeeded Kieran McGowan as chief executive in 1999.

A nationwide bank strike that continues for seven months is not the ideal economic background against which to launch a new state agency which hopes to persuade foreign investors to set up industry. The IDA's establishment as a non-civil service state agency in April 1970 could hardly have taken place at a less opportune time. The national bank strike which started that month continued until November 1970 and was a grave embarrassment, very difficult to explain to potential investors. However, it was the first of two bank strikes in a decade that was disfigured by bitter industrial disputes. These ranged from strikes in the ESB in 1972, which led to power failures and industrial shutdowns, and culminated in 1979 in postal and airline strikes.

The Northern Ireland conflict, and the risk of a spillover of violence into the Republic, was a besetting fear through the decade. In December 1972, two bombs exploded in Dublin, killing two people and injuring 127 others. In May 1974, further car bombs in Dublin and Monaghan resulted in a further thirty-one deaths and 150 persons injured. In October 1975, Dr Herrema, Managing Director of the largest foreign employer in Ireland – Ferenka Ltd in Limerick, a subsidiary of the Dutch AKZO group – was kidnapped by the IRA. He was held for over a month, until rescued by the gardaí. And then in July 1976, the British Ambassador to Ireland was assassinated.

If those traumatic events induced days of despair and anguish in the IDA, Michael Killeen was temperamentally well suited to counter them – he was a natural optimist. His instinct and example was to 'put the head down' and get on with the job of promoting Ireland, irrespective of the problems. By getting close to the key decision-taking individuals in a foreign company, he believed the IDA could rationalise the perceived problem – whatever it was.

On the other hand, Ireland's entry into the EEC in 1973 had greatly enhanced the country's attraction as an industrial location. For the IDA, it became a key selling point. Community membership gave investors guaranteed entry to a market of 250 million people. No longer was Ireland an isolated island with uncertain access to some European markets. To capitalise on the new opportunity, the IDA accelerated its promotional drive in two ways. It developed a direct marketing approach to foreign companies involving individual presentations. The IDA also sought to raise Ireland's business profile by a sustained advertising campaign, highlighting the country as the most profitable investment location in Europe.

In its early years, the new IDA derived great satisfaction from the beginning of large investments in the new man-made fibre industries: the Italian Snia Viscosa nylon plant for Sligo (1971), the UK Courtaulds polyester plant for Letterkenny (1973) and the Japanese Asahi Chemical company's acrylic plant for Killala (1974). Other high-profile companies to locate here were Gillette-Braun to Carlow with 1,000 jobs, the pharmaceutical companies Syntex to Clarecastle, Merck Sharpe and Dohme to Clonmel, and Warner Lambert to Dublin. Clearly, the IDA machine was working.

However, adverse external developments impinged heavily on the IDA's success in industrial-development promotion. The 1973 oil crisis, when the OPEC states dramatically raised energy prices, hit IDA promotion badly in 1974 and 1975. The resulting world recession cut demand sharply and raised inflation. Faced with adverse economic conditions, the major international companies became more risk-averse. They were unwilling to make new investments overseas while global demand remained depressed. The number of foreign projects negotiated by the IDA fell by half, dropping from eighty in 1973 to some forty in 1975, before the upturn finally began. By the end of the decade, the Irish economy had recovered, and in 1979 the IDA had negotiated the highest volume of foreign investment ever – 14,000 projected jobs. That was twice the level of the nadir year of 1975.

The late seventies were heady days as the IDA captured the emerging stars of the electronics industry. One such was the US microchip company Mostek from Dallas, Texas. It chose Ireland to manufacture its chips for the European market and built a showpiece plant in Blanchardstown, Dublin. I was deputed in 1979 to go to New York with the Minister for Industry and Commerce, Des O'Malley, for the official announcement. This we organised jointly with Mostek at a press launch in the Pierre Hotel before a full house from the American business media. The Mostek decision proved critical. It gave the IDA an opportunity to speak with greater confidence about an Ireland now capable of supporting high-technology investment. That same year, two more success stories of the emerging computer world – Wang Laboratories of Massachusetts with their word-processing range and Verbatim of California – picked Ireland as their European base.

Our euphoria was short-lived. Just before the dawn of the

new decade, the seeds of a second and even deeper recession were being sown. Once more, in June 1979, the oil-producing countries raised energy prices. In August 1979, Lord Mountbatten was murdered by the IRA, adversely affecting the industrial-development climate. Inflation took off again in Ireland, as elsewhere, reaching 20 per cent in 1981.

*

In the autumn of 1980, Michael Killeen, who had been managing director of the IDA for just over a decade, announced his intention to resign. He wanted to make a career in the private sector. After a public competition open to all comers, I was selected to succeed him. That transition year of 1980 benefited from the positive international mood of preceding years as negotiations for a cluster of outstanding industries matured. It was just before economic recession struck a second time in less than a decade. As high interest rates eroded investor confidence worldwide, the multinationals again retrenched, and foreign investment once more dried up.

Before that happened, the glamorous Apple Computer, led by industry guru Steven Jobs, chose Ireland as its European production base. Apple was a real coup for the IDA. As the pioneer of the personal computer, Apple's investment decision had a major demonstration effect within the electronics industry. It put Ireland on the map in Silicon Valley, California, for Apple was one of the most admired companies in the fast-growing high-technology sector.

Earlier in the spring of 1980, during a four-month Eisenhower Fellowship study tour of emerging-industry sectors in the USA, my wife Mary and I visited the Silicon Valley area north of San Francisco. Declan Collins, the IDA man based there, acted as our guide. As we toured the 'new age' industrial parks of the Valley, Declan pointed out the individual companies established in Ireland. 'We have that one,' he exclaimed, spotting the distinctive Apple and Verbatim logos or, 'We haven't that one yet,' as he gestured towards Intel, which was to come some ten years later. Apple's decision during 1979 to locate in Ireland was such a source of pride that we stopped and took photos standing in front of that famous logo – the multicoloured apple with a bite taken out of it. I still have them!

The other big projects of 1980 included Bausch and Lomb plastic lenses for Waterford and the IMED medical equipment company (now Donegal Healthcare Ltd) for Letterkenny. Kostal of Germany established a car electronics plant in Abbeyfeale, and Fujitsu of Japan began the test and assembly of microchips in Tallaght, Dublin. All these new plants prospered, enhanced the name of Ireland with their peers and have contributed handsomely to jobs and economic growth ever since.

But on succeeding Michael Killeen, little did I know that the famous IDA pipeline was just about to peak. The world recession deepened and US economic growth, which provided the motor for about half the foreign inward investment, remained depressed. At home, inflation averaged 16.6 per cent over the four years 1980–3 inclusive, and the economy actually contracted in three years – 1982, 1983 and 1986. The domestic business mood become more pessimistic as markets deteriorated, taxes increased, the public-sector deficit kept on rising and there was a net contraction of manufacturing employment.

The mood of depression and despondency became infectious. As employment continued to fall up to 1986, the killer comment from journalists attending IDA briefings held to announce new projects – say for 500 jobs – was the riposte, 'It's only a drop in the ocean.' The IDA saw the challenge of the 1980s as keeping the flag of Ireland flying internationally in the face of all adversity. Like any commercial business, the Authority knew it must keep pushing the 'brand' in the market place. Otherwise, when the economic clouds finally lifted, Ireland would lose out, and more than three decades spent building up our industrial-development reputation would go for nought.

Nevertheless, it was tough. In late 1981, for example, the IDA organised a prestigious evening seminar in the campus of Stanford University Palo Alto, which is right in the heart of Silicon Valley. We were doing well until the dreaded subject of the Irish inflation rate was raised during the question-and-answer session. It was not easy to defend a 20 per cent inflation rate, particularly to an American audience.

As the recession intensified, unemployment rose, and the battle for investment between European countries became more aggressive and much 'dirtier'. Increasingly, other industrial-development agencies used a wide variety of spoiling tactics to win new investment at our expense. In 1983, the IDA discovered that rival agencies, bidding for the same projects, were sabotaging our promotional efforts. Some of the larger EEC member states – Britain and France were the main culprits – had suggested to potential investors that publicly funded purchases of their products might be blacklisted if the new investment was located in Ireland.

In other instances, doubts were even cast on the assurance of Ireland's free-trade access to European and global markets. This threat implied difficulties either with the customs authorities or, in the case of multinational drug companies, in meeting national health regulations. In particular, the computer and healthcare industries were very vulnerable to such suggestions, as public purchasing of their products represented a big slice of the market. In other cases, the IDA found itself up against unexpected competition in financial packages, where countries accumulated a range of regional, sectoral and local financial grants to circumvent EEC guidelines.

These new scare tactics represented a covert form of protectionism that came to a head in 1982. Privately, a dozen firms with which the IDA was then in negotiation had told us of their experiences. They even gave us copies of the financial packages offered. This threatened to undermine the foundation of Ireland's pitch to investors, namely, that although we only had a home market of 3.5 million, our membership of the EEC was a guarantee of full and unimpeded access to the larger 250 million European market.

However, once any doubt was sown in the investor's mind on the validity of the Irish assumption, companies had to weigh up the risks involved carefully. The IDA brought the details to the Department of Industry and Commerce, which, in turn, tabled its concerns with the European Commission in Brussels. The Commission response was to request that the companies involved should provide details of their individual complaints before it would launch an investigation. As a result both the IDA and the companies found themselves in a 'catch 22' predicament. By lodging an official complaint to the Commission about a country, the company would be jeopardising its hopes of ever winning business or support there.

The government's concerns were so great that the Taoiseach, Garret FitzGerald, brought the issue to an EEC Summit meeting in Stuttgart, in June 1983. In a formal statement on his return, he said he had raised with the heads of state and government 'the case of new forms of protectionism to influence the location of mobile international investment' and pointed out 'the distortions caused by the procurement policies in some states, and to the increasing use of technical and health regulations as forms of protectionism'. However, these threats to Ireland were not satisfactorily dealt with until the single-market initiative was launched by the European Commission with considerable fanfare in 1985. This set about removing by 1992 the very non-tariff barriers that the government and the IDA had complained about.

As the recession deepened in the early eighties, global unemployment rose as capital replaced labour. Increased automation and greater use of computer technologies meant fewer were employed, as productivity rose and costs fell. By 1982, among Europe's OECD member countries, some 16 million people were jobless, and unemployment was forecast to rise for a further two years. IDA staff, in their worldwide contacts with companies about future investment plans, found a common pattern of response emerging. Many were under pressure to reduce unit costs by investing in the most advanced technologies and thereby reducing the numbers employed in production. But for a state agency whose prime focus was to get industries with the highest job content for Ireland, this was not the happiest of messages. And it prompted a reassessment of strategy.

In response, I launched a complete policy rethink within the IDA which involved every staff member, and I brought in the McKinsey Consulting company to facilitate the re-evaluation. The end result was the IDA Strategic Plan for the decade 1982–92. I unveiled, publicly, the essence of this new approach in the most significant speech of my career, at a conference in Trinity College, Dublin, in 1983. The occasion was to mark the bicentenary of the Dublin Chamber of Commerce. Privately, I had felt such a gathering provided the ideal historical backdrop to outline a new response to the profound industrial changes under way.

The preceding speaker was Dr Tony O'Reilly, President of

Heinz Corporation, who gave a witty and brilliant speech about the power of branded products. In his final anecdote, he recounted hearing an Australian radio broadcast description of a car break-in and theft. It listed the final item stolen as a bottle of Baileys Irish Cream – a testimony to the worldwide success of the Baileys brand. For any speaker, Dr O'Reilly is a hard act to follow. As I set out to unveil a 'Growth Policy for the Future', I hoped my listeners would settle down and be in a receptive mood for such a serious theme.

The message was that the IDA should focus on attracting industries that could achieve high output growth using the best technology available, while maximising their spending on Irish services and materials. In this way, the IDA would maximise the gains for the economy, both through jobs within the company and via the related service employment that would be created in consequence. Our judgement was that the most technologically advanced firms would be the most successful in the market place. We believed the jobs would follow that success. This marked a reversal of the IDA's traditional approach of attracting the most labour-intensive industries, since labour was in abundant supply in Ireland.

This new strategy provided a logic for the IDA to favour companies with the most advanced production facilities, even if these were not the most labour-intensive in a sector. It also offered a basis for judging a company by its total job impact; whether directly, on its own premises, and indirectly, through its suppliers. In this way the IDA would get the best total job result by encouraging firms to source the greatest possible share of their services and materials in Ireland. Electronics, computer software and special emerging opportunities in biotechnology and healthcare were the foreign industries I listed as meeting the high-growth criteria.

This focus on high-output, high-technology companies as the key to getting jobs got the official seal of approval in the government White Paper on Industrial Policy in 1984. In time, indigenous Irish business saw the spending power of the foreign companies on printing, freight, catering and components. The multinationals were a source of good business and supported jobs in their companies. Unfortunately, public or media comment rarely focused on these spin-off benefits to Irish companies, except when a foreign industry was facing closure. Nevertheless, their economic impact within Ireland remains considerable. Figures in the IDA Ireland annual report, 1998, based on 1997 data, estimated these companies spent some £8 billion, out of total sales of £22.6 billion. Thus some 35 per cent of the value of all sales by these companies was retained in the Irish economy.

Despite the depressing effect of recessionary economic conditions between 1980 and 1986, the IDA introduced two particular initiatives that were to produce lasting benefits. The first was a new International Services Programme. This was specifically designed to attract the booming new service-sector companies that were highly employment-intensive. As a distinct area of new investment, this sector needed both a different promotional approach and a different range of incentives than manufacturing industry. Since 1981, legislation was in place enabling the IDA to give employment grants, as capital grants were of little benefit to those companies. In all we had twelve target sectors, including data processing, software development and publishing houses.

The expanded concept of International Services brought IDA staff through the doors of a wider and more varied range of industries. It soon produced results, with the arrival of an IBM Software Centre (1983), Lotus software (1984) and Microsoft software (1985). By their presence, all three helped establish, over time, a world-class base for software companies in this country, and by their subsequent expansions, they have created thousands of jobs in Ireland.

At the same time, the IDA took a second significant initiative. It launched an international advertising campaign in 1983 that was radically different in look and tone from anything else, anywhere. In conjunction with McConnell's Advertising Agency and after detailed research, we introduced the 'We're the Young Europeans' theme. The IDA switched the focus of attention away from tax incentives and finance and, instead, highlighted Ireland's educated youth and European Community membership. The advertisements, which featured students in Trinity College and a close-up of a graduate class in University College, Dublin, had a remarkable impact on our business audience. The campaign ads were mentioned frequently in conversations with IDA staff. Whether by design or good fortune, the business leaders associated Ireland with the very assets – human capital – they regarded as critical to success: bright, educated young people. And these were just the qualities that served to distinguish Ireland from her European competitors in the battle for industrial development.

Despite the recession, the IDA continued to win prize projects such as the first Japanese pharmaceutical company, Yamanouchi in 1985, and the Fruit of the Loom textile company for the Inishowen Peninsula the following year. Foreign companies typically had created about 6,000 net first-time jobs a year. However, the recession took its toll, and between cutbacks and closures there was a net drop in jobs in the foreign sector in four of the seven years 1980 to 1986 inclusive. In just one day in May 1983, the closures were announced of the AT&T-owned Telectron factory, employing 800 in Tallaght, and the Black and Decker plant, with 270 workers in Kildare. The loss of 1,000 jobs in a single day was a double-whammy blow. These years witnessed many false dawns of economic recovery. The economy contracted in the two years 1982 and 1983 and made a modest recovery in 1984 before a further year of negative growth in 1985.

For an organisation like the IDA, which thrives on optimism and confidence in Ireland's economic future, and where the staff convey their convictions to prospective investors, these were difficult times. Throughout, my primary aim was to keep staff motivation and morale high, given the prevailing mood of pessimism. So, at successive IDA annual conferences – the rallying time for the year ahead – I used a chart to illustrate how the Irish public mood oscillates between melancholia and euphoria. The prevailing mood of pessimism was overdone and I predicted that on the first signs of the upturn, we would swing back, quickly, to a more euphoric state of mind.

But 1986 provided little relief from the gloom, with business confidence still depressed. The IDA Annual Report for the year summed up the scene as follows: 'High real interest rates, depressed domestic demand and unfavourable exchange rates created a generally difficult environment for industry in 1986.' The general election announced in January 1987 brought the world media to Ireland, and their coverage reflected both the atmosphere of gloom and the sense of economic crisis. Whether the foreign journalist spoke to a taxi driver, an economist or a journalist in Ireland, the message re-transmitted in the international media was one of unmitigated disaster. In the face of such a gloomy consensus, the IDA version of Ireland sounded like a fairy tale. It was a tough time.

The nadir of international coverage came in a special feature in the influential *Economist* magazine on Ireland in January 1987, entitled 'How the government spent the people into a slump.' The survey opened with an old photograph of a poverty-stricken family with the headline, 'In Hock, Out of Work'. The final flourish concluded, 'Yet the next government will most probably be formed by Mr Haughey and his rural-based Fianna Fáil supporters longing to hand out money after four years in opposition. Irish bankers fear that, to their shame, the International Monetary Fund may have to step in to impose stringency that their own politicians cannot muster.'

When viewed through the eyes of a national investment-promotion agency, there could scarcely be worse international coverage. It was close to 'turn out the lights time' in the IDA. But, as it transpired, the *Economist* conclusion was correct in only one aspect. Charles Haughey became Taoiseach in March, and Fianna Fáil proceeded as a minority government. But he did so with the support of the Fine Gael opposition, combining tough fiscal policy measures with some innovative tax changes and investment incentives. These policy measures laid the foundation for what was to become the Celtic Tiger economy. In all of this, there was a special irony and significance. For just ten years later, in 1997, the *Economist* again analysed Ireland in depth, and the storyline was very different. This time, the Irish economy featured as the magazine's cover story, and the praise was as lavish as the criticism had been harsh, just a decade earlier. The economy had become 'Europe's shining light' and the article contained a glowing analysis of the anatomy of the 'emerald tiger'.

*

In March 1987, Ray Mac Sharry became Minister of Finance in the new Fianna Fáil minority government for the second time in four years. Elsewhere in this book, he describes the nature of the policies pursued, and the political decisions taken by the new government to revive the economy. The IDA Annual Report for that year succinctly summed up the dramatic change in the economic climate achieved within twelve months. It noted that 1987 'was truly remarkable for the speed and extent of the improvement in the business environment in Ireland'.

Taoiseach Charles Haughey and his advisers had come into office hostile to the IDA, if only to judge by some obviously inspired media leaks about the fate awaiting the organisation. There was little trust or confidence extended to the IDA in pushing ahead with the proposed International Financial Services Centre in Dublin.

Then the IDA Chairman, Joe McCabe, and myself were summoned to government buildings for an intensive review of all our policies with the Taoiseach, Minister Ray Mac Sharry, Albert Reynolds, Minister for Industry and Commerce, and Pádraig Ó hUiginn, Secretary of the Taoiseach's Department. At the start of the meeting, which was directed by the Taoiseach, the atmosphere was tetchy. I wondered if the IDA and its staff were to be the 'fall guys' for the poor employment outlook. We had prepared an outline written presentation of IDA plans for each sector of industry, outlining the companies we were targeting, and with which we were then in negotiations. As we worked our way through the sectors, the atmosphere thawed. It seemed there was a growing realisation that these IDA fellows knew what they were about after all and had positive plans in place. We came through the inquisition successfully and Haughey in subsequent conversation with me summed up, with obvious approval, our foreign-investment policy as 'high-tech, high-productivity, high-skill'. It was a very accurate rendering.

As the new government cut public spending to help stabilise the public finances, it looked to all state organisations to raise productivity by doing more work with less money and fewer people. Given the mood of fiscal austerity, the IDA felt it too should respond to the spirit of the times. So we came up with a number of changes: first, a commitment to win more jobs, and second, a unilateral decision, to seek one hundred staff redundancies. In addition, we tightened up on the grant-giving conditions for industry. These now became legally repayable, if target job numbers were not achieved. For a proud organisation like the IDA, the decision to seek redundancies was traumatic. Nevertheless, the target was reached in three months, by the end of 1987. The Minister for Industry and Commerce, Albert Reynolds, paid a handsome public tribute to the organisation's response at the launch of revised policies in 1988 when he said:

> I want to take this opportunity to compliment the IDA and its management team for the professional manner in which the organisation took on board the cuts in its current and capital budgets for 1988. The IDA has regrouped its personnel and organisation structure to align with the new industrial-policy objectives. What the IDA is committing itself to achieve is an improved performance in terms of jobs and industrial growth for a lesser input from the public purse.

Throughout 1987, the rapid pace of the Irish economic recovery accelerated and won greater international recognition and publicity. The IDA capitalised on the better performance, and the number and quality of projects in the agency 'pipeline' improved greatly. Within two years, the IDA had secured a cluster of high-calibre companies. These included, from the US, Motorola and Teradata computer firms locating at Swords; Intel and Stratus computer companies at Leixlip and Blanchardstown and Electronic Data Systems in Dublin. SCI computer sub-assemblies set up in Fermoy and Puritan Bennett Healthcare located in Galway. From Japan came Fujitsu Isotec, a printer-component project, and from Switzerland came the Sandoz (now part õf Novartis) pharmaceutical plant for Cork.

The Motorola and Intel investments were viewed in the IDA as outstanding coups. These were household names in their industries and primary targets of every European investment agency. In fact, the IDA had pursued both companies for over a decade. Motorola was a world leader in mobile communications – pagers and mobile telephones – and would make a selection of these products in Ireland. By 1998, it had 1,600 on its direct payroll in Ireland. Meanwhile Intel was the dominant manu-facturer of microprocessors – the intelligent chip at the heart of electronics – and had chosen Ireland as its European base for the complex 'black art' of microchip manufacture. By 1998, Intel directly employed 3,500 staff, had invested £1.8 billion and that year opened its 'FAB 14' to make its latest microchip. This was done in the largest industrial premises – 800,000 square feet – ever constructed in Ireland. The Intel investment put Ireland into the premier league in the international electronics industry.

Intel, as the world leader in manufacturing microprocessors for computers and electronic devices, was the most prized target for European investment agencies. By the late eighties, though it had almost $1 billion in sales in Europe, Intel had no production plant within the European Community. Previously, the electronics company had decided to locate a plant in Israel. And while staff at Menlo Park, the IDA's office in Silicon Valley, California, had routinely maintained contact with the firm, there was no sign of interest in securing a European base, unlike most other US electronics companies which had done so. However, Intel's senior people had periodically attended IDA events.

Since 1978, the number of transistors in the chip, which

drives most PCs, has increased from 29,000 in the 8086 processor in 1978 to 7.5 million in the Pentium twenty years later. This rate of exponential growth reflects what has come to be called Moore's law, after Intel's Gordon Moore. He claimed that the power of microchips doubles every two years or so, requiring Intel to build new high-volume plants for each new generation of chips.

In March 1989, we got the news that Intel had appointed a nine-person team to examine seven countries in Europe as a location for investment in two distinct projects: one was to make microprocessors (semi-conductors) and involved 1,500 jobs, and the other was to make computer systems, with 1,000 jobs. It was possible that the two projects could be located in different countries, since different staff divisions in Intel were responsible for the respective developments. Consequently, each had individual preferences for the ideal location for their own project.

The IDA organisation went to 'red alert' status to compete for the project, and we assembled a team of fifteen people from many parts of the organisation to handle the contest: IDA staff in the US, the Dublin-based electronics division, the regional offices in Ireland where the industry might be located, and our property, legal and tax specialists. Kieran McGowan as director of the foreign industry division of the IDA coordinated the team and its key players, including Martin Cronin, head of the electronic group; Frank Ryan, the key Dublin-based project officer; P. J. Daly, director of US operations for the IDA; Tony Jones the West Coast director; and Gerry Kehoe, the executive with the most direct interaction with Intel's head office.

We faced two challenges right from the start. First, the IDA had to convince Intel that Ireland could support such a large and sophisticated investment – a mammoth task in its own right. Second, we knew we faced major obstacles in convincing government departments that the IDA should support a full-scale semiconductor-manufacturing (technically wafer-fabrication) plant. And of course there was the international competition. There were seven other European countries on Intel's list for on-site investigation: Scotland, Wales, France, Germany, Austria, the Netherlands and Spain. In the Intel team's visits to Ireland, all aspects of a potential project were scrutinised.

Early on, Intel was attracted to a sixty-acre industrial park along the Leixlip–Maynooth road which the IDA had acquired and developed some five years earlier. Its executives noted the housing and population growth in neighbouring towns, and the plans for the new M50 motorway. But what about planning procedures and possible delays? Since the price of microchips keeps falling as new generations of more powerful chips come to market, then clearly unscheduled planning delays affecting building and production could have catastrophic consequences for the commercial success of the plant. Once again, other players for Ireland Inc played their part. Gerry Ward, the Kildare County Manager, and his top engineer, John Carrick, reassured the company of their full support in speedy processing of the planning permission, and in securing other facilities like water and road access. It was obvious that the Kildare chiefs could neither guarantee planning approval nor avoid delays arising from public objections. However, their equally obvious commitment and enthusiasm kept Leixlip as Intel's preferred site.

Another query was the political development of the European Union and the achievement of a genuinely free single market. Peter Sutherland, then the Irish Commissioner in Brussels, met the nine-person Intel team on a Sunday night in Dublin's Shelbourne Hotel to brief and reassure them. In the course of its evaluation, Intel was undoubtedly impressed with the development of the electronics industry in Ireland over the preceding twenty years and the sophistication of the support services available, such as Irish transport carriers, architects and builders.

Intel then cut the shortlist to four: Scotland, Wales, Austria and Ireland. But there was one big question mark still hanging over Ireland's claims. The country did not already have an example of a large-scale producer of microchips. So how could the IDA satisfy the company that Intel could get the experienced engineers that were needed to produce them? Other countries had such plants in operation. So to eliminate this weakness in the Irish case, the IDA commissioned Amrop International, a specialist consulting group, with a brief to locate Irish engineers who were working abroad and had relevant experience in the semi-conductor industry. Within five weeks, over 300 Irish engineers, mainly in the US, had been identified and individually contacted; each of them had between three and seven years' experience in the production of volume semi-conductors. The formal report handed to Intel had the positive finding that over 80 per cent of the expatriate engineers would return to Ireland if given a good career opportunity with a quality company. This report was crucial in satisfying Intel that Ireland could satisfactorily host an advanced microchip plant.

However, we were still in an international contest. Even if Ireland technically could do the job, there remained the issues of the financing and profitability of the development here, by comparison with the other locations. The financial negotiations were arduous, not least because the IDA faced an immense hurdle in making the case for Intel to government departments. The IDA already had on its files a formal letter from the Department of Industry and Commerce which directed it not to support large-scale semi-conductor plants. Both Chairman

Joe McCabe and myself had sought – before Intel came on the scene – to get this general directive rescinded, but we failed. We knew that if we wished to back such a plant, and then seek departmental and government approval, we would do so against the background of a distinct lack of official enthusiasm or goodwill. This hostile official attitude to the semi-conductor industry had hardened in the wake of two disappointments in 1985. The Mostek semi-conductor plant at Blanchardstown, Dublin, had closed in November 1985 with a loss of some 500 jobs. The collapse in world prices for its memory chips, which were bought and sold as a standard commodity, proved its undoing. However, Intel's microprocessors were much more complex, with distinct proprietary features.

The second disappointment was the decision in 1985 of an Intel competitor, Advanced Micro Devices (AMD), to defer its plans for an £180 million facility at Greystones, County Wicklow. This plant was intended to employ 1,000 people, half of them graduates, in making its proprietary microchips. The IDA had also fought a tough battle for the AMD project, and its indefinite postponement was heartbreaking.

Joe McCabe and myself shared a common view that Intel was a world leader in its products, that its intelligent microchips would be at the heart of the electronic and computing revolution and that if Ireland could win the Intel project, this would complement perfectly the electronics-industry strategy that had been put in place. We resolved to take the internal negotiations on the Intel financial package to the limit. My guidance to IDA staff, who were aware of the official reservations, was to press ahead and forget about the politics of it. In any event, the likely scale of IDA financial grants to Intel would demand the most serious evaluation. The grant package of £87 million, which, even though it was spread over ten years and entailed 2,600 high-quality jobs, was equivalent to 80 per cent of the government capital grant of £109 million to the IDA in 1989. And that sum had to cover both investment in Irish business and foreign industry. How could the IDA justify putting such a sum into one company? If the IDA did this, what about its budget for small business? Clearly, these were the questions raised.

As Kieran McGowan liaised with the Intel team, he faced other tough questions. If Intel expanded subsequently, would it get equal treatment with other companies? Would the 10 per cent tax rate continue after the year 2000, the terminal date then set. In the torrid negotiating atmosphere, we managed to get satisfactory assurances back within days.

Intel then cut the shortlist to two locations – Scotland and Ireland. During the final phase, the Irish team of the IDA, industrialists, bankers, educationalists and local authority person-nel did everything within their power to secure the project for Ireland. More outside consultants were appointed to assist the IDA in the commercial evaluation of the project. The analysis proved positive. The IDA approved the deal and both Minister O'Malley and the government departments were coming around strongly to favour the project. Then came the last week of negotiations, and day after day and long into the nights, the sessions to resolve the remaining difficulties and the outstanding details continued. We got word that British Prime Minister Margaret Thatcher was to intervene, personally, in a last-minute bid to sway the investment to the United Kingdom. But Ireland had done her homework. The availability of skills, a low corporate tax rate and financial support were edging us ahead in the race.

The decision went Ireland's way. There was unconfined joy, excitement and pride among IDA staff everywhere. It reminded me of the atmosphere almost twenty years before when the IDA had won its first computer project, the Digital (DEC) project that went to Galway. The Intel investment was officially announced at a packed press conference in the IDA's headquarters at Wilton House, Dublin on 3 October 1989, in the presence of Gordon Moore, chairman of Intel, with his top executives, and Michael Smith, Minister for Science and Technology. This was just seven months after Intel had commenced the active evaluation of its European location. Intel would establish its European manufacturing base in Ireland, putting both its computer systems and its semiconductor facilities on the same site in Leixlip. And it would introduce a level of advanced technology few previously thought could be undertaken here, at least on such a scale. Undoubtedly, what pushed Ireland ahead in the tight race at the finish was the attitude of the Irish workforce. Intel admired the 'can do' attitude of the Irish. The company was convinced the Irish would make this investment a success.

The Intel project represents the most successful investment of taxpayers' money by the IDA in the thirty-year history of the organisation. No other overseas investment has exceeded the benefits and return to Ireland generated from the Intel project. Not surprisingly, 1989 became known at the IDA as the year of Intel. It also proved to be a watershed year for the attraction of high-technology investment.

ALBERT REYNOLDS

In 1987, as the new Minister for Industry and Commerce, Albert Reynolds, had already had a successful business career before going into politics. He brought a vigorous private business style to the promotion of investment. On missions to the USA and Japan in his first two years as minister, he established an immediate rapport with business audiences and while 'on the road' with IDA, he refined a growing number of promotional aphorisms and sales pitches. These had immense appeal to his audiences, implying a rare government understanding of business. They included 'Today's profit is tomorrow's capital', 'Your success is our success' and 'I'm a bottom-line man.'

While Albert Reynolds was on these overseas missions, the IDA resident executive would take the Minister's official biographical note and use it when formally introducing Minister Reynolds. Nick Kendellen, the IDA Director in Chicago, was so good at massaging the official version for his US audience that we in the Irish team thoroughly enjoyed the warm-up and introduction. Albert Reynolds had started with a chain of ballrooms, set up C and D Petfoods and bought a local Longford newspaper. But in Nick's version, the Minister had started his business career in the entertainment industry, diversified into the food industry and latterly become a publisher – it was an impressive range of industries even by US standards.

Earlier, as Minister for Posts and Telegraphs in 1979, Albert Reynolds had laid the foundations for a revolution in Irish telecommunications. In 1979, he announced a £1.25 billion state investment in the most advanced phone system available, a digital-based network. Almost overnight, Ireland moved from having one of the worst phone services in the world to one of the best. Where once there were 160,000 customers waiting months for a phone connection, soon the queues had disappeared, and phones were available virtually on demand.

The move allowed the IDA to target a whole new range of industries where a first-class phone service was the key factor. These ranged from software to call centres and customer support and other data-related services. Ireland's edge in this telecommunications area helped the IDA persuade many of the new high-technology companies to locate here.

Having managed the IDA through the six years of recessionary times – from 1981 to 1986 – I was then fortunate enough to experience three years of sustained economic recovery, from 1987 to 1989. This allowed the IDA to get back to its winning ways. I felt then that it was time for me to move on. For me, the Intel investment and the company's decision to favour Ireland was a recognition of the industry strategy created and executed through IDA leadership over the previous twenty years. But, in particular, it was a testimony to the promotional skills, persistence and negotiating ability of the IDA staff. And it was as fitting an end to my regime as I could dream of.

I also felt a strong obligation to try and ensure the IDA remained a dynamic and entrepreneurial organisation in its national work of promoting Ireland. Having built up a strong management team in the IDA, it was time to give them a crack at the top job. I talked to Joe McCabe, the IDA Chairman, and agreed a formal announcement (November 1989) of my intention to resign and hand over to a successor in June 1990.

No sooner was my resignation signalled than I got a call from Taoiseach Charles Haughey to visit him in his office in Government Buildings. After greeting me, and settling down with a cup of tea, his opening words were, 'What nonsense is this about you leaving the IDA?' I explained my conviction that I had made my contribution over the past decade, and that now it was time to appoint a successor, in the interests of the continued freshness and vitality of the organisation. He thanked me for my work for the country.

His words were particularly encouraging for me, given his earlier scepticism about the IDA on coming into government. Subsequently, he arranged for my appointment to the Custom House Docks Authority in 1990. There I continued my involvement with the emerging International Financial Services Centre in Dublin until that Authority came to an end in April 1997 and was succeeded by the Dublin Docklands Development Authority.

At the IDA, Kieran McGowan was selected as the new managing director with effect from June 1990. He had first joined the so-called old IDA in 1967 when it was still part of the Department of Industry and Commerce. He knew every aspect of the foreign investment business. Kieran is blessed with a combination of temperament and talent. His boyish charm, complete integrity and great ability to communicate and get on with people are complemented by a sharp mind and great decisiveness. Under his management, the IDA was to enter a golden era of success.

The management transition year in 1990 proved to be a boom year, with the economy expanding by some 8 per cent, the fastest growth rate for more than twenty years. But outside Ireland, the economic clouds were gathering once more; the combination of the Gulf War in 1991 and recession in Britain and the US saw growth drop to a modest 2 per cent to 3 per cent annual rate to 1993.

In 1991, Minister for Industry Des O'Malley instituted a further review of industrial policy, this time with the aid of an advisory group headed by Jim Culliton, chairman of Cement Roadstone Holdings. The Culliton Report advocated splitting the IDA, with one division specialising in foreign investment and another to provide services for indigenous industry. The end result, after some years of debate and experiment, was the creation of three agencies incorporating differing elements of the old organisation. Today IDA-Ireland specialises in promoting foreign investment. Enterprise Ireland focuses on assisting indigenous industry, while Forfás is concerned with policy advice.

Kieran McGowan opted to stay with the foreign-investment

mandate, and from January 1994, when the first organisational rejigging was carried out, he became chief executive of IDA-Ireland, but with one difference. The 'A' of IDA was now downgraded to 'Agency' from the original 'Authority' that had featured in the IDA brand name since 1950. The bureaucracy was finally getting its own back!

The organisational carve-up was effected during 1993. For IDA staff it was a year of disorientation as colleagues saw the organisation split into three separate organisations, dividing former colleagues in the process. But from the following January, McGowan marshalled and motivated his troops in his new Agency. The results were impressive: a progressive increase in new jobs in foreign industry with a marked acceleration from 1994 onwards.

The US market was buoyant and Europe's demand remained strong for the high-tech products coming from the foreign base in Ireland, so the draining effect of job losses was limited. The Irish economy bounced back to a 7 per cent growth rate in 1994, the year it first won renown, internationally, as the Celtic Tiger, with inflation remaining low, and the debt burden falling.

The leading personal-computer manufacturers, Dell and Gateway 2000, chose Ireland as their European production and customer-service centres. And Compaq, whose production base was lost to Scotland in a tight investment competition, returned to Ireland to set up a 600-job customer-service centre. It served to illustrate the merit of the IDA philosophy of never giving up on a company, even when it seems to have chosen another country as its preferred European location. The case of Hewlett Packard (HP) also illustrates the point. It remains one of the most admired companies in the computer and computer-printer business. Scotland was its long-established European base. However, IDA persistence was rewarded finally in 1995 when

Hewlett Packard decided to establish a new plant in Leixlip to make print-toner cartridges for its bestselling printers. Initial plans were for a plant with 1,200 people, but HP was so impressed by its Irish experience that in 1996 the company announced a further jobs expansion. The decision was taken even before construction of its first factory was completed.

Recent years have seen a cluster of 'mega-projects' secured annually, and on a scale previous IDA generations could scarcely imagine – eight projects with over 500 jobs each in 1996 alone. In that year, IBM Corporation decided to establish the largest single new project ever in the history of IDA, at Mulhuddart outside Dublin – 3,000 jobs to provide customer-support services for IBM customers in Europe. This was a stunning achievement for Kieran McGowan and his team.

The IBM decision also reflected the fruits of IDA tenacity over many years. Since 1970, the IDA had pursued the world's largest computer and services company, but without success. The US multinational simply was not interested then. Prevailing company policy had assured IBM employees of lifetime employment. Effectively, this meant the company would invest in a new project only if the domestic market was capable of sustaining the jobs of the IBM employees. And, because of the small size of the domestic market, this rationale ruled Ireland out of consideration for any export-oriented investment.

However, in 1983, the IDA managed to circumvent this traditional company restriction when, with the help of the Irish-based sales company, a 100-person Software Development Centre was established. It was set up to meet IBM's in-house development needs. The company's positive experience of Ireland through this centre, the choice of Ireland by so many leaders in the computer industry, the more open IBM philosophy of its new Chairman Lou Gerstner and the IDA's persistence over more than two decades eventually produced results. All these factors helped to secure the 3,000 IBM jobs for Dublin in 1996.

Kieran McGowan has also had remarkable success in establishing Ireland as a European telemarketing centre. The Agency's intention of exploiting this sector was clearly signalled in the 1991 Annual Report which referred to the traditional approach of 'continuously identifying or creating new market opportunities'. One of the business areas being analysed was listed as telemarketing. It is a classic case history of the IDA in action.

The analysis identified the kinds of companies – airline, hotel and car-rental reservations – that could benefit from a centralised European telecentre. This would both save costs for the company and give customers a better service. Then the key ingredients of the 'package of attractions' were identified and put in place with the help of the government and Irish support services. The mix involved competitive telecommunication charges, young people with Continental European languages, attractive offices, employment grants and favourable tax rulings. The IDA took the resultant call-centre package, went out into the global market place to the target companies and has been most successful in a short period. Some 7,000 people are employed in the new call centres, ranging from airlines like American Airlines and Lufthansa–United Airlines to computer manufacturers Dell and Gateway, and their evolution to e-commerce centres is already evident.

INDUSTRIAL POLICY 1950–98
A CHRONOLOGY

1950   Industrial Development Authority (IDA) is established within the Department of Industry and Commerce to initiate proposals for industrial investment from domestic and foreign sources.

1952   Undeveloped Areas Act establishes a grants board (An Foras Tionscal) awarding non-repayable cash grants for industrial-development projects in designated areas of the west.

1956   Industrial Grants Act extends qualifying area for grants for new industry to the rest of the country.

1956   Finance Act introduces Export Profits Tax Relief (EPTR) with 50 per cent tax remission on profits, increased to 100 per cent relief two years later.

1958   Relaxation of the Control of Manufactures Act – designed to keep control of industry in Irish hands.

1958   Export profits exemption for business at Shannon Airport until 1983.

1959   Shannon Free Airport Development Company (SFADCO) awarded grant-giving powers.

1960   Finance Act extends period of EPTR from ten to fifteen years.

1964   Control of Manufactures Act repealed. No restriction on foreign direct investment.

1965   Anglo-Irish Free Trade Agreement: free trade in most manufactured goods to be completed by 1975, via annual 10 per cent tariff cuts.

1969   Industrial Development Act provides for merger of An Foras Tionscal and IDA as a single new independent state agency – the Industrial Development Authority – outside civil-service structures. Major rationalisation of industrial promotion and grant incentives.

1969   Export Profits Tax Relief extended to 1989–90

1973   Ireland joins the European Economic Community (EEC).

1978   Government abolishes EPTR and replaces it with a special 10 per cent rate of corporation profit tax for all manufacturing industry from 1981–2000. Those qualifying for export-tax relief before 1981 continue to benefit until 1990.

1981   Industrial Development (No. 2) Act for the first time gives the IDA the power to give 'employment grants' unrelated to building and machinery investment. Also, it allows the Minister to designate the specific types of service business that would qualify for these new grants.

1982   Telesis Report: a major review of industrial policy criticises over-reliance on foreign industry and favours a better balance between overseas and indigenous industry. Telesis recommends a substantial reduction in the level of grants to foreign firms. And it favours the Department of Industry and Commerce over the IDA in the formulation of industrial strategy.

1984   Industrial Policy White Paper rejects Telesis finding on reduced grants for overseas firms but accepts a recommendation for greater discrimination in grant levels.

1987   Financial Services Act establishes International Financial Services Centres in Dublin, to be marketed internationally by the IDA. Profits of qualifying activities carried out from the Centre are taxed at 10 per cent until 2005.

1990   Government extends the 10 per cent corporation profits tax rate to 2010.

1992   Culliton report on industrial policy for the 1990s. Recommends a shift from grants to equity for indigenous industry, with the grant-aid budget for mobile international industry squeezed further. Also favours a stronger Departmental role in developing industrial policy, with one agency (IDA Ireland) responsible for attracting foreign investment, and a new agency for the promotion of indigenous industry.

1993   Industrial Development Act establishes three agencies: IDA Ireland for overseas industry; Forbairt for indigenous industry, and Forfás, as the policy advisory and coordination board for industrial development and science and technology.

1998   Agreement with European Commission on universal 12.5 per cent corporation tax for all trading companies from 2003. All existing commitments to the 10 per cent tax rates for manufacturing industry to the year 2010 to be honoured. The current 28 per cent standard rate will be reduced by 4 per cent annually, for 2000, 2001 and 2002, and by 3.5 per cent for 2003, giving a 12.5 per cent rate at that date.

1998   Industrial Development Act establishes Enterprise Ireland as the new development agency supporting indigenous industry. It incorporates Forbairt, An Bord Tráchtála (the Export Board) and certain activities of FÁS (state training authority). IDA Ireland remains responsible for foreign industry.

11

HOW THE IDA OPERATES

Padraic White

The IDA annual conference, held every January in a Dublin hotel over two or three days, was one of the key events in the Authority's working year. There, executive directors, managers and overseas personnel reviewed their past twelve-month perform-ance and unveiled any major initiatives planned for the year ahead. As a young executive, I listened in awe as the Californian-based staff told us of the wondrous ways of West Coast USA, of tilt-up factories built in weeks, of exotic landscaped business parks and of the hot new companies favoured by the venture capitalists.

However, the end of each annual conference had a most entertaining but deadly serious ritual. During Michael Killeen's tenure he had instituted a system whereby targets for new foreign projects and projected new jobs were set for the year ahead. But invariably at the conference the total of projected investments and jobs included in the individual plans presented by the various directors never quite matched Killeen's original overall figure.

So in the final session Killeen engaged in some public

bargaining with the directors, perhaps to make up a difference of, say, 3,000 in the numbers. Having got some initial offers he might turn to Ted O'Neill, his trusted director, and teasingly inquire, 'Ted, do you think you could make up the 1,000 missing.' Ted was – and still is – an inveterate smoker. Usually, he had the head down and spoke in a quiet voice, even in a small group. He would take a puff and then, in an almost inaudible voice, say, 'All right, Michael.' With that, the conference was over, the target was committed and all headed for the exit – and the nearest bar – to consider the dynamics of another annual conference. This management structure created by Michael Killeen proved its worth and has endured with some refinements to this very day.

Quite deliberately, he had created within the IDA a very structured organisation. At each operational level, there were prescribed procedures to be followed, and precise delegated powers of decision established. In addition to the monthly meeting of the new Authority under its first chairman, John H. Donovan of Esso Ireland, Killeen introduced weekly meetings with his executive directors and with the board of the IDA. The latter took decisions on all investment proposals. In addition, he held a monthly management meeting with his divisional managers.

This layered structure was used to make decisions with fast turnaround times and to create a sense of direction in the new organisation. It also gave Killeen different arenas in which to encourage and cajole his executives into producing better performances. So at the monthly management meeting, a dozen or so of the top executives, with their varied public- and private-sector backgrounds, would report progress on meeting the year's job targets. Early on, the IDA had developed a monthly pipeline of projects. It contained all industrial prospects likely to come on stream from anywhere in the world. Projected jobs materialising within twelve months were then assigned a probability factor. This monthly barometer of job prospects quickly became a key feature of IDA life – with the staff mood changing as the jobs pipeline emptied or filled. It also served as a remarkably accurate leading indicator of industrial prospects.

From the outset, the challenge facing the IDA was how to attract just the right type and scale of foreign investment to fit Ireland's needs. It was quick to apply a fresh approach, with the brainpower required for the effort coming from a strong planning and research section, headed by Ray McLoughlin. This also served as the intellectual powerhouse of the IDA. The planning unit generated new ideas and concepts that were fully tested against the natural scepticism and day-to-day experience of those who were on the road and seeking investment for Ireland in a tough marketplace.

Shortly after joining the IDA, I remember, quite vividly, attending a briefing session where Ray McLoughlin demonstrated his 'closed loop' system of industrial planning. He began his exposition by defining the national economic and social objectives of the country. Then he set out the criteria for selecting industries, whether in terms of Ireland's location or capacity to attract inward investment. First, foreign target companies were identified and their likely investment requirements assessed. The outcome was then measured against Ireland's ability to meet the development needs of those companies. The whole exercise yielded valuable insights into the necessary marketing, negotiation and selling approaches to attract such investment. As the strategy was implemented, progress was monitored and refinements were introduced as required – hence the term 'closed loop'. It became the subject of much light-hearted comment throughout the organisation.

The basic template so laid out was compelling. Its logic was to target with rifle-shot precision individual companies that met specific criteria, then go directly to them and make the case for locating in Ireland. Here was a proactive, not a reactive approach to industrial development. It was the opposite of waiting passively for investment applications – still a very prevalent practice in investment agencies – or else relying mainly on seminars, conferences or public relations to generate a response.

The new IDA also created task forces, where three or four executives went on the road for six weeks, perhaps to Sweden, Holland or the United States. The task force would be based in a local hotel, in cities where the IDA did not have offices, and would be preceded by an advance man whose role was to phone the target companies unsolicited and then talk his way into securing an appointment for the IDA team. It was the 'cold calling' approach. Some were wizard cold callers: Richard O'Farrell was fluent in Continental languages, had a confident and distinguished speaking voice, and was a master of the telephone art. These armies of cold callers, and the commando-style task forces fanning out across the world, laid the ground for Ireland's dramatic success in getting new industries later in the 1970s.

Once again, both the scale and logistics of the whole operation was breathtaking. In the first full year (1971) of the direct-marketing approach, IDA executives made presentations to 105 different target companies. Next year, they increased this to 775 in thirteen countries. And, by 1973, a staggering 2,600 presentations to individual companies were made across the world. The homework underpinning this promotional effort was equally impressive: the target companies were selected from within industrial sectors and from company directories, with custom-built presentations prepared for each team. No fewer than 4,000 direct presentations to target companies were made in the five years to 1974. At that time, Brendan Swan, the marketing expert, introduced the idea of 'king-size presentations' to the IDA annual conference. This involved identifying potential investors and then hand-tailoring individual presentations to convince them to locate new investment here. It meant setting out detailed investment proposals to selected companies, and suggesting why some of their specific product lines should be manufactured in Ireland. The exercise even included financial projections. And of course, all showed a fine profit.

The fruits of this enhanced marketing exercise came through quickly, and the IDA knew this intensive and more focused approach could pay off. The west of Ireland benefited from the arrival of Digital in Galway, Cross Pens and Square D electronics in Ballinasloe and Baxter Travenol healthcare in Castlebar. These new industries were truly the wonder of the Western world. In parallel, the Authority sought to make Ireland better known in the international business world. It did so by a sustained advertising campaign that raised Ireland's profile internationally and highlighted the country as the most profitable investment location in Europe. The campaign involved placing 300 to 400 advertisements annually in the opinion-forming printed media.

The IDA also invited business journalists to Ireland as part of a planned programme each year and organised a full schedule of meetings for them with ministers, industrialists, union leaders, economists and Irish journalists. They paid their own way – it was a good test of their genuine interest. For example, in 1974, sixty journalists came and subsequently produced some 550 articles. Promotion seminars were organised throughout the world to brief investors. By 1979, the IDA had trebled the number of its overseas offices to eighteen, both as a way of spreading the Irish investment message and gathering local intelligence about companies expanding overseas. Mobilising full political support behind the IDA's promotional efforts abroad was critical to the organisation's success in attracting foreign industry. Michael Killeen would agree a schedule of foreign missions. These would be led by the Industry Minister of the day, and occasionally the Taoiseach. Gradually, through this kaleidoscope of promotional approaches, knowledge of Ireland, its attractions and incentives, was established in the key markets.

RAY MCLOUGHLIN

Ray McLoughlin brought the same clarity of vision and strategic thinking to industrial-development strategy that he had displayed on and off the rugby field. As head of the IDA research unit, he analysed how best to attract foreign direct investment to Ireland and identified the key factors for promotional success.

His analysis, outlined in an article in Administration *(Spring 1972, Vol 20 No 1), remains as valid today as when it was first written, and was rooted in his practical experience in the IDA. For Ray, successful industrial development began with an appraisal of the mutual needs of those involved – the state and the potential industrial investor. Each needed to secure a perfect industrial-development fit. The State's concern is for high quality jobs, well distributed throughout the country, and at the lowest cost to the taxpayer. The IDA's role is to act as the middleman and facilitator in helping to secure them. It targets prospective companies, identifies their investment needs and matches their requirements with the native skills and resources available here.*

To work successfully, the approach requires a continuing back-up programme to ensure the necessary capital resources, infrastructure and educational skills are available to meet the demands created by the IDA's own marketing and selling efforts. It is a dynamic process that requires continual monitoring of the results achieved, both to measure the overall effectiveness of the programme and to fine-tune it, as and when required.

Ray McLoughlin saw the selection effort as a key element in the marketing activity:

> *In selecting industries, it is important to put our eggs in the best baskets. We therefore direct our interests to those product and industry areas which offer the best prospects of high economic benefit in relation to the initial economic cost. This selection process has got four elements:*
>
> 1 *Pick those that meet basic economic and social criteria such as, not too capital-intensive; high male labour content; high use of native raw materials and services; low scale factor.*
>
> 2 *Pick those that offer the best chances of commercial stability and therefore economic stability, by reference to commercial criteria such as high profitability; strong growth both in output and international trade.*
>
> 3 *Pick those with high dependence on scarce human resources, such as skilled people, because it implies a greater commitment and tie.*
>
> 4 *Pick those which can take advantage of natural resources and therefore enable us to conserve other resources.*

From 1969 onwards, violence in Northern Ireland cast a dark shadow over the whole island of Ireland as an investment location. In response, the IDA made greater use of 'site visits' to counter business fears. The adverse effects were most severe in 1971, when new investment commitments dropped by a third. So, getting investors to visit the country and to see for themselves that the Republic of Ireland was stable and safe for business became more important than ever.

A commitment to make such a 'visit' is significant. It means the foreign company, at its own expense, considers the Irish investment prospect sufficiently interesting to send one or more executives for a week or so to explore the country's economic attractions. The IDA site visit is at the very heart of the conversion of a tentative prospect to an agreed industrial-development project. Once a company expresses an interest in visiting, the IDA foreign-based staff flash the news to their Dublin-based counterparts and, jointly, they arrange a detailed tour.

Typically, this IDA itinerary will include a number of possible regional locations, with visits to other foreign industries for an open dialogue on doing business in Ireland, followed by meetings with support services, such as accountants, banks and solicitors. It may extend to discussions with county managers in relation to land or roads, or with university staff to review graduate availability. The full itinerary provides an airport arrival-to-departure schedule, but the IDA has always gone further. One of its staff is deputed to accompany and assist the incoming foreign visitors throughout their Irish visit

The site visit is a make-or-break exercise and may be the result of years of quiet cajoling by IDA staff abroad. The investor who suffers a bad experience or is simply not impressed is most unlikely to make an investment here. Each year, there are some 500 visits by potential investors, and the expertise and effort required to organise these trips efficiently is daunting. As the foreign industrialist travels through Ireland on his reconnaissance, he moves from the jurisdiction of one IDA Regional Manager to another, each of whom wants to win the project for his or her area. And so the managers go to great – and creative – lengths to ensure the investor has the best experience while under their 'roof'.

Certainly, creativity was needed in those early days when roads were bad and restaurants and hotels of reliable high quality were limited. In addition, there was a much smaller base of successful foreign companies to introduce to the visiting investor. So, from sheer necessity, the regional managers carved out another Ireland. They developed their own network of hoteliers and restaurant owners who could be relied upon to give a first-class service and not let the side down. Managers had their own routes, which, even if longer, were used to avoid run-down industrial estates and public eyesores. And they relied on friendships with local managers of foreign industries to give up some of their free time and join in the selling effort for Ireland over lunch or dinner.

But sometimes, even with the best planning, disaster struck. In 1987, the president of the Korean corporation Saehan Media visited Sligo to decide whether to locate a videotape-manu-facturing operation with a possible 800 jobs in a large empty factory in the area. A special plane was chartered to get him to the town. Éamon Howley, the IDA Regional Manager, was there to greet him on the tarmac at the new regional airport at Strandhill, ready to drive him to see the vacant factory. Unfortunately, when they reached O'Connell Street in Sligo, the narrow street was completely blocked by traffic. Saehan Media anticipated having 1,000 container journeys a year, and the prospect of having the articulated trucks navigating the congested O'Connell Street put the whole project in danger. It was a tough day for the Regional Manager.

And so it was that building the long-spoken-of second bridge in Sligo became a condition of the first Korean industry in Ireland locating in the town. In fact, that request for government approval to fund the bridge was included in the same document as the IDA request for authorisation of financial support for the new industry. In any event the new bridge in Sligo was completed in 1990, but for commercial reasons the Korean company did not move in until 1992.

The new IDA has from the very first day of operation in 1970 regarded the careful management of site visits as a critical part of the 'loop' in securing investment, and was determined to minimise the risk of failure. As the typical investor will also be visiting a number of other countries in Europe, there is a competitive edge to the itineraries and pressure on IDA to ensure the Irish experience is the best.

In 1971, Digital Equipment Corporation, then the pioneer in mini-computers, proved to be among the first big successes of this new approach. The corridors of IDA headquarters in Lansdowne House buzzed with excitement on hearing the good news: 'We've got Digital – 1,000 jobs in Galway.' I can still recall the sense of exhilaration felt at that announcement. Even those in the IDA not directly involved took pride in what was a major breakthrough for the organisation. Digital was the first of the new electronics companies to set up in Ireland, and its presence heavily influenced many major multinational computer hardware and software companies to establish here in later years.

For the IDA, beating the investment challenge became a driving goal that, increasingly, defined the ethos of the organis-ation. It was epitomised by a 'Win the project or die' philosophy. In 1998, an external consultant doing an in-house study of employee attitudes wondered aloud to IDA Chief Executive Kieran McGowan whether the same aggressive approach he had found fifteen years earlier still existed. On completion of the survey, he found that the positive spirit remained as strong as ever. As McGowan has noted, 'One of the most positive aspects of the IDA, throughout all its life, is the way this determination to do the business and secure the investment makes things happen.' A competitive nationalism has been part of the organisation's success from day one. IDA staff talk of playing for Ireland against other countries, and during the difficult, recessionary eighties, I encouraged the staff to recall that they were serving the country, not just holding down a job.

Today Ireland is well established as a prime European location for investment by the world's leading corporations – with 26 per cent of all greenfield investment projects from the US into Europe locating here. It was not always so. For many years, there was a clash between how American business perceived Ireland and the changed economic reality that the IDA sought to project, but which foreign investors were slow to recognise.

It was reflected in the clash of images. For quite a few Americans, Ireland remained a romantic misty isle peopled by characters straight out of *The Quiet Man* and full of bog roads with stray donkeys. To the IDA, Ireland had become a vibrant modern economy, and the ideal export base for foreign multi-nationals aiming to penetrate the European market. The IDA had a hard fight, and it took a long time to dispel that dated image of the country.

Particularly from 1970, the new IDA set out to convince its critical audience, the Fortune 500 type companies whose leaders were likely to invest in Europe, that there was indeed another Ireland. It was a businesslike place that could coexist with the Ireland of their imagination, the rural, undeveloped, windswept island on the edge of Europe. Advertising was one of the 'hidden persuaders' used by the IDA, and the promotional message also changed with the times. From the start, the IDA engaged McConnell's Advertising Agency in Dublin as its adviser, and over the years its managing director, John Fanning, became something of a guru on the subject of national-promotion advertising.

The advertising campaign was not intended to stimulate

applications or direct enquiries; investors do not normally respond in this manner. It was designed to create both a favourable impression of Ireland's suitability as an industrial base, and to provide a background awareness of the country's investment potential. So when the IDA executive phoned a target company or met one of its senior executives, then at least he could hope for a positive awareness of Ireland. The media campaign would secure a receptive audience for the Irish sales pitch, rather than executives having to rely entirely on a cold-call approach.

In John Fanning's analogy, advertising provides the air-cover while IDA troops on the ground engage in the combat, fighting for investment. The initial advertising sought to highlight what were considered Ireland's eye-catching advantages. The ads proclaimed 'No tax and no red tape' and 'Double your after-tax profits'. Highlighting the tax benefits was seen as a logical way of differentiating our product in the market place. But the IDA pledge to cut through bureaucracy with the promise of 'no red tape' was not designed as empty marketing rhetoric. The detail of the ads spelled out the commitment, namely that the IDA:

Will organise the whole thing.
Will give you all the details.
Will see you get the fullest benefit of Ireland's big industrial advantages and incentives.

The IDA assigned staff to accompany and assist the potential investor throughout the entire exploratory visit to Ireland. A network of key contacts in different areas – government Departments, the Revenue Commissioners, individual industrialists and their national business organisation (CII/IBEC), Congress of Trade Unions, universities and colleges, banks, telephone and electricity agencies and local authorities – was in place. They were willing to offer help and advice where necessary. This facility enabled the IDA to deliver on its marketing promise. So the investor found a welcoming response from all parts of the state bureaucracy, even from regulatory agencies like the tax authorities, or the Central Bank. For many, it was a refreshing and unusual experience.

After the June 1972 referendum, when voters endorsed Irish membership of the Common Market by a five-to-one margin, the new advertising message was adjusted and became 'More Profit in the Common Market' and 'Ireland – the most profitable location in the Common Market'.

.

*

I was appointed head of the IDA Planning Division in 1975, and I encouraged the young economists there to come up with economic material or analyses that could provide the IDA's front-of-house staff with a competitive edge in promoting Ireland's advantages. I was very aware that it would help our standing internationally if we could deliver some winning angle to the executives knocking at the doors. Just two years later we stumbled on a set of statistics that became central to the IDA message and have remained so ever since.

In the course of trawling through the US Department of Commerce magazines for useful pointers to the investment intentions of US companies, Dan Flinter (later to become Chief Executive of Enterprise Ireland) came across the results of an annual survey of investment abroad by American companies. He did a few calculations and discovered the return on US investment in Ireland came to 29 per cent, or over four times the EEC average. I took the results to the IDA's management meeting, where the figures were greeted with great enthusiasm. Overnight, these became a key marketing aid for IDA executives, particularly in America. The survey figures were used in advertisements showing a pencil encircling the 29 per cent figure. The caption read simply, 'The highest return on US investment in the EEC', with a footnote attributing the source to the US Department of Commerce. The ads made a big impact on readers, so much so that McConnell's won a series of advertising awards from *Business Week* magazine. The IDA economists visited the US Department of Commerce periodically to be fully briefed on the interpretation and calculations. They always received a warm welcome; the staff there were chuffed to see their own research used to such telling effect.

After more than twenty-five years, the returns for US investors today are of much the same order of magnitude and remain part of the core IDA message. And, since that discovery, I doubt if any speech made by an Irish minister to an American business audience did not feature the line in the script which read, 'Ireland has the highest return on US investment in the European Union – 29 percent. These are not our figures – they come from your Department of Commerce.'

The recession of the early 1980s led to even more intense competition among European investment agencies. Once again, it was time for Ireland to differentiate itself in the market place. So, in 1982, the IDA set out to find a new basis for projecting Ireland as an investment location. McConnell's organised a questionnaire survey of senior business executives in the US from a selection of industry sectors that had become IDA targets. A sample of the respondents were then interviewed in-depth.

The survey results showed we had succeeded in one of our top objectives – to raise the profile of Ireland as a potential location in Europe for investment. But the in-depth interviews uncovered a big problem, one of credibility. The claim to be the most profitable location in Europe was too much at variance with the traditional American view of Ireland as a tranquil, rural, backward country. Quite simply, it was not believable. It clashed with the image the IDA sought to project, that of making Ireland the European base for the best of the US electronics, computer and software companies. In John Fanning's view, it was hard to compete with repeated showings of *The Quiet Man* on American television.

Our initial response to the credibility gap was to investigate it more fully. So the IDA commissioned detailed qualitative research among the top decision-makers in foreign companies which had recently decided to invest in Ireland. In reaching that decision, they had compared Ireland with the alternative European locations. The research brief was to pinpoint the main reasons for choosing Ireland. When the data was analysed, the results were unequivocal. The primary reason for locating here was the quality of the workforce and the availability of highly qualified graduate staff. In the opinion of industrialists, Irish educational standards had emerged as a real strength.

Niall McIvor was spearheading the IDA work on the new advertising theme and, together with John Fanning, we pored over the research findings to find the clues to producing a persuasive new presentation of Ireland's attractions. We added another element, namely the relative youth of the Irish population. By comparison with the ageing population of other European countries, some 50 per cent of the Irish population were under the age of twenty-five. Ireland's membership of the EEC, with access to its large market, was the bedrock business rationale for investing in Ireland. In deciding to combine these findings into a new campaign theme, 'Ireland – Home of the Young Europeans', we hoped we had hit on a winning formula.

The actual advertisements were different in look and tone

from anything else then in vogue. The first series featured pictures of young people, and comparative statements such as 'People are to Ireland as oil is to Texas' and 'People are to Ireland as champagne is to France'. The subsequent and most sustained series featured photographs of young people in different educational settings, including students pictured on the stairway in Trinity College and a close-up of a graduate class in University College, Dublin. The most daring one showed a group photograph of graduates with their degree parchments with the caption 'Hire them, before they hire you'.

The 'Young European' theme was launched in March 1983 in the key IDA markets, using the *Wall Street Journal, Business Week,* The *Economist,* radio commercials and outdoor poster sites in the US. A pan-European campaign involving business magazines with a wide international circulation was also used. About £1 million was allocated to the annual campaign. It represented a change in focus away from industrial incentives and finance and towards underlining the country's educated youth and EEC membership.

However, because it was so different from previous IDA advertising themes, the marketing staff remained sceptical of this 'soft focus' theme of youth and education, as opposed to the traditional hard-edged financial-style advertisements of the past. Undoubtedly, there was a risk in moving from a proven winning theme to the new untried and softer approach. An additional problem was that if IDA staff were sceptical and lacked confidence in the Young European theme, they were unlikely to advocate and support it in dealing with clients.

To tackle this internal credibility gap, we commissioned a special film for briefing IDA staff, narrated by broadcaster Pat Kenny. The documentary explained the research and logic of the new marketing approach. It was shown internally on various occasions and helped provide a rationale for the Young European campaign. Later, the World Bank's Foreign Investment Advisory Service (FIAS) used the video as an example of a research-based national-investment promotion.

The impact of the Young European campaign was positive right from the outset. It became a talking point in many discussions with client companies. Their top executives still recalled it, many years after the campaign had ceased. The relevance of 'young educated people' as the key to business success was cited increasingly by the leaders of the companies coming to Ireland. It was heartening to realise that the Young European theme, selected from a mass of data and considerations, was right on target as far as the investors were concerned and that its relevance and power increased with the passing years. In time, this would come to differentiate Ireland from her European competitors for mobile investment.

The advertising budget was one of the victims of the budgetary cutbacks from 1988. The IDA sought to sustain the 'young educated staff' theme in its media activities and in presentations to business audiences. However, as the world leaders in the high-tech sectors increasingly chose Ireland as their European base, the need to spread the message through advertising diminished. The Celtic Tiger took on a momentum of its own in the world's media and became well known. Nowadays, the IDA uses occasional advertisements to promote Ireland or a particular target sector and maintains a permanent display in Dublin Airport which arriving passengers can scarcely miss. The Young European campaign posters still hang in the reception areas of IDA Headquarters in Dublin, but they have done their job.

*

In the battle to attract overseas investment to Ireland, no financial weapon has been more important than tax in convincing new industry to locate here. It remains the IDA's unique selling point, giving Ireland a critical advantage in winning new investment. The idea, though first developed in 1956, was not fully exploited until 1970, when the newly revitalised IDA, under Michael Killeen, redesigned it into a unique world tax advantage. The incentive was packaged and presented in a simple graphic message – 'no tax' or 'double your after-tax profits' – one which the Authority sold aggressively through advertisements and seminars. As well as the initial tax exemption, there was a second and highly significant concession. This was a government commitment to a twenty-year benefit period (fifteen full years' exemption and five years' partial). When combined, these provided a uniquely attractive package: zero tax, allied to a long-term time horizon for its operation.

In 1956, the first year of the new exports-profits tax exemption, if the approach was similar, it was much more low-key. Ted O'Neill, then executive director of the original IDA, recalls going with the Minister for Industry and Commerce, William Norton, on an industrial-development mission to Bonn, Germany. There they put forward Ireland's attractions as 'tax incentives plus financial grants plus access to the United Kingdom market'. Although the incentive applied only to profits on exports, it was attractive, since foreign companies normally exported all their production from Ireland.

The Export Sales Tax Relief provision – allowing a 50 per cent tax exemption on export sales profits – was introduced in the Finance Act of 1956. It was extended in 1957 and 1958, with manufacturing companies given a fifteen-year 100 per cent exemption from tax on export profits and a further five years of tapering relief. The focus on encouraging exports by offering tax incentives applied to both Irish and foreign companies. It was further evidence of the new realisation that the old policies of relying on the protected small home market had failed.

The virtue of the scheme as marketed by the IDA was that it was simple and easy to understand. Above all, it sent two very strong signals to the international business community. Clearly, the country was pro-enterprise in the way it rewarded rather than penalised profits, and second, the twenty-year tax horizon showed that Ireland favoured a long-term approach to investment. No other country that was competing for mobile foreign investment could match it.

It became Ireland's unique selling point. But if the IDA teams had a compelling sales pitch to attract the multinationals, they had relatively few other advantages at that time. Once such a clear tax benefit was established, the challenge in future years was to retain the competitive edge it provided for as long as possible.

In the negotiations for Ireland's entry to the EEC in 1973, the export tax provision first came under close external scrutiny. Favouring exports so explicitly meant it offended the EEC treaty requirements of non-discrimination. But the Irish negotiators under Minister for Foreign Affairs Dr Paddy Hillery secured an outcome that met IDA requirements. The compromise ensured that commitments made to foreign companies could be honoured in full, and the tax incentive would continue until a Community-wide review of state aids to industry had taken place. There was an audible sigh of relief in IDA Headquarters in Lansdowne Road.

It was four years before the much-heralded EEC review got under way in earnest. In 1977, the European Commission started an ambitious exercise to identify, measure and set ceilings on regional aids. As Ireland was regarded as a single region by the Commission, all the industry aids had to be transparent and on the table. In response, the Department of Industry and Commerce set up an inter-departmental task force to plan Ireland's strategy during the Commission scrutiny. As manager of the IDA Planning Division, I was asked to represent the organisation on the task force. At meetings with Commission officials and other member states, Ireland's incentive regime was clearly under threat, particularly from those countries that were losing out to the IDA in the battle for new foreign investment. However, it was sobering to realise that the Commission and its officials, not governments, had the real power in deciding whether state aids complied with the EEC Treaty. Nevertheless, the stakes were high.

The task force, with government backing, decided on a twin-track approach. In dealing with the Commission, it would negotiate the most favourable ceilings and rules on aids, such as financial grants. And, while accepting that the days of the export tax incentive were numbered, it would seek the longest possible transition period for new investors. In addition, it would insist that all commitments given to existing companies were fully honoured.

In Brussels, at the multilateral meetings, there was no mistaking the look of satisfaction on the faces of our industrial-development rivals as we signalled the end of the export tax incentive. However, any forced ending of a long-term low tax concession – our unique selling point – for new investment would have had disastrous consequences. And since the Commission showed no great concern for the Irish difficulty, we would have to find our own solution.

As the task force negotiated the best deal from Brussels on the state-aids review, it secretly embarked on the search for an answer to the puzzle. How could we find a way through the

Treaty of Rome that would be as close as possible to tax exemption, and yet not fall foul of the Commission, and the state aids regime? The task force spotted a gap. It noted that the EEC did not control normal company tax rates, simply because there was no agreement in place on tax harmonisation. Any such agreement would require a unanimous vote of the member states. So if Ireland had a low tax rate for manufacturing industry that applied to all profits, whether from domestic or export sales, or whether the company was Irish or foreign, then this could become an effective substitute for the doomed export tax incentive.

At this point, members of the task force argued strongly on the optimum level of any new manufacturing tax incentive. The higher the rate set, then the more revenue would be generated for the state in the years ahead. But fewer jobs would also be created in consequence. A high tax rate also meant a greater risk that foreign investors would be alienated and Ireland's reputation as an investment location would be undermined. The honourable compromise was to go for a 10 per cent tax, guaranteed for twenty years to recipient companies. It gave the state the prospect of handsome revenues based on 10 per cent of the highly profitable companies the IDA would attract. And as existing companies came to the end of the exports tax incentive they would move on to the 10 per cent level, and thus add further to state revenue.

The end play came on 20 December 1978, when the Minister for Industry and Commerce, Des O'Malley, took a flight to Brussels on an important mission. He told the EEC Commissioner for Competition Policy, Raymond Vouel, that Ireland would cease to offer the exports incentive from January 1981, and secured agreement to the transitional arrangements in the intervening two years, thus enabling a smooth transition to the new 10 per cent tax regime. He then walked down the corridor in the Berlaymont building to meet the Commissioner responsible for taxation, Irishman Dick Burke. There, as a matter of courtesy, he informed him that Ireland would be introducing a new 10 per cent tax applying to all manufacturing industry from January 1981. The twin-track approach had come to fruition.

However, the IDA was left facing a fresh challenge. It had to fine-tune Ireland's appeal to foreign investors. Acceptance of a zero tax in place for twenty-five years had to be replaced by international recognition and acceptance that the new 10 per cent tax was still a powerful incentive. It was a calculated gamble, fraught with danger, and, if badly received, with significant downside risk for the economy. The IDA feared it would be seen as signalling that Ireland planned, progressively, to take more tax from foreign companies, once the new rate was established. If this was the case, investor confidence would be greatly undermined.

The IDA worked out a detailed plan to market the new 10 per cent tax and sell it positively to investors. An advertising campaign in the international business media carried a simple message with – by international standards – a still remarkable promise, 'Maximum 10 per cent tax guaranteed to the year 2000'. Thankfully, the reception to the new message was universally positive and we moved seamlessly to the 10 per cent tax regime and the twenty-year horizon. The incentives remain to this day, the unique and essential foundation stones of Ireland's foreign-investment boom.

It has always been a core IDA principle that Ireland should offer the investor the longest possible time horizon on the predictability of taxes. For the investor, able with confidence to forecast a tax-rate liability some ten to twenty years ahead, can also estimate the net return on his Irish investment. And in that way he can plan on reinvestment and expansion with greater assurance. Since no other country has been able to match such a long-term commitment, Ireland retains a unique advantage that reflects a deep understanding of investor needs.

However, with the passing years, the expiry year of 2000 for the 10 per cent tax loomed ever closer. As it did, the number of guaranteed years available to the prospective investor dropped, progressively, from the original twenty-year period. By 1988, with twelve years remaining, the IDA embarked on detailed research to prepare a case to put to government for the incentive tax to be installed after the year 2000. Plant Location International–Price Waterhouse were asked to assess Ireland's competitiveness by comparison with other European countries. Their brief was to take into account taxes, financial grants and costs and to examine investments in different sectors. At the same time, the IDA began a confidential survey of existing foreign companies in order to forecast corporation-tax revenue after export sales relief was abolished in 1980, with their transition to the new 10 per cent rate.

When we assimilated all the results and considered the best possible future tax regime for manufacturing, the IDA favoured an extension of the 10 per cent tax for another ten years to the year 2010. The international study had demonstrated it was still necessary to retain our competitiveness, while the confidential survey proved that a 10 per cent tax would also deliver a hefty revenue to the state.

The outcome of the general election of June 1989 introduced a new and unexpected hazard to the IDA ambition of securing a further time extension to the 10 per cent tax regime. The election proved disastrous for Fianna Fáil – the party lost seats and broke a 'core value ' in forming a coalition government with the Progressive Democrats led by Des O'Malley, who, once again, was back in the Department of Industry and Commerce, and the political boss of the IDA.

The new hazard for the IDA was that any new extension of the 10 per cent tax would obviously have to be promoted at the Cabinet table by Minister O'Malley. However, he was now leader of a party with a core policy of cutting the personal tax burden. The party's pre-election policy proposed a 'minimum tax' for every business entity, irrespective of any allowances or off-sets, as one source of funding for the personal tax concessions. The notion of a new law to override normal tax deductions, when coupled with the uncertainty over the rate of the minimum tax, suggested a radical break with the existing 10 per cent low tax regime used to promote foreign investment. At that very moment, the IDA was seeking to extend the rate for another ten years. By coincidence, O'Malley had piloted the original 10 per cent tax through government and the European Commission a decade earlier.

The IDA Chairman Joe McCabe embarked on a campaign of communication and persuasion, stressing that an extension of the tax regime beyond 2000 was an utter necessity for the foreign-investment programme. While this might appear a distant date, it meant that companies negotiating large-scale investments with the IDA in 1989 might get into taxable profits by 1995, allowing for building time and initial losses, and so in reality they might see Ireland as offering only five years of a low tax. McCabe argued the case with O'Malley on a number of occasions during their regular Minister-and-Chairman liaison meetings.

We went directly to meet Seán Cromien, Secretary of the Department of Finance, to get his support for our proposals. We disclosed that the IDA survey had shown that the Exchequer would get an additional £220 million by 1992 from companies making the transition to 10 per cent from the exports tax exemption, and from companies in the new Financial Centre in

Dublin. This imminent 'bonus' was equal to 72 per cent of the total corporation tax paid in the year 1989–90. Seán Cromien was surprised at these findings, and somewhat questioning about their accuracy, although the department had no available figures itself. He did arrange for the Revenue Commissioners to make their own calculations subsequently, and the IDA figures were fully vindicated.

We also had to counter a strong argument by the civil servants that the extension could not be done without the permission of the European Commission. In the IDA, we could not see any legal or any other reason for going to Brussels and asserted this view equally forcefully. Within the IDA, we were conscious of the pressures on the government to reduce personal taxes, and that seeking a further ten-year span of low tax for the manufacturing sector could be a tough decision for Ministers. But we had done our homework, and later in 1989, we were thrilled to hear that Minister O'Malley had triggered the procedure for sending the IDA tax proposal to government, and that subsequently the Cabinet backed the IDA proposal with the full support of the Minister for Finance, Albert Reynolds. The following year, the government announced that it would extend the 10 per cent tax rate to 2010. Once again, we were back with a twenty-year horizon.

The timing was also fortunate, as the IDA was putting strong emphasis on persuading companies to invest before the completion in 1992 of the EEC single market. This was designed to sweep away hidden barriers to trade and investment within the Community. International companies were worried that the single market would be tantamount to 'Fortress Europe', and many thought it wise to invest before any fortress doors slammed shut. Mind you, the IDA executives did not seek to disabuse them of this view and from 1990 on, they were able to make

Ireland's case as the ideal location within the European 'fortress', greatly helped by the tax-incentive extension to 2010.

As the 1990s advanced and the new millennium loomed, the future of the 10 per cent tax was back on the agenda. But this time there were some new considerations. There was a growing demand to extend the 10 per cent tax to the indigenous service sector. The hotels and tourist industry, among others, argued that they were also creating jobs and generating tax revenue based on exports. The standard 40 per cent corporate tax rate that applied generally to services was viewed, increasingly, by policy-makers as a disincentive to local enterprise. At the same time, the 10 per cent tax regime for the new financial centre in Dublin was due to end in 2005, and there were severe doubts whether the EU Commission would agree to roll over its special advantages. But above all, a 40 per cent standard corporate tax rate coexisting with a 10 per cent tax rate for manufacturing was seen as a source of distortion and inequity between different sectors in the economy.

In response, Forfás – the state's industrial policy and coordination board – masterminded a study of the options. It found that a low corporate tax rate in the range 10 to 15 per cent for all sectors was possible in Ireland. Very few countries could contemplate such a radical change because of the possible loss of state revenue. However, Ireland was able to do so because the existing 10 per cent tax regime had become such a dynamic source of revenue. And in early 1997 the Rainbow government (Fine Gael, Labour and Democratic Left) announced its intention to introduce an across-the-board 12.5 per cent standard tax for all trading companies in Ireland from January 2006 and to enter into discussions with the EU Commission on the proposal.

It was a breathtaking move by any standards, but it also required careful nurturing to bring it to fruition. When the new government of Fianna Fáil and the Progressive Democrats was formed in June 1997, it supported the 12.5 per cent tax concept and set about negotiating Commission acceptance. The government needed the EU agreement to honour all existing commitments to companies that had been guaranteed the 10 per cent tax to 2010. But since the usefulness of a low tax to foreign investors depends on its recognition by other countries, clearly the goodwill, in particular, of other European countries was essential. Some were annoyed because of Ireland's success in attracting foreign inward investment, including consolidation of European plants into Ireland. And while the EU Commission could not object to a member state deciding its own standard tax rate, it was pressing for the rapid removal of the discrepancy between the varying Irish company taxes.

The end result was that the government agreed to advance the introduction of the universal 12.5 per cent tax for all trading companies to 2003, with the guarantee that all existing commitments will be honoured. Then Ireland will be the only developed country in the world taking only 12.5 per cent in tax on company profits, irrespective of sector, size of business or nationality. The country will justly merit the title of the Enterprise Isle.

The story of the development of such a distinctive low tax, favouring enterprise and investment, stretches back to the original export incentive measure in 1956. It has been central to our continuing ability to attract foreign investment. When the after-tax return on investing in Ireland was compared with other European alternatives, the result made a persuasive case for this country over more than four decades. The tax advantage helped overcome so many of our natural disadvantages of size and location, such as our distance from Continental markets, and the small size of the domestic market for a company's products.

*

When disaster strikes and a foreign company closes, with major job losses, the IDA finds itself in the firing line. The Agency is seen as responsible for bringing the company to Ireland, and so when the company fails, the wrath of the public and the focus of media attention is turned back on the IDA. It must explain and justify its decision and save the company. If all else fails, the IDA has to find a replacement industry.

Whenever this happens, the latent native suspicion of multinationals also comes to the surface with a vengeance. In any country, the stronger the sense of nationalism – as in Ireland – the greater the expectation that native industry has the necessary enterprise, skill and finance to make the investment and create the jobs. So, viewed from such a narrow perspective, foreign investment is a second-best choice. It implies that Irish entrepreneurs have failed and are inadequate. According to such critics, the multinationals, on encountering global trading difficulties, chop the foreign branch plant as a first resort. In the early days of the IDA, such attitudes were widely prevalent in Ireland, especially during the recession years of the 1980s, when many such closures occurred.

Since then, I believe Irish attitudes towards foreign companies have softened and become more supportive for a number of powerful reasons. First, the Irish plants are no longer one of a number of vulnerable branch plants. Increasingly, these are now largely the European base for a whole product range. Second, the management in place there is virtually all Irish. And third, indigenous Irish business, as sub-suppliers, experiences directly the benefits of the foreign sector through the £8 billion spent annually on wages, materials and services.

Even now, however, hostility to foreign companies can spring to the surface on the basis of a single closure announcement. The Seagate company closure of its 1,400-job computer hard disk plant

Tánaiste and Enterprise Minister Mary Harney at the Baxter Healthcare plant in Castlebar in 1999, announcing 300 new jobs for a company that refused to die in 1987, when it first faced closure. With the minister are Tom Mulqueen, general manager, manufacturing, at Baxter and Eric Beard, chairman of the company's European board.

Tomas Ó Cófaigh, former governor of the Central Bank. Ó Cófaigh was one of the 'three wise men' involved in marketing the IFSC globally. His personal friendships with key European central bankers proved to be a trump card.

Dermot Desmond,who managed to sell the IFSC concept to Taoiseach Charles Haughey.

Albert Reynolds: A government decision taken in 1979, when Reynolds was Minister for Posts and Telegraphs, to make a major investment to update the country's telecommunications system was critical to Ireland's future economic success.

Former Fine Gael leader Alan Dukes, whose Tallaght Strategy in 1987 was one of the keys to national economic recovery, with current Labour leader Ruairí Quinn, who, as minister in the Fine Gael–Labour coalition in the mid-1980s, backed a study into the establishment of a financial-services centre in Dublin.

Minister for Finance Charlie McCreevy: His success with Enterprise Minister Mary Harney in negotiating with the European Commission a 12.5 per cent corporation tax from 2003 for all trading companies secured Ireland's advantage as an industrial-investment centre.

IDA chairman Michael Killeen – second from right – and Padraic White, managing director, hosting a meeting in June 1984 with US President Ronald Reagan and top executives from American companies located in the west of Ireland.

As Michael Killeen retires in 1981, he hands the key of his sixth-floor office to his successor, Padraic White.

Minister for Science and Technology Michael Smith (right) and Padraic White at the press conference in October 1989 to announce Intel's decision to locate in Ireland.

The Intel plant at Leixlip, County Kildare.

Padraic White on his appointment as IDA managing director in 1981.

Kieran McGowan, who succeeded Padraic White as head of the IDA.

PEOPLE ARE TO IRELAND
AS CHAMPAGNE IS TO FRANCE.

The Irish.
Europe's youngest and fastest-growing population. Educated, talented, flexible, innovative.

Ireland.
A member of the European Common Market. Noted for its favorable government attitudes towards business. The most profitable industrial location in Europe for U.S. manufacturers.

Ireland. Home of the Irish. The young Europeans.

IDA Ireland ♣

INDUSTRIAL DEVELOPMENT AUTHORITY
The Irish government's industrial development agency has offices in DUBLIN (Head Office),
Tel. (01) 686633, LONDON (01) 699 5941, TOKYO (03) 262 7621, HONG KONG (5) 939637,
SYDNEY (02) 233 5999. Offices also in Cologne, Stuttgart, Hamburg, Munich, Paris, Amsterdam,
Copenhagen, Milan, New York, Chicago, Houston, Los Angeles, Cleveland, San Francisco,
Boston, Fort Lauderdale, Atlanta.

"WE'RE THE YOUNG EUROPEANS."

IDA

One of the highly successful series of IDA ads on the 'Young Europeans' theme that were used to great effect in the 1980s.

in Clonmel in 1997 resurrected the old questions: should we continue to rely on foreign industry, and how can we make sure they do not close? In the latter instance, Kieran McGowan, as IDA managing director, found himself defending not only the Seagate closure but the entire strategy of attracting foreign investment.

The rise and fall of industries and companies is an inevitable part of industrial development. As markets and technology change, those who fail to adapt cannot hope to survive. It means the foreign-investment story in Ireland also includes disasters, near misses and even some Lazarus-style recoveries.

The closure of the Ferenka factory outside Limerick city with the loss of 1,400 jobs in 1977 was an unprecedented industrial disaster. The factory was the largest foreign employer in Ireland and its closure was traumatic for the workforce, the city of Limerick and for the IDA, which had attracted Ferenka to Ireland. The parent company was the AKZO group from the Netherlands. It had built a massive factory of over 300,000 square feet at Annacotty in 1969 outside Limerick city and rapidly recruited the 1,400 staff to produce steel cord, then being introduced to tyre manufacture. But from the start, there were management-union problems.

The IDA, concerned by the labour-relations difficulties at the plant, commissioned an independent assessment of the Ferenka operation. In the judgement of Ted O'Neill, the IDA Director responsible, the report was 'a damning indictment of the management of the plant'. O'Neill travelled to Amsterdam to meet the company owners in the early 1970s and left the highly critical document on the table, but without comment. Shortly afterwards, the parent company appointed Dr Tiede Herrema as the new Managing Director. Immediately, he set about improving the company's fortunes and opened a dialogue with Ted O'Neill on Ferenka's difficulties.

On the morning of 3 October 1975 Dr Herrema was due to meet O'Neill in his Dublin office to discuss some new ideas about the Dutch company's future. He never showed up. It was the day the IRA kidnapped him. Dr Herrema was released almost a month later by the kidnappers, after gardaí surrounded the house where he was being held and negotiated his release. The nightmare experience of Dr Herrema did nothing to enhance the commitment of the Dutch parent company to resolve the problems at their Irish plant. In 1976 Dr Herrema was replaced, and the company was closed in 1977. Ted O'Neill is of the firm view that Dr Herrema could have saved the Ferenka plant. In the event, the closure and loss of 1,400 jobs gave foreign investment a bad name for years in Ireland. The retort, 'Are they going to do a Ferenka?' became the code language of sceptics of any foreign company in Ireland.

There were no takers for the Ferenka plant in Limerick – until John DeLorean arrived in Ireland the following year, with his gull-wing car venture. Early in 1978, the IDA staff in our Chicago office, whose territory covered Detroit, the home of General Motors, learned of a contest between Detroit city and Puerto Rico to be the location of the DeLorean 'dream car' project. The news was relayed to Seamus Cashman, IDA's North American Director, who was based in Park Avenue, New York, and he orchestrated the moves to get Ireland on the agenda as a contender. Between February and July 1978, the IDA system went into overdrive in advancing, evaluating and making decisions on the DeLorean car project.

DeLorean came with a formidable reputation, based on his career in General Motors, America's largest – and legendary – car maker, where he had become vice-president in charge of car and truck production. If anyone knew about the car industry and the opportunities it offered, John Delorean should. His plan was to manufacture a fashionable sports car with a brushed-aluminium finish and gull-wing doors for a niche market neglected by the big manufacturers. The planned 2,000 jobs made it the largest single project, in employment terms, considered by the IDA up to that time. And when the detailed analysis of the project was reviewed in IDA Headquarters in Dublin, the project seemed to fit the recently closed Ferenka plant like a glove. In one move, the lost jobs in Limerick could be more than replaced.

The IDA management and board had checked out his market projections, and support from US car dealers and financiers was also assessed. DeLorean came to Dublin to see Ireland for himself and advance the negotiations. I was then head of planning in IDA and, while not involved directly in the DeLorean project, I recall the buzz and bustle it generated in the Lansdowne Road headquarters – not every day was a 2,000-job project within grasp.

In March 1987, the IDA Authority formally considered a report on the DeLorean proposal. There, it agreed in principle on the outlines of the deal to be negotiated for its location in the former Ferenka building in Limerick. Shortly afterwards, however, doubts began to surface. Rumours in the IDA corridors suggested that US dealers might not be as committed to buying the cars from Ireland as had first appeared. Doubts surfaced too about the strength of American financial backing for the project. The car was at a much earlier stage of development than had been realised. Even within the IDA team handling the proposal, differences of opinion opened up. These concerns reached such a pitch that Michael Killeen called a special meeting of the Authority members in early April. It was so sensitive that it was held, not in the IDA offices, but across the road in Jury's Hotel, Ballsbridge.

John Kerrigan, the Dublin-based coordinator for the project, was dispatched to the USA, and he spent his Easter there doing further research on the project. His 400-page analysis was considered at the IDA Authority's meeting in mid-May and a financial package of $44 million was approved for submission to the Cabinet. The Authority noted the exceptional job needs of the Limerick area in the wake of the Ferenka closure but instructed that the risk factors be brought fully to the notice of the government. The Cabinet backed the deal and the approval was signalled to DeLorean.

Then, DeLorean overplayed his hand. He returned to the negotiating table and demanded further improvements in the deal. He even rang John Kerrigan at his Dublin home at midnight to say that he had been contacted by Northern Ireland about the project. Kerrigan interpreted the call as another pressure tactic.

The original decision to back him had involved Killeen and his colleagues in a fine balance between the large job benefits for Limerick and the considerable risks of a new car project. When DeLorean came back for more, the doubts came to the fore. Killeen was losing confidence in both the viability of the project and in DeLorean himself. Now, he wanted out of the project. However, there was one problem. The Authority had given a formal offer to DeLorean, and once accepted, it would be binding on the IDA. These were tension-filled days. Michael Killeen decided to treat DeLorean's bargaining ploy as tantamount to rejection of the IDA offer. At a meeting of the Authority on 14 June 1978, he advised the members that the company had said the offer was unacceptable. The meeting agreed that the offer would be withdrawn and negotiations terminated, subject to legal confirmation that this was reasonable and subject to the Minister's agreement. And so, the IDA offer was whipped off the table with the full agreement of Minister Des O'Malley, in whose Limerick constituency the project was to be located.

De Lorean may well have suspected that the game was up with the IDA because we now know that on 12 June, two days before the fateful Authority meeting, he had brought his project one hundred miles north to Belfast, where he introduced it to the Department of Commerce with the benefit of the appraisals and projections that resulted from his negotiations with the IDA. On 3 August 1978, Roy Mason, Secretary of state for Northern Ireland, and John DeLorean announced agreement on the car project at a press conference in Belfast. A new half-a-million square-foot factory would be built at Dunmurry on the outskirts of Belfast. I recall, as if it were yesterday, DeLorean's graphic promise that 'we aim to move from cow pasture to production within eighteen months.' Full-scale production of cars commenced in February 1981, and at its peak the DeLorean company had 2,600 workers making the gull-wing cars. A year later, the company hit the financial rocks and went into receivership in February 1982, closing its doors for good in October that year. Just over 8,000 of the dream cars had rolled off the line in its short history.

As controversy and fraud allegations engulfed the DeLorean project in Belfast, there was a common view among IDA staff that if DeLorean had gone ahead in Limerick, the resulting scandal and loss of public funds would have finished off the IDA. It did leave its own scars and led to a shake-up of the organisation. It threatened to kill off the IDA's willingness to back large projects in the emerging electronic and software industries. But thankfully, the ghost of DeLorean was successfully exorcised and normal IDA service resumed in subsequent years.

In Northern Ireland, many litigation proceedings were taken to recover the £70 million of public funds invested in the project, including investigations of alleged fraud involving DeLorean and others with a Swiss company. These proceedings did bear fruit and by 1998, a total of £47 million had been recovered.

*

The scale of the recession in the US and Europe in the early 1980s made market conditions difficult for international business and reduced the profitability of companies. This led to wholesale cutbacks, both in employment and new investment. Jobs were shed both at the parent plants of companies and at their foreign subsidiaries. Ireland did not escape. One particular week in May 1983 provided the most memorable illustration of the downturn – and one that remains etched in my memory. Two of the most prestigious companies in the world made a decision to close their operations in Ireland. AT&T, the US telecommunications giant, and Black and Decker, the US brand leader in DIY tools, announced the closure of their Irish plants.

AT&T had acquired the Telectron plant in Tallaght, Dublin, which employed 800 people making specialist small telephone exchanges. It was one of their first European acquisitions and the company appointed as head of the Irish operations an American with no international experience whose approach did not suit his new responsibility. The order book deteriorated, the company was losing money and in April 1983 it announced it was going to cease operations in Tallaght. I took the unusual step of issuing a public statement requesting a suspension of the decision until the IDA had had a chance to discuss it fully with the parent company in the US.

Normally, by the time a company goes public with a job loss or closure announcement, the IDA will have gone to the limit in exploring every avenue to get a better outcome and accepted that, realistically, there was no alternative. However, in this case, we were far from satisfied that we had a satisfactory dialogue with the AT&T representatives in Ireland, bearing in mind the gravity of some 800 job losses. So Minister of State Eddie Collins, David Hanna, the IDA manager responsible, and myself made the long trip to California to meet James Olsen, chairman of AT&T's international operations and vice-chairman of the entire AT&T company itself, in a last-ditch effort to save the jobs in Tallaght.

The setting was the La Quinta resort hotel, a complex with Spanish-style villas in Palm Springs. There, the giant company was having its last annual get-together of corporate heads before the enforced break-up of its operating companies into 'Baby Bells'. We made our way through the holidaymakers for the high-noon meeting with Chairman Olsen and two senior aides. We brought with us a package of proposals to turn the business around: advancing Irish government purchasing of its equipment, assisting in the marketing of Telectron products abroad and identifying sub-contract business with the electronic companies in Ireland.

Olsen pointed to the fact that the business was not there to sustain the workforce. During a tough two-and-a-half-hour session, we pressed for the retention of at least a nucleus of manufacturing business in Tallaght, until the markets picked up and the order book improved. There was little sentiment or goodwill for us to draw on as the company had inherited a troublesome industrial-relations situation in the Tallaght operation. Olsen and his executives withdrew to consider our proposals. During the next half-hour, as we anxiously awaited the company verdict, we were torn between hope and pessimism regarding the outcome. In the event, Olsen returned to say a reprieve would only prolong the agony. The plant would close after all. Our mission had failed.

On the very day – 5 May 1983 – that we returned to Ireland, as the news of the failure of our Californian mission was confirmed publicly, Black and Decker also announced the closure of its new factory in Kildare and the loss of 270 jobs because of poor markets for its DIY workbench. In response to media queries about the run of factory closures, I dubbed it the 'blackest week' for industry in Ireland. The front page headline in the *Irish Times* the following day captured the mood of those times: 'Nearly 1,000 lost jobs in "blackest week" of slump.' The fact that two such leading US companies – AT&T and Black and Decker – could not manage to make a success of their Irish investments gives some measure of the severity of the international recession. Subsequently, the IDA supported the conversion of both premises into Enterprise Centres for small business.

One closure that did conform to the traditional picture of callous action by a multinational was the shutdown by Hyster on 10 June 1987 of its automated materials handling plant in Blanchardstown in Dublin. The IDA had secured the project after the toughest possible negotiations with company chairman Bill Kilkenny. Hyster, based in Portland, Oregon, and the second-largest fork-lift-truck manufacturer in the world, already operated a plant in Coleraine, Northern Ireland. The new project for Dublin had all the most desirable characteristics one could wish for in a new investment. Ireland would become the company's global centre for the design, development, marketing and manufacture of the automated warehouse handling project. The public announcement five years earlier, in May 1982, had predicted 450 jobs by 1987 and 1,500 in ten years – the bulk of the IDA's financial support was linked directly to the employment, training and research activities of the Irish workforce.

The new project seemed a logical extension of Hyster's well-established fork-lift trucks, used in warehousing, providing a complete automated warehousing system with automated vehicles. The markets and economics of the new development had been researched in great detail. The success of the project was seen by the company as central to its future. By early 1987, the company employed 225 young Irish staff in a fine new building in the attractive Snugborough Business Park in Blanchardstown, Dublin. But from an early stage the company lacked adequate finance to support the new project, while market demand for Hyster's new equipment failed to materialise as expected. In addition, the manager sent over to take charge of the Dublin operation experienced friction with his Irish staff. The IDA was engaged in intense discussions with the parent company on ways of restructuring the Irish operation when the company told us at 5.30 PM that it was closing down the following morning, Wednesday June 10. Hyster's Dublin-based manager learned the bad news only at 2 AM on the morning itself.

When the Irish staff began arriving for work at 7 AM, they found that the American staff had locked the main doors and staff entrance and were handing out typewritten notices, informing them of the termination of the business. However, the workers discovered an open side door, pushed their way inside and started a sit-in until they got a satisfactory redundancy deal.

As a way of ceasing operations, the company's action was callous and indefensible. Once more, I went out front with press briefings and radio interviews to explain an industry closure, a task all the more difficult in this instance because of the regrettable fashion in which the company had handled it. Another source of annoyance was that they had gone through with the announcement while the Minister for Industry, Albert Reynolds, was actually in the US on an investment-promotion trip. In his absence, Minister for Finance Ray Mac Sharry dealt with the Hyster bombshell before an angry Dáil.

In the IDA, we set down one dominant criterion in the search to find a replacement industry. It would have to be such a blue-chip project that the chances of a repeat failure in the same plant would be close to zero. In the event, we found the perfect substitute later in the same year. Thermo King, which already had a successful operation in Galway making truck refrigeration units, selected the former Hyster plant as an added production centre. It continues to operate there.

But the Hyster closure had aroused widespread public resentment and led to questioning of the wisdom of the entire foreign-investment policy. The debate became so intense, so one-sided and so hostile to foreign investment that I decided to tackle the issues raised head-on, while the storm was still raging. In a speech in Athlone some days later, on 15 June 1987, entitled 'Foreign Industry – A Proud Record in Ireland', I attempted to redress the balance by strongly defending the performance of foreign industry overall and then setting out the significance then of their employment and economic contribution. A few days later, the *Irish Times* in an editorial entitled 'Emotional Backlash' supported my basic theme by stating that 'the occasional failure is inevitable and must be seen in perspective . . . against the solid record of so many enterprises which have set up within the state.' The subsequent performance of the foreign sector amply justified the case I made then in the eye of the anti-foreign-industry hurricane.

Once a multinational makes a public announcement to close a plant, that decision is rarely reversed. But, in the case of the Baxter Travenol Healthcare plant in Castlebar, that is exactly what happened. Baxter Travenol was one of the first big successes of the new IDA. The deal was negotiated in 1971 and was designed to create over 1,000 jobs in a magnificent new premises on the outskirts of Castlebar, styled as 'laboratories' by the company. The main product was blood therapy bags. The company also opened a sister plant in Swinford to produce intravenous catheters. At first, everything went well, and employment at the company's two facilities reached a peak of 1,500.

But the policy of regular rotation of its US-based managers produced a lack of management continuity, with each manager leaving problems for his successor to handle. As a result, the industrial relations climate in the large Castlebar plant deteriorated. The company also tended to be early to settle wage deals in national pay rounds, and usually at high rates. These developments left the US parent company increasingly disenchanted with the Castlebar operation. And so, by the time the company adopted the more universal policy of appointing Irish general managers, the industrial difficulties at the plant had become entrenched.

In the difficult economic conditions of the early 1980s, governments in Europe and the US, in their bid to curb overall public spending and rising deficits, focused particularly on health expenditure to secure savings. These pressures hit the parent Baxter Travenol corporation severely in 1984, as its sales, profits and share price all dropped sharply. As Christmas loomed, the company executives came to the IDA with the bad news. They wanted to close the Castlebar plant entirely, with a loss of 700 jobs, although the Swinford plant, with its 180 jobs, was to be retained and expanded. Healthcare cutbacks in the company's markets meant Baxter had excess manufacturing capacity in Castlebar's main line of blood-therapy products. It had chosen the company's French plant as the preferred centre instead. According to the company, productivity at Castlebar was lower than at any other of its European operations. So when the difficulties arose, Castlebar, unfortunately, had neither economics nor sentiment in its favour, as far as the parent company was concerned.

The IDA philosophy in closure situations is to win the maximum time from the company before any final shutdown. This gives an opportunity either to try and secure a greatly reduced operating presence by a foreign company or to find replacement industries to absorb the jobs being lost. With the strong support of Minister John Bruton, Baxter Travenol agreed to phase out the operation over two years, an unusually long period. The deadline for total closure was set for December 1986. However, the winding-down process was to start within three months, with the initial loss of 450 jobs by October 1985. The company agreed to cooperate fully with a special IDA Action Group, which was leading the search for replacement industries.

On 3 January 1985, I held a press conference to outline fully the background to the closure and to seek publicly local support for the IDA's endeavours to attract replacement industries. There would be little hope of getting any other company to come to Castlebar if there was a poisonous attitude towards multinationals. So, immediately after the shock closure announcement, I sought community and worker support, through an interview with David Hanly on RTÉ's *Morning Ireland* radio programme.

In addition, I wanted to avoid an emotional backlash against the company and to keep its goodwill as, privately, we intended to use the time before total closure to attempt to reverse the decision. The Castlebar community played it smart. And while there were the inevitable post-mortems and great sadness at the individual redundancies, there was no general public bloodletting at Baxter's expense.

The search for replacement industries continued over the next two years. A special promotional brochure was produced in cooperation with Baxter. The IDA had an advance factory available adjacent to the factory and later acquired from the company some two-thirds of the premises vacated following the initial redundancies. In the meantime, Baxter in the US had written to 500 companies, making the case for investment in the Castlebar area. And in the town itself, a 'Jobs for Castlebar' campaign was launched, under the chairmanship of the Urban Council Chairman, Paddy McGuinness. This too cooperated closely with the IDA in the search for new industry. However, new industries were slow in coming.

Throughout, the IDA had a close and trusted alliance with Bernard Collins, the Irish general manager at the Baxter plant in Castlebar, both in seeking new industries and in the more difficult challenge of reversing the total closure. Bernard and the 250 staff still left by late 1985 set out to demonstrate that they could reduce costs at the Castlebar plant and be as competitive as any of Baxter's rivals in the product still in production there – water and glucose solutions for the intravenous treatment of patients.

By dint of a heroic collective endeavour, which was palpable on a visit to the plant, and undeterred by the imminence of the closure date in December 1986, the remaining staff gradually brought down the unit costs of production. Their first break came in February 1986, when the company announced a reprieve of a further year before closure. While publicly the reason given for the deferral was related to the takeover by Baxter of another big US healthcare company (American Hospital Supply), I believed it had also begun to take note of positive changes by the Castlebar staff.

Productivity at Castlebar continued to improve and, armed with the results, Pat O'Brien, the IDA Director, and myself travelled in May 1987 to the parent-company headquarters in

Chicago. There we presented the case for a reversal of the decision to close. We were mindful as we made our pitch that a senior executive from the company's headquarters (Charles Ebling) had stated publicly after the initial announcement that he 'was not aware of any set of circumstances that might arise in the future that could make us reverse the decision'.

Shortly afterwards, the word came through to us from Chicago – the Castlebar plant and its 250 staff would be saved. The good news became public knowledge on 4 June 1987. It was with a great sense of satisfaction that the IDA issued a formal statement that day, congratulating the staff at Baxter Travenol in Castlebar, then led by manager Donal O'Dwyer, on 'their outstanding performance in improving efficiency and quality, culminating in the company's decision to remain in full production'. The replacement-industry initiative bore some modest fruit that year also with the approval by the IDA of three new companies for Castlebar planning to employ over one hundred people (Cable Products, Johnson Industries and Amagruss).

By May 1999, now renamed Baxter Healthcare, the company was employing 610 people in Castlebar and was spending £44 million annually in Ireland on wages, raw materials and services. In that month, Baxter further deepened its Irish commitment by announcing the creation of another 220 jobs in Castlebar. This brought the total there to 830 jobs, where – not so long ago – there were to be none. Castlebar had become the company's centre of excellence for renal solutions for kidney-dialysis treatment, supplying the entire European market.

And so the wheel came full circle, with its decision to set up a new centre in Dublin, employing eighty people, to provide the company with European-wide support services in finance, purchasing, information technology and logistics. Tánaiste Mary

Harney fully appreciated the historic significance of the investment for the company. Announcing the expansion, she 'congratulated the management and workforce at Baxter Ireland, as it was their immense effort that had won this investment'. The battle to retain the Irish lifeline to Baxter back in 1985–7 had more than paid off.

12

THE MUSCLES OF THE CELTIC TIGER
THE IDA'S WINNING SECTORS

Padraic White

The IDA approach to targeting sectors of industry was set out
in Ray McLoughlin's 'closed loop' model in 1970, and its logic
continues to this day. As an industrial-development strategy, it
is easy to state and hard to execute: first, identify the sectors and
sub-sectors that are growing and would provide a good fit for
Ireland; second, find the best companies in those sectors; and
third, persuade them to come here. However, one must also
develop the human skills and support facilities to meet their
operating requirements. And that means investment in education
– human capital – as well as physical infrastructure, like
telecommunications and roads.

Consequently, the IDA has always been scanning the world
business horizon for the emerging sectors and niche areas of the
future. Once a sector is targeted, the challenge is to spot the winning
companies within it, before they become household names, and also
before the world's other development agencies have beaten a path
to their doors. And of course, there is always room for a good project
that may not be in the priority technological areas.

The IDA's Winning Sectors

Michael Killeen was convinced that the electronic and pharmaceutical sectors were right for Ireland. He was influenced by two pioneering papers produced under the auspices of the National Science Council. The new science organisation, chaired by Professor Colm Ó hEocha of University College Galway, started life in January 1968, two years ahead of the IDA's reorganisation. The Council was another manifestation of the search for new ways to secure Ireland's economic development. It was designed to promote science and research related to the country's economic development and to create links, which were weak in those days, between the academic world and industry. The Council's Research and Development Committee was headed by a director of Irish Ropes Ltd, Joe McCabe (who later became Chairman of the IDA). It commissioned specialists from the University of East Anglia to produce proposals for technology sectors which Ireland could exploit successfully, and where its academic and technology effort should be developed. They came up with electronics and fine chemicals (including pharmaceuticals) as two winning sectors.

While Killeen was figuring out his approach in his first year in office as head of the IDA, McCabe brought him the papers on the two sectors. He went through the background thinking in detail and received a strong endorsement of the strategy from Killeen. This episode reveals another clue to the puzzle as to how the IDA identified two target sectors, electronics and pharmaceuticals, which were to prove so successful in Ireland, despite the lack of a domestic industrial tradition or specialisation in the universities.

It is interesting to observe the winners and losers in hindsight. The man-made-fibre industry sector was badly hit by the oil-price rises in 1979, and today there are two main survivors – Unifi Ltd in Letterkenny and Wellman Ltd in Cavan. In the

1970s, as oil exploration in the North Sea and in Irish waters intensified in response to energy-price rises, interest grew in oil-production platforms, and plans were well advanced for an industry to make them at Killala, County Mayo. The IDA carried out a worldwide search in the mid-seventies for a company to develop a zinc smelter which Minister for Industry Justin Keating believed was necessary to secure the full benefits of the discovery of large zinc deposits. Proposals from the New Jersey Zinc Company were publicly unveiled subsequently, but the smelter never materialised.

Clothing and textile companies – for example, Wrangler, Bluebell, Farah Jeans and Burlington Industries' four textile plants – did provide thousands of jobs. But when faced with changes in fashion or tough price competition from Asia, they either closed or cut back their operations. Within the IDA, a much-debated question over the years was the judgement call required on the merits of a company that employed, say, 500 workers for five or six years and which, through expenditure in the Irish economy, had contributed more than any state grants received.

In the high-technology area the IDA backed many companies that were regarded as the stars of the sector, but, when consolidation and maturity in the industry occurred, they fell by the wayside. What is most encouraging, however, is that the IDA's investment portfolio also included most of the ultimate winners. Three foreign-dominated sectors ultimately emerged as the most successful and have contributed most to Ireland's economic growth: healthcare (pharmaceuticals and medical devices), electronics and software. In many cases, the original company names have changed, as the parent company was either taken over or merged following a consolidation within the industry.

*

The healthcare industry makes products to improve human health and well-being and to help provide a better quality of life. However, within the sector, there are two quite different types of company. The pharmaceutical wing makes drugs and medicines, or ingredients for them, while the medical-device wing makes tangible products such as catheters, syringes and dosage-measurement devices. There are over 150 foreign companies in the overall healthcare industry, employing more than 25,000 people directly and responsible for some 20 per cent of Irish exports.

The pharmaceutical industry has proven to be the first sectoral success of Ireland's industrial promotion. Its development dates back to about 1960, and its evolution can be traced to the decision of a Danish company, Leo Laboratories, to establish in Dublin. Today over sixty companies operate within this sector, employing 12,000 people and accounting for 18 per cent of Ireland's manufactured exports. Another of the 'founding members' was Squibb Linson, a US-owned company which in 1964 settled in Swords, County Dublin. It serves as an exemplar of the longevity, vitality and level of corporate change within the Irish pharmaceutical industry. When the larger US pharmaceutical company Bristol Myers, itself a long-standing elusive target of IDA promotions, acquired Squibb Linson's US parent, it found itself with an Irish manufacturing subsidiary for the first time. Through this acquisition, Bristol Myers came to learn at first hand about Ireland, with some beneficial consequences. In 1998, it decided to establish a new pharmaceutical plan in Dublin's Mulhuddart, as well as expanding the Swords plant – the investment was a hefty £300 million, with 500 additional jobs to be created.

Another early arrival was the Pfizer Corporation. In 1969, it first agreed to establish a plant in Ringaskiddy, County Cork.

The decision was heavily influenced by Irish-American Jack Mulcahy, a senior vice-president of the company and a strong supporter of investment in Ireland. Pfizer now has three plants on its Cork site, where the active ingredient for its best-selling Viagra – an anti-impotence pill – is also manufactured. In addition, it has a licensed Pfizer Bank in the International Financial Centre in Dublin.

The Warner Lambert company from the US went into production in Dun Laoghaire in 1970 and was an influential flagship company in subsequent years. Its continued vitality is demonstrated by its four plants in Ireland, in Dublin and Cork, which employ about 1,000 people. To the IDA, the pharmaceutical sector became a natural focus for its direct-marketing approach to companies. A relatively small number of world leaders were easily identified and targeted. The attractions were clear. Pharmaceuticals required large capital investment which, in turn, this ensured that a company locating here was more likely to have a long-term commitment. The IDA used the presence of the growing number of multinational drug companies as an advertisement to help win others. Undoubtedly, for such a profitable sector, the tax relief provided a very real benefit that heavily influenced their decision to invest in Ireland.

The early fruits of the intense marketing initiatives in the United States were the decisions in 1973 by Syntex to establish a manufacturing plant in County Clare (subsequently acquired by Roche, the giant Swiss company). Merck Sharpe and Dohme came to Clonmel, and SmithKline French located in Cork. These decisions by leading US pharmaceutical companies to choose Ireland as their European base for selected product lines and to settle in regional locations in the country offered early proof to the IDA of the value of its sectoral focus, its company targeting and marketing and its regional philosophy.

Allergan Corporation provided a good example of the marriage of international marketing and the commitment to regional development within Ireland. In 1976, the company, from Orange County, California, decided to establish the European base for its contact-lens solutions in Westport, a town on County Mayo's Atlantic coast with a population then of 3,000 people. Allergan has underpinned the economic progress of Westport and its hinterland by directly employing 1,000 people and by its substantial purchases of printing and other services from the area.

Highlights of the pharmaceutical industry in Ireland in the 1980s include the commitment of the US company Schering Plough to Ireland. At Inishannon, County Cork, it makes Interferon, which is a copy of a protein found naturally in low levels in the human body and is used to treat a variety of conditions, including hepatitis C. That decade also saw the location of the Dutch-owned Organon in Dublin and the first new pharmaceutical plant by a Japanese company in Ireland – the Yamanouchi investment at Mulhuddart.

A small number of individual companies in the pharmaceutical industry have been at the centre of environmental controversy over the years. Environmental objections may be to the composition of effluent, the nature of air emissions or odours. In July 1998, a local farmer, John Hanrahan, won a protracted and widely publicised case against Merck Sharpe and Dohme in Clonmel on an appeal to the Supreme Court. The court found that, as a matter of probability, there was a causal relationship between the ailments of animals on Hanrahan's farm and the factory emissions. It was a classic David-against-Goliath struggle – the small man against the giant multinational. In the aftermath of the Hanrahan case, there was a palpable public suspicion of the pharmaceutical industry and of new investments, particularly if these included incinerators.

In the Cork city area, which had attracted pharmaceutical industries to the Little Island area and to Ringaskiddy, local opposition to the industry was very strong. It was provoked by the persistence of unpleasant smells in the air there. These odours varied in intensity with wind direction and were attributed, variously, to different companies. The IDA played a mediating role in these conflicts, responding to community concerns and also encouraging the companies to clear up the air pollution, while trying to maintain Ireland's reputation as welcoming pharmaceutical investment.

Peace between the industry and the Cork communities was eventually achieved. The companies made the necessary investment to get rid of the nuisance smells, and the national Environmental Protection Agency was set up with strong licensing powers. However, during this turbulent time relating to environmental issues, Ireland lost a number of first-class investments because of the controversies.

The Schering Plough company pulled out of a planned investment in the Clonmel area in 1976. Beecham's did not proceed with an industry planned for County Clare. The loss in 1987 of a $250 million investment, which the IDA had negotiated with the US-based Merrell Dow pharmaceutical company, was particularly heartbreaking. Merrell was one of the few remaining 'big league' players in that sector not then in Ireland. It had decided to locate in the Cork city area but, because of the Ringaskiddy controversy, instead chose a site in the pastoral area of east Cork, near Killeagh. However, local hostility to the project was so great that the proposal was abandoned.

It was devastating news. Losing a hard-won investment was bad enough, but the potential damage to the IDA strategy of making Ireland a base for the pharmaceutical industry was too much to contemplate. Though Merrell, in its formal statement abandoning the investment, left the door open to consider Ireland in the future, the IDA believed a first-rate company had been lost for good. Fortunately, the cavalry came over the hill shortly afterwards in the form of the Swiss pharmaceutical company Sandoz. In 1989, it finalised negotiations with the IDA for a £170 million-plus investment in the Ringaskiddy area – in the face of the most intense opposition to the pharmaceutical sector.

The company had experience of tough environmental battles, following an accidental spillage into the River Rhine from one of its plants. Sandoz assigned a formidable and experienced man, Winfried Pedersen, to help win community support for the project and secure planning permission. During that time, it showed patience and great understanding for the concerns of the local community and Sandoz got planning clearance. By 1990, plant construction was well under way. The company, now part of Novartis, the largest pharmaceutical company in the world, had demonstrated that with the right approach, Ireland was still a viable location for new pharmaceutical industries.

Overall, the foreign pharmaceutical sector has had a remarkable record in Ireland. There has never been a plant closure, and among the 12,000 workers employed, some 30 per cent are graduates. It exports more than three times the value of its imports and in 1998 contributed an estimated £235 million in corporation tax. Since almost every top pharmaceutical international company has a substantive investment in Ireland, growth will largely come from more investment and support for administrative services from the existing base of companies. Currently, sixteen of the top twenty pharmaceutical companies globally have manufacturing operations in Ireland.

The other segment of the healthcare sector is the medical-devices industry. In many ways, this is a dream industry, in terms of its ultra-clean facilities, laboratory-style image, employment growth and scale of investment. Its development is linked to the continuing world need for medical treatment. There are seventy foreign companies employing 11,500 people directly in this area. Exports exceed £1 billion a year and the industry has put down deep roots in Ireland's economy. Over one-third of all the materials it needs are sourced domestically, and some 40 per cent of companies are carrying out product development here.

The first wave of medical-device companies came mainly from the US and were attracted in the early 1970s in response to the saturation targeting of the new IDA. These included two Chicago-based companies, Baxter Travenol, which set up in Castlebar, and Abbott Laboratories, which invested in Sligo and Donegal. The founding members also included Hollister in Ballina and Becton Dickinson in Drogheda. They became showpiece industries providing stable jobs in beautifully designed premises conveying a new image of industry. They were willing to locate in the less-developed western and midland regions, and their presence transformed the economic prospects of their adopted towns. The early success of the medical-devices strategy was powerful proof to the IDA that its systematic approach in selecting sectors and companies, marketing to them directly and offering a full support service in Ireland actually worked. Ireland encountered severe competition from low-cost emerging countries such as Puerto Rico and Mexico in the 1980s but still managed to attract star companies that have prospered, including CR Bard in Galway, Bausch and Lomb in Waterford, Mallinckrodt in Athlone and Sherwood Medical in Tullamore.

The 1990s have brought a further surge of new medical-device companies to Ireland, averaging four annually. One of the IDA coups was the attraction of the US company Boston Scientific to Galway in 1994 – employment there and at its subsequent Cork investment is scheduled to reach 2,000. The majority of the world leaders in the medical-devices industry are now in Ireland, well-distributed in thirty-five different locations, the majority in the less-developed western and midland areas. The companies make high-margin products which can be delivered within twenty-four hours to most markets in Europe. The industry will continue to expand in terms of investment, exports and jobs.

*

Electronics represents the largest single foreign-industry sector in Ireland and has been at the heart of the rapid transformation of the country's economic and job prospects. Its landscaped, airy buildings, state-of-the-art technologies and cosmopolitan Irish workforces are synonymous with the emergence of the Celtic Tiger economy. It contributes 30 per cent of Irish exports, employs some 28,000 people directly and spends £2,000 million each year in Ireland on wages, local goods and services. Employment has increased every year.

The vision of making Ireland a world-class centre for the new electronics industry evolved within the IDA in the mid-1970s. There was no indigenous electronics industry and Ireland's potential was spotted as the IDA continued to search for new investment sectors while its staff in the American market place watched and mingled with the pioneers in Silicon Valley in California and on Route 128 in Boston.

The pre-history of the electronic industry goes back to the development here in the 1960s of a trio of American companies, all still in operation today. Two were subsidiaries of General Electric (GE) – EI at Shannon (1963) and Ecco (now Harris Ireland) at Dundalk (1966) – and the third was the Core

Memories company, based in Coolock, Dublin (1967), now known as Data Products Ltd. The GE companies produced semiconductors of the times ('discreet' ones as distinct from the current 'integrated' variety) and the Coolock company made 'memories' for large computers. The remarkable survival capacity of these early companies in a constantly changing technological sector is highlighted in the person of Frank Toal. He joined Ecco, Dundalk, at its start-up in 1966 and thirty-three years later was managing director in the same plant!

These early companies introduced young Irish engineers and technicians to the nascent electronics technologies and to the disciplined management philosophy of the US multinationals. The path of one of these engineers, Frank McCabe, illustrates the evolution of the industry in Ireland and the crucial role played by individuals, both Irish and foreign, as they moved between companies.

McCabe, a graduate of mechanical engineering from University College Dublin, was the first operations manager of General Electric's semiconductor plant in Dundalk. Later, he became the Irish-based chief of GE's electronics business in Europe and moved in 1970 from Dundalk to manage its sister plant in Shannon. On joining Digital Equipment Corporation (DEC) in Galway in 1979, he was responsible for the company's entire European manufacturing. Five years later, he moved to its Massachusetts head office as senior vice-president. Then, he completed the circle by returning to Ireland in 1994 to head up Intel's operation, with the added responsibilities of vice-president of technology and manufacturing for Intel worldwide. Indeed, the two General Electric plants acted as the most prolific training centres for Irish managers who were subsequently recruited by other incoming multinationals, which were eager to recruit those imbued with the distinctive GE philosophy and culture.

The first fruit of the new IDA electronics strategy was the decision in 1971 of Digital Equipment of Massachusetts (DEC) to put its mini-computer manufacturing into Galway. This was the era of young, fast-growing mini-computer companies, and the Digital example was used by the IDA in its marketing to secure many of the industry's rising stars. These were attracted to Ireland to gain access to the European market and responded to the country's package of educated young people, financial grants and tax incentives. The decade ended with Wang Laboratories of Lowell, Massachusetts, trailblazers in electronic word-processing, announcing in December 1979 its plan to make computers in Limerick and employ 1,600 people.

In the same month, Michael Killeen publicly set out the IDA vision of the industry in a speech to the Royal Institute of Chartered Surveyors entitled 'The Electronics Revolution – Its Impact on Ireland'. He calculated that employment in the electronics industry had doubled to 10,000 people in the six years to 1979 and predicted that 'electronics would be the biggest single source of new jobs in coming years.' He listed fourteen separate sub-sectors of the industry – such as integrated circuits, scientific instrument and terminals – which the IDA had selected as targets. Electronics exports had risen dramatically to account for 20 per cent of Irish manufacturing exports by 1978.

But the sheer scale of the employment needs of the electronics companies the IDA had negotiated with between 1977 and 1979 presented an unexpected crisis. When the numbers of electrical engineers and technicians were added up in the companies already signed up, the employment requirement far exceeded the numbers coming out of the Irish universities and regional colleges. In 1976, the IDA had negotiated electronics projects with 1,600 jobs, but in the following three years it secured a wave of electronics industries with 18,000 projected jobs. These were heady days of success but when the IDA got down to figure out the skill implications, the conclusions were stark. The country was producing 100 electrical engineers and 200 electrical technicians a year, but the industry needed four times that volume each year to meet the expected demand. Since it takes between two and five years to educate technicians and engineers, an immediate national response was needed if we were to continue to promote electronics investment, never mind find the skilled people for the industries already under construction and beginning recruitment.

In his speech Killeen was signalling publicly the extent of the crisis – as well as the graduate opportunities. In fact, the IDA had already taken steps through 1979 to redress the situation. It briefed the Higher Education Authority, which included representatives of the universities, individual college heads and government departments on the impending graduate crisis. The IDA invited the Higher Education Authority to a special presentation in Lansdowne House. I can still recall the starkness of the gap between the lines showing the expected graduate outflow over the coming five years, and the IDA projection of demand based on its negotiations with companies.

This was the most dramatic interaction up to then between the IDA and the education authorities and government in seeking to adjust graduate output to fit the rapid changes both in technology and the mix of foreign industries. The government and the colleges responded immediately, and with enthusiasm, to the crisis. As a short-term solution they proposed to convert science graduates to electronics qualifications via one-year conversion courses, and for the medium term they expanded or added new courses. By autumn 1979, the Higher Education Authority was given more funds and fourteen special conversion courses and fifty-eight new or expanded courses in electrical engineering were under way. The story of such a rapid response by the educational authorities to industry's needs is so rare internationally that the IDA relayed it to prospective investors many times. It offered reassurance that Ireland would deliver the skills needed.

A further serious drawback to building an electronics industry in Ireland was the outdated telephone network. It was the old electro-mechanical system, quite unsuited to the data-transmission needs of the electronic and software companies. In addition, there were long waiting lists for new phones. For the IDA, this was a serious impediment to its efforts to promote Ireland as a European base for foreign electronics companies. The cavalry again rode to the rescue when the Minister for Communications, Albert Reynolds, announced in 1979 radical plans for a new state telecommunications agency and investment in a modern digital-based system.

A fully automatic service would be available in five years and – miracle of miracles – waiting times for phones would be cut to six weeks. The ministerial words were no sooner spoken that the new promised land of digital phones on demand was added to the IDA gospel around the globe.

TELECOMS

Taking key strategic decisions at the right time has been critical to the success of today's Celtic Tiger economy. This is particularly true in telecommunications, where Ireland has experienced two distinct revolutions within a short time: the first in 1979, when the government decision to upgrade the telephone system was taken, and the second in 1998, when the government accelerated the full liberalisation of the whole telecommunications market. This opened the way to competition, while other measures were designed to place Ireland in the front line of the development of electronic commerce.

In both cases, failure had served as the catalyst for change. Some two decades ago, the phone system was the weak link in the IDA's marketing efforts to attract foreign investment. At any industrial-promotion seminar that the IDA organised abroad, the poor state of the phone was the greatest single complaint from foreign industrialists. And not surprisingly. The average success rate of dialled trunk calls from Dublin was just 59 per cent. Only 39 per cent of calls to the Dublin operator were answered within a minute.

At home, when the IDA sought to raise the issue directly with the Department of Posts and Telegraphs, the response was hostile. On one such occasion, I accompanied Michael Killeen to an ill-fated meeting with the Secretary of the Department, Proinsias Ó Colmáin. It was a chilly encounter. Ó Colmáin questioned the IDA's right to voice the slightest criticism or advance the mildest suggestion. Any sentence beginning with the proposition that 'The Department should consider' was dismissed as improper interference.

However, in 1978, within a year of that meeting, the report of the Review Group of Posts and Telegraphs was published. It accepted that the deteriorating condition of the phone service constituted a 'crisis', both for the public and the economy. A year later, Albert Reynolds, as Minister, announced a £650 million investment to build a digital-based network. A new state agency, Telecom Éireann, was established to run the service on a commercial basis. Michael Smurfit became its first chairman.

It allowed the IDA to proclaim that, outside of France, Ireland now had the most advanced digital-based telecom system in Europe. The Authority could now target a new range of industries where first-class international telecommunications was a key factor. These ranged from software development to call centres, customer support and data-related services. For the IDA, these knowledge industries became a major new source of job creation.

Ten years later, another series of interrelated developments had a lasting influence on the subsequent development of the electronics industry. One of the IDA target segments was integrated circuits, or ICs as they were called, and one of the bright new stars was Mostek. Before Mostek, Ireland's experience in the semiconductor industry primarily revolved around the activities of Analog Devices, Limerick. Some years previously, it had established a semiconductor-assembly operation at Raheen Industrial Estate. Analog effectively markets its products in a niche sector of industry and in subsequent years was to extend greatly its activities in Ireland. Today Analog in Limerick employs up to 200 semiconductor design engineers and is responsible worldwide for the design production and marketing of its C-MOS technology products.

But Mostek was different. It represented IDA's first investment and experience in the attraction to Ireland of high-volume semiconductor production. The Dallas company was a pioneer in making memory chips known as RAMs – Random Access Memory. When it set up in Dublin in 1979, Mostek's presence raised Ireland's standing in the electronics sector. But it also presented a considerable challenge to bring together all the skills necessary to produce these microchips in Ireland. In the event, Mostek developed an admirable operation at Blanchardstown and was a flagship of Ireland's technical prowess until the collapse in memory chip prices led to its closure. But it had demonstrated Ireland's ability to support such technological industries. Today, both NEC and Fujitsu of Japan operate volume semiconductor-assembly operations here, at Ballivor, County Meath, and Tallaght in Dublin, respectively.

Mostek's arrival also prompted interest in creating the research and education back-up to support our national aspiration to become a player in the microelectronics industry. And so in

1979, the government announced funding for a research centre in University College Cork. Professor Gerry Wrixon set up the new National Microelectronics Centre, which became part of the IDA itinerary ever afterwards for almost every prospective investor in the sector. When Ireland had little by way of a credible base of advanced industries, or technological showpieces, Professor Wrixon and his staff were an indispensable part of Ireland's industrial-promotion team. In all these ways, a series of decisions were taken in 1979 – on education, telecommunications and research facilities – which were to prove crucial in the following decades in the creation of the electronics industry in Ireland.

The 1980s opened with another spectacular coup for IDA – the decision of the glamorous Apple computer company, led by industry leader Steve Jobs, to establish its European manufacturing base in Holyhill, Cork city. This plant has survived innumerable corporate changes and cutbacks as Apple Corporation struggled in the market place in the 1990s – it remains Apple's only European production base, employing some 450 people. Other big-name companies to follow Apple to Ireland were Amdahl, a producer of large-frame computers at Swords, County Dublin, and Verbatim, the market leader in floppy disks, which set up in Limerick. The output of graduate engineers and technicians in the 1980s continued to grow in response to the crisis decisions of 1979. And, in turn, they enabled the production of more-complex electronic products in Ireland, such as the process-control equipment manufactured by Measurex (Waterford) and Accuray (Dundalk).

The IDA electronics division used a see-through model of a computer to identify every component in it. Then, systematically, it canvassed the makers of each individual component, such as keyboards, hard disks, cables, computer mice and sub-assemblies. The decade closed with Ireland successfully inducing two companies the IDA had pursued for over a decade to locate here – Intel's microprocessor plant and Motorola's communications-products plant.

As the 1990s opened, Ireland had proven its credibility as a front-runner in Europe for the most sophisticated foreign investment in electronics and computers. Companies commented on the high calibre of the engineers, computer-science graduates and technicians being produced. Dell and Gateway 2000, the new pioneers of personal computers which are sold directly to the public, both chose Ireland as their European base. So did the leaders in workstations, Sun Microsystems, and in database software, Oracle. Computers and telecommunications converged, exemplified by the boom in the Internet, and the IDA moved to attract the new leaders in these segments, such as 3Com, Cabletron and Bay Networks, which was subsequently acquired by Nortel of Canada.

Ireland's investment in new digital-based telecommunications gradually became available in the 1980s. The IDA then combined three elements in a new promotional package: first, Telecom Éireann's technical advantage; second, its low charges for volume users; and third, the availability of staff with a range of European languages. It was designed to attract the marketing, customer and technical-support services of the computer and electronic companies establishing in Ireland. And so today, if you live in Europe and want to order a Dell, Gateway 2000 or Compaq computer, your telephone call will come through to Irish-based staff speaking in your language.

Ireland's status was further enhanced by the IBM decision in 1996 to invest over £200 million in a European centre at Mulhuddart in Dublin to employ 3,000 people in a project to make electronic components and provide customer-support services. The achievement in securing annually over 20 per cent of new US electronic companies investing in European countries during the 1990s is a further testimony to the company's international status in the electronics industry. In the present decade, the industry has tripled to 28,000 the numbers directly employed there and is set to increase further in the years to come. Today, twenty of the top twenty-five US high-technology companies have substantial operations in Ireland. A critical mass of investment from technology companies has been secured, against strong international competition. IDA's score sheet in this sector now lists IBM, Intel, Hewlett Packard, Compaq, Xerox, Dell, Nortel, Ericsson, Matsushita (Panasonic), Philips, Siemens, TDK, Lucent and Hitachi – a who's who of the high-technology world.

The rapid pace of expansion in electronics and international services based in Ireland created capacity constraints as the decade came to a close – both in qualified staff and in 'broadband' telecommunications capacity with other countries to carry Internet volumes of data. In 1997 the IDA privately and publicly signalled the dangers to investment promotion posed by a shortage of qualified staff for the electronic, software and teleservice industries. The government responded with a series of decisions to increase by 1,000 the output of teleservice staff and the creation of a £250 million Technology Fund.

We had become so convinced of our superior telecommunications service that it came as a shock when a Forfás report in 1998 pointed out that we had fallen behind by not continually investing in its capacity to carry large volumes of data at sufficiently high speed. The report said that £200 million needed to be invested to meet the requirements of international and local companies in broadband networks that enable maximum information transfer – like television pictures. And it recommended that the opening up of the Irish telecommunications market to full competition should not be delayed until 2000.

The seriousness of the telecommunications issue for Ireland's reputation as an investment centre was brought forcefully to public attention in May 1998. Newspaper reports claimed that Ireland had lost out on an expansion of Microsoft's European Internet site because of the company's concern over Telecom Éireann's broadband capacity. Ireland, so often on the winning side in recent years, took the analysis of telecommunication failings to heart and the Microsoft loss served as a wake-up call. If Ireland failed to catch up, the country's reputation as a leading European centre, not only for the electronics industry but for international service companies, would be in jeopardy. Our hope of becoming a top location for e-commerce companies would be dashed.

*

The promotion of Ireland as a base for international services operations has been developed and refined by the IDA continuously since 1970. It now comprises one of the three most important areas of inward foreign investment. The introduction of new computers and electronic systems has led to a reduction in manufacturing employment in the world's leading economies. At the same time, jobs in services in those economies – where the IDA was seeking investment – have grown as a proportion of total employment. Manufacturing industry provided the traditional focus of IDA promotion, and certainly government departments and banks seemed much happier putting money into tangible assets, like bricks and machinery. A common view was that only manufactured goods, which were visible, tradeable and exportable, really added to the wealth of the country.

However, if services include every business which is neither farming nor manufacturing, how do you identify those that should be targeted by a national investment-promotion agency? For there are thousands of service activities in other countries – advertising, energy, shops and laundries – from which to choose. Selecting those that would bring additional jobs and benefits to Ireland is not an easy exercise and presents some difficult choices. How would you justify supporting foreign services attracted here, while not backing financially indigenous service companies? These were the issues which the IDA grappled with over the years in seeking out a defensible basis for promoting and investing in foreign service companies.

The IDA first launched its Service Industry Programme in July 1973 with two priority target sectors, namely, engineering consultancy and computer services, including software production. The express aim was to attract companies from abroad to establish a base in Ireland from which to sell their services either globally or as a substitute for services that were then imported. The expected benefits were good-quality jobs and a positive contribution to the balance of payments from export earnings. The idea had emerged from the IDA's own planning division or 'think tank'. There, a small group led by Páid McMenamin, observing the expansion of service employment and the con-traction of manufacturing jobs in the US, the prime target for Ireland's investment drive, had proposed in 1972 that the IDA should target the service companies. The proposal was rebuffed at first, but in early 1973, McMenamin sent a two-page synopsis to IDA executive directors. And this time approval, for a pilot approach to international services, was given.

Engineering and related consultancy services were included because of a hitherto unused and neglected legislative provision in the tax code that allowed export earnings on these services to qualify for tax exemption. Ireland was in her first year of EEC membership and, in deference to the treaty restrictions on aids to exports, the tax concession was applied only to profits on consultancy projects in countries outside the Community. In the case of computer services, the Revenue Commissioners were prepared to grant tax relief if there was a physical product, like a tape or disk, which they would treat as a manufactured good. The IDA used its existing range of capital and training grants as best it could for the new service companies, although these incentives had been designed for manufacturing industry, where construction and plant costs were the dominant costs. And so the IDA set out across the world to promote the new concept. By the end of 1974, six new service projects had been negotiated, with a total of 370 possible jobs.

The dramatic rise in oil prices from 1973 created two related opportunities: the newly acquired wealth of the Middle East oil-producing countries led to major capital investment in their own economies and a demand for foreign technical expertise, while the higher oil prices spurred the search for new commercial wells. One of the early successes was the decision by a US consultancy company, Jacob's Engineering, to set up in Ireland and recruit Irish staff for its international assignments. One of its first undertakings was to design and manage a potash recovery plant in Jordan. By 1980, the IDA was able to report that over a hundred service projects had been approved and then employed 3,000 people, mostly graduates of third-level colleges.

In 1979-80, it was time to look at ways of broadening the range of international services being promoted, and IDA scanned many possible target sectors. It was also evident that the traditional capital grants for machinery and factory construction were of little benefit to a service company renting office space, having little capital spending but giving valuable jobs to graduates. We came up with proposals for a new type of incentive, an employment grant, which would be paid for each person employed.

The proposal to introduce employment grants and to target a wider range of international services which would qualify for these grants was backed by the Department of Industry and Commerce. A year later, the necessary legislation was passed. The Industrial Development (No 2) Act, 1981, gave the IDA the legal power to award employment grants and enabled the minister to designate the specific categories of service sectors that could qualify for these grants. Based on the IDA recommendations for an extended range of target services, the Minister designated twelve sectors, including data processing, software development, healthcare services, recording services, administrative headquarters and publishing houses. Significantly, in the light of subsequent events, the list also included financial services.

Since the EEC had prohibited discrimination in favour of exports, one of the written and legal requirements was that the project would create 'added value' in Ireland. This, the IDA interpreted as meaning either creating exports or saving imports. In September 1981, the IDA unveiled its expanded International Services Programme, complete with new sectors and incentives. New business parks with office accommodation were especially designed for the expected services at Plassey Park, Limerick, and Leopardstown, Dublin, and later in Waterford, Dundalk, Sligo, Galway and Cork. With this tool kit, the IDA executives began to incorporate international services into their normal promotional activity. (The main adjustment in later years was the amendment to the tax code from 1984 to make a wide range of computer services eligible for the low tax rates applicable to manufacturing companies in cases where they had received employment grants from the IDA.)

Success quickly followed the new initiative. In 1982, the IDA announced that two of the top software suppliers in Europe

(Cincom and Informatics) were establishing software centres in Ireland. For years, the IBM company was a natural target of IDA promotion but no progress was possible because the company philosophy in those days was to put manufacturing into a country only if the home market could support the workforce – this cautionary approach was linked to IBM's lifetime employment guarantee at the time. By sheer persistence, the IDA won IBM interest in the new international service opportunities in Ireland, and in 1983 the company agreed to establish a software-development centre with a hundred people in Dublin to do specialist work for IBM itself. The success of the centre influenced IBM's decision to locate its 3,000-job campus project in Ireland fourteen years later, in 1996.

The decisions by Lotus corporation and Microsoft to locate here were critical in putting Ireland on the international software map. In 1984, Lotus set up its European centre for software development in Dublin, and a year later, Microsoft chose Sandyford, Dublin, as its European production and distribution centre.

In the case of Microsoft, P. J. Daly, head of the new IDA service initiative, recalls the tough competition with the Neuchatel canton of Switzerland. Microsoft's financial director came to Dublin, still undecided between the two locations. Though he was impressed with the low 10 per cent tax rate, the IDA could not come up with an available premises to meet the company's urgent needs. An overnight solution was found when architect Brian O'Halloran produced an alluring sketch plan for a fine new Microsoft headquarters in the Sandyford Industrial Park, ready for occupation in five months. The decision was in Ireland's favour.

Like most of the fast-growing new companies coming out of the US, Microsoft was not well known internationally. Daly recalls, with some amusement, fielding some typical queries from IDA board members when he sought approval for the project: 'Who is Microsoft?' and 'Will they be around in twelve months' time? They now directly employ 1,500 people in Ireland and dominate the world's PC-software market.

The challenge for the IDA in promoting newer service opportunities – like call centres – lay in convincing companies that they could save costs and provide a better service to customers from Ireland than anywhere else. Starting with a blank sheet in 1992, Kieran McGowan and his colleagues made Ireland a market leader in pan-European call centres, including reservation centres, customer service, technical support and telemarketing.

Having spotted the opening, they put together a 'persuasion package' comprising people, competitive telecommunications, employment grants and the 10 per cent tax and went out to persuade companies of their vision. By 1996, there were 26 teleservice projects employing over 3,000 people and growing rapidly. These included a 600-person American Airlines reserva-tion centre, a Hertz car rental reservation centre with 200 jobs, an ITT Sheraton Hotels reservation centre, and a Citibank customer-support service initially employing 1,000 people and expanding by a further 1,300 in the coming years. But because of a weak tradition of foreign language learning in Ireland, a high proportion – 40 per cent – of the linguists in the teleservices companies are from outside Ireland. By the end of 1998, there were 27,000 employed full time in the foreign-owned international services, including financial services in Ireland, according to the official survey.

Another niche area under development by the IDA is the concept of promoting shared services such as administration, accounting and invoicing. There, a company with a number of

European offices, factories or outlets would centralise these functions in Ireland and benefit from cost savings and greater efficiency.

The next big opportunity in international services will arise from the boom in Internet use for communications and electronic commerce. The Forfás agency has estimated that 25,000 new jobs could be created in Ireland by 2010 based on the growth of business transactions on the Internet. And before leaving the IDA, Kieran McGowan pledged the IDA to making Ireland the Internet capital of Europe and a centre of global electronic commerce. The missed Microsoft opportunity of May 1998 had shown one thing clearly: the speed of change in Internet activity had outpaced Ireland's capacity to respond. But the lesson was not lost. The result was orchestrated national action – through ministers, individual government departments and the state agencies. One early sign that positioning Ireland as a leader in e-commerce was firmly on the government agenda was the innovative inclusion in President Clinton's visit to Ireland in September 1998 of a public signing with Taoiseach Ahern of a joint US–Ireland communiqué on e-commerce. This set out common principles to guide the development of the new activities, for example, that taxes on e-commerce should be consistent and non-discriminatory.

The high-profile public ceremony in the Dublin facility of Gateway Corporation, one of America's leading PC makers, featured the first-ever digital computer-based signing of an agreement between two countries and provided a positive pro-Ireland signal to IDA's target e-commerce companies in the US. Another signal of Ireland's urgent intent to get into the e-commerce ring was Minister Mary O'Rourke's decision to bring forward by a year the complete deregulation of telecommunications services to 1 December 1998. On the chosen deregulation day, twenty-one companies could brandish their new general telecommunications licences awarded by the independent Director of Telecommunications Regulation, Etain Doyle.

In mid-1999, a series of linked government measures was announced, designed to get Ireland into a leading position in the race to become the country of choice in Europe for electronic-commerce business. These included a deal with the Global Crossing company of America to provide dramatically enhanced telecommunication connections between the US, Ireland and twenty-four European cities. The pay-off promised is fifteen times the telecom capacity out of Ireland at one-tenth of the existing costs. The trans-Atlantic cable would surface in the first National Digital Park, dedicated to e-commerce companies. This is being developed by Citywest Business Campus and IDA Ireland on a 100-acre site on the outskirts of Dublin. The regional centres would be included in the e-commerce world through investment of £70 million – with EU support – by telecom and cable companies, which would bring the enlarged broadband network to them.

An enlightened legal framework to support this virtual world of international commerce was unveiled and put on the Internet, and public reaction was invited before the legislation was finalised. It included, for example, the measure provided for authenticating electronic signatures and giving legal status to electronic contracts and writings. The history of Ireland's foreign-investment success illustrates the powerful role of committed individuals with a particular vision in galvanising a government to take action, and the e-commerce saga is no exception. One such perpetual visionary is Dr Edward Walsh, the first President of the University of Limerick. He developed a first-class electronics and engineering faculty there and led the campaign to persuade the government to support the new National Digital Park.

As he presided at the official opening of the Digital Park in July 1999, I recalled my successful collaboration with him, fifteen years earlier, in developing the concept and reality of Plassey Technological Park in Limerick. This was based on forging links between the firms setting up on the IDA's land bank, which happened to be adjacent to the university, and the resources and skills of the university itself. The national e-commerce and Internet infrastructure now being put in place should enable IDA-Ireland to succeed in its ambition to make Ireland a leading European centre for the extensive range of new-age industries needing these facilities.

*

Few passions can match regional passions, particularly the west of Ireland brand, about the location of foreign industry within the country. As a native of County Leitrim, I was familiar with the fear of rural neglect, to the benefit of Dublin, and talked myself into a job in the IDA's new regional planning team when I first joined the organisation in 1970. I was fired up with fury against the regional strategy of Colin Buchanan and Associates published in September 1968. This proposed a 'growth centre' strategy where development and industry would be deliberately focused on a small number of the larger cities. According to growth-centre theory, these larger cities would achieve more self-sustaining economic growth and attract more sophisticated business services. The benefits would 'trickle down' to the smaller towns in the region. But all the other cities and towns not listed by Buchanan translated the recommendations as equivalent to their death knell from neglect. They certainly did not buy into the trickle-down theory!

The 'centralists', who favoured centralisation of development and jobs, were pitched against the 'dispersalists', who favoured a greater dispersal of investment and new industry to the smaller towns and rural areas. The west of Ireland triumvirate of John Healy, Jim Maguire and Ted Nealon were all newspapermen and generated immense firepower in favour of the west through skilful use of the media. John Healy's book entitled *Death of an Irish Town* (1968) was an evocative portrayal of the decline of the rural area around his native Charlestown, County Mayo. It had a profound impact in favour of the rural areas and for a greater dispersal of foreign industry than envisaged in the *Buchanan Report*.

The new Industrial Development Authority (April 1970) found itself right in the midst of this regional battle. Since it was the state agency with responsibility for delivering the new industries, expectations of its performance were high. Above all, it was given the legislative mandate 'to foster the national objective of regional industrial development'. Michael Killeen was a west of Ireland man (he was born in Donegal and moved to Galway as a schoolboy) and had an instinctive empathy with regional aspirations. He responded to the organisation's regional mandate by setting up a separate Regional Division and creating a dedicated team with planning and economic expertise under Tom O'Connor, former Limerick County Manager. Killeen committed the IDA to the publication of regional industrial plans, one for each region outside Shannon, and to a transparent statement of the pace of new investment which the IDA would target in each region. The Shannon Development Company had already shown how a specific development plan could be developed for a single region, namely the mid-west region.

I was a member of that first IDA regional planning team. We came down firmly in favour of bringing jobs to the people and of a much greater dispersal of industry than had been favoured in the Buchanan report. The IDA was convinced, from its first-hand experience of foreign investors, that industry could be persuaded to settle in the smaller cities and towns. However, there was more to regional development than industrial investment and the government had still to make its mind up on overall regional policy, taking account of a plethora of reports, including the *Buchanan Report*. How far should the population of Dublin and the main cities be encouraged? What did priority to the less developed regions in the west and midlands mean in terms of investment in roads, airports and sanitary services?

While the media debate on these issues was orchestrated by the Healy-Maguire-Nealon trio, an equally tough and spirited battle was in progress behind the closed doors of government departments over the recommendations that should be put to the Cabinet on regional policy. I have never seen civil servants approach any subject so sharply divided, in this case between those who favoured concentration of industry and investment and those who wanted dispersal in the interests of the small towns and rural areas. I have never seen facts so readily suborned to suit personal ideologies as in this interdepartmental contest. My recollection is that the Department of Finance ended up writing their own full-scale report of dissent – they were 'concentrationists' to the core in Merrion Street.

The upshot of this struggle for the regional soul of the government was a government statement in May 1972 outlining – bravely, it must be said – the regional strategy to be pursued over the next twenty years. Dublin's development was to be assisted only to match its own natural population increase – in other words, official plans should not support net migration of people to Dublin. Expansion would be facilitated in the main regional centres of Cork, Limerick, Waterford, Galway, Dundalk, Drogheda, Sligo and Athlone. But those who feared the neglect of the smaller towns took heart from the government commitment to 'relatively large expansion of towns in areas remote from existing major towns'. The official statement went further in responding to pleas of the west in saying that regional policy should also 'provide for the maximum spread of development through all regions and so minimising population dislocation through internal migration'.

This gave the 'green light' to the IDA's desired regional balance of industry and in the following month, June 1972, Michael Killeen unveiled the nine volumes of the first IDA Regional Industrial Plans. These reports were the essence of transparency and public commitment. The plans committed the IDA to the creation of 55,000 new jobs in the following five years to 1977. They set out forty-seven separate groups of towns and made a commitment to create a specific number of new jobs in each group, within the national target of 55,000. The sentiment of favouring less-developed regions was converted to a commitment to increase the manufacturing base in the west by some 50 per cent and that in the south-east region by 16 per cent.

The IDA then went on to put its plans into action. It bought lands and built advance factories in scores of towns throughout Ireland. It set about marrying the energies of its executives hunting for industry in California or Germany with the public commitment to reach new job targets in specified towns throughout Ireland. The many foreign industries employing thousands of people in the smaller cities and towns in Ireland are the fruits of that IDA regional commitment. For example, you will see thriving industries stemming from those original plans well represented in a series of towns along the west coast, including Letterkenny, Donegal town, Sligo, Castlebar, Westport, Ballinasloe and Tuam.

The record shows that the 55,000 new jobs were created in the five years to 1977 and that substantial increases in net manufacturing employment were achieved in the less-developed regions: the west (Galway and Mayo) saw an increase of 60 per cent, the midlands saw an increase of 35 per cent, the north-west (Sligo and Leitrim) was up 34 per cent, while Donegal, which was badly affected by the violence in Northern Ireland, had a 15 per cent growth in manufacturing jobs. By contrast, the well-established industrial regions in the east suffered as a result of free trade and the after-effects of the 1973 energy crisis.

The IDA felt it had proved the sceptics wrong about its ability to attract industry to the poorer regions. The successor to the pioneering Regional Plans was the IDA Industrial Plan 1978–82, published in 1979, which combined a policy for national growth industries with a very specific regional policy. The regional component retained the concept of Town Group Targets – a bias in favour of the poorer regions – and upped the target for new state-aided jobs to 75,000, including the mid-west and Gaeltacht areas. The new plan was launched in the heady days of 1979, a boom year for IDA and the economy, and followed seventeen regional consultative conferences with local authorities, farming organisations, industrialists and trade unions – the most extensive consultations ever undertaken for an IDA plan.

Unfortunately, Ireland was moving into a period of high inflation, recession and drops in employment, and although the IDA reported that over 80 per cent of the new jobs had been achieved by the end of 1982, this was overshadowed by the even bigger job losses and the general economic gloom of the period. Because of the overwhelming sense of national economic woes, the regional dimension dropped down the national agenda and the IDA did not publish or commit itself to such specific regional and urban job targets as were last found in its Industrial Plan of 1979. Internally, the IDA maintained a priority town listing of unemployment 'black spots' and job needs and every monthly management meeting reviewed projects in the pipeline for these black spots and considered what could be done to steer emerging projects to them.

The regional passions dimmed all round and remained largely dormant until the acceleration of IDA-backed new industries from 1994 and the regular radio announcements of mega-projects for the Dublin area prompted a reawakening of regional demands for their share of the new investment. These increasingly insistent demands led to the regional distribution of industry coming back strongly on the IDA agenda, as evidenced in the words of IDA Chairman Denis Hanrahan in the 1997 annual report. There he noted that 'considerable attention has been given to the need to achieve a more equitable distribution of inward investment throughout the entire country.' And he acknowledged that 'certain imbalances were occurring with the east (particularly Dublin) attracting an inordinate amount of new overseas investment.'

The country has been divided into two regions for the purpose of European Union funding and eligibility for differing levels of state grants. The more favoured region (called Objective I areas) comprises thirteen counties in the west, midlands and border area with Northern Ireland. The IDA responded to the regional demands in mid-1999 when Chairman Hanrahan committed the organisation to doubling the national share of jobs from new foreign-investment projects going to the priority counties – from 25 per cent to 50 per cent over the next five years. We are witnessing a rerun, some thirty years on, of similar regional policy issues to those first triggered by the *Buchanan Report*.

The debate on selecting and investing strongly in the original list of Buchanan growth centres is back on the agenda of government. The last time out, following the government decision on regional policy in May 1972, the IDA took deadly seriously its mandate to foster regional development via industry and laid out its response and focused the organisation on achieving the results. But there was little evidence that other contributors to the holy grail of 'a comprehensive regional policy' did their bit. Hopefully, history will not repeat itself.

*

This story of the emergence of the Celtic Tiger economy has focused on the foreign-investment segment of the industrial economy in Ireland, as this segment provided the dominant stimulus to new investment, jobs and exports by comparison with indigenous industry. Native industry went through its own version of a 'long march' from the thirty-year comfort zone (1932–66) of protection behind high tariffs and import restrictions, through the turbulent transition to a low tariff regime introduced by the Anglo-Irish Free Trade Agreement in 1965 and substantially completed by 1980 as a consequence of Ireland's membership of the European Economic Community from 1973.

The casualty rate among Irish industry in this progression towards free trade was horrendous, even though detailed analyses of the threats facing each sector were done in advance and government adaptation and re-equipment grants were given to affected companies. At the time of EEC entry, half the employment in indigenous firms was in sectors facing full free-trade competition, like textiles, clothing and footwear. By 1980, one out of four jobs was lost and in the bigger companies with over 500 employees, the losses were even more devastating – one out of two jobs disappeared. In other words, the stars of the traditional Irish industrial firmament were grievously, if not mortally, damaged and in a weak position to proceed with investment and job creation. The recession, inflation and economic gloom of the subsequent years 1980–6 involved falling home demand and were not conducive to a renaissance of native industry. Like many other aspects of Ireland's economic story, the revival of Irish indigenous industry can be traced back to 1987.

The IDA had a unique perspective and influence on Irish industry since the organisation had state responsibility for the promotion of both foreign and indigenous industry for some twenty-four years, right up to January 1994, when responsibility for Irish industry was transferred to a separate state agency. (Forbairt and subsequently, from mid-1998, Enterprise Ireland). From its foundation, the IDA had taken the then-novel and embryonic concept in Ireland of specifically promoting small native firms, and it championed the Small Industries Programme for firms with up to fifty employees. In conjunction with the County Development Teams, based in the local authorities, the IDA had gone into the villages and byways of Ireland seeking out the local entrepreneur. A refinement in the form of the Enterprise Development Programme was introduced in 1978. This was tailored to the needs of senior executives or academics who could develop companies with greater growth potential but which also needed much more money.

This combination of responsibility in one organisation for encouraging a small two- or three-person local company, while negotiating 1,000 job projects from the world's biggest corporations, created a diverse and rich dialogue within the IDA on the contribution to Ireland of these different approaches. It also led to a focus on maximising the spend of the foreign companies on Irish goods and services and to 'linkage' with local firms.

In its work with the larger local firms, the IDA moved gradually from funding a discreet physical investment which could create jobs to looking at the overall strategy and growth of a company. We called it the company-development approach. Initially, it was a hard gospel to advocate to government and the public because a company might have to reduce jobs – and do so with IDA funding – before it could become profitable and then expand jobs. Today, the purpose of intervention by Enterprise Ireland is to help companies get a competitive advantage, which they can sustain, thereby finding the key to more sales, exports, profits – and jobs.

The revival of Irish indigenous industry has been succinctly charted by Eoin O'Malley of the ESRI. Since 1987, there has been a substantial improvement in the employment, output and exports of Irish industry. According to O'Malley, the improvement is without precedent in twentieth-century Ireland but has also been stronger than that of industrial countries generally. Local business has benefited from the business confidence and economic growth in this period and, in turn, contributed positively to their longevity. The revamped official industrial policies for native industry have also borne fruit.

The foreign industries have made an outstanding contribution to the emergence of a healthy local industry and to prosperity in virtually every service activity in Ireland. By 1998, they were spending £9.4 billion on Irish wages, materials and services – more than double the spend of five years earlier. In addition, the foreign companies introduced thousands of Irish managers to their software, electronic, computing, manufacturing and financial know-how and to their advanced management philosophies and practices. It goes back to General Electric's influence in the mid-1960s. These Irish managers, in turn, armed with the experience, insights and confidence gained in a multinational company, increasingly went on to start or join new Irish companies and are prominent as leaders of Ireland's fast-growing indigenous companies.

13

THE IDA: KEYS TO SUCCESS

Padraic White

The IDA is one of a small number of national investment-promotion organisations which have been demonstrably successful in promoting foreign investment to the benefit of their country. Others in the premier division include the Economic Development Board of Singapore, the Industrial Development Centre of Taiwan, the Malaysian Industrial Development Authority, the Costa Rican Development Agency, the Chilean Board and the Locate in Britain Bureau (and its participating bodies such as Scottish Enterprise, the Welsh Development Agency and the Industrial Development Board of Northern Ireland).

Almost every country in the United Nations has an agency or official entity with a mandate to promote foreign investment. The vast majority are ineffective. It is interesting to note that most of the successful agencies are in countries with relatively small populations, such as Singapore, Ireland, Dubai, Costa Rica and Taiwan. Even in the case of Britain, the driving forces are the individual country or regionally based investment agencies such as Wales or the north-east. They usually have a strong sense of national or regional cohesion and motivation. The larger the home market in a country – like Mexico – the more that investment will come anyway to serve that market and the less the need to put state resources specifically into attracting investment. The opposite applies to the smaller countries, like Ireland, with an island-wide market of only 5 million people, where the domestic market is marginal or irrelevant to the investment decisions of foreign industries.

Yet smallness of population, national cohesion and acute employment needs are not sufficient prerequisites for the emergence of successful investment-promotion agencies. Most countries know the 'formula', for it has been studied and advocated by organisations such as the World Bank's Foreign Investment Advisory Agency. But only a handful of countries manage to create or replicate the winning combination. I believe that Ireland was fortunate in its Camelot-like 'shining moment' in 1969–70, which moulded the new Industrial Development Authority and its role within Irish administration and society. The template laid down then has remained essentially the same over the years. The precise industrial targets naturally change over the years, but the IDA process of searching out the emerging growth niches and then tracking down the emerging star companies has varied little.

The common bond and sense of national purpose between the senior civil servants and Michael Killeen, the IDA's pioneering managing director, gave the new organisation a healthy start in life. This was reflected in the powerful mandate and tools extended to the IDA to do the job in its founding legislation in 1969. The confidence vested in the IDA is powerfully illustrated in its responsibility to act under the minister 'as a body having national responsibility for the furtherance of industrial development'. Legislative mandates are one thing but earning respect and the right to a national role are entirely different matters. Killeen did this brilliantly. He was convinced that in the interests of a professional presentation of Ireland to the outside world the IDA should be the sole promoter abroad of investment. But to achieve this, he had to persuade every ambitious city or its mayor that rather than going on a solo run internationally they should leave it to the IDA. His commitment to regional plans and targets was one answer. Another was the network of regional offices throughout Ireland. He led the way in forging alliances with local authorities and other key contributors to development, such as the universities and colleges. In return, the IDA came to win for itself the title of undisputed international champion of Ireland's investment attractions. Another key to the IDA's success was its wide vision of the many elements needed for successful investment. It identified and researched critical support services for industry, such as telecommunications, port capacity and graduate and skill availability, and campaigned for improvements. It worked hard to create public and political support for its mission. One tangible manifestation of its success here is the solid party-political support over the decades for maintaining low taxes for foreign investment.

The accretion of international credibility has, of course, been interrupted from time to time by domestic problems such as inflation, labour disputes or fears relating to Northern Ireland. Nonetheless, as a broad generalisation, with each passing year, as the base and sophistication of foreign industry grows, so does the credibility of the country for investment. It becomes less a question of, 'Why should we go to Ireland' and more one of, 'Why are we not in Ireland.' For this reason, the IDA has been able to reduce progressively the level of financial grants for industry over the past twenty years.

Success has many fathers and one subject of argument has

been the relative significance of the IDA's role in bringing in foreign investment versus that of already existing attractions such as skilled labour, tax incentives and industrial grants. In my recollection, economists generally regard the investment flows as a function of the business environment. It is impossible to demonstrate quantitative relationships between the IDA role as an organisation and investment success. I believe, however, that the overwhelming reason for Ireland's success in foreign investment is due to the IDA's role for a number of reasons. First, from its very start the organisation devoted immense effort to campaigning for a sufficiently attractive business environment. It influenced changes in graduate output and better telecommunications and pioneered American-style business parks in the days when the private sector was not convinced of their merits. Moreover, it exercised a key influence on successive governments to modify but retain a powerful and distinct low-tax regime as part of the foreign-investment package. Second, the mix of public servants and private-sector staff who formed the heart of the IDA were exemplified by a 'can do' culture and the degree of patriotic fervour they brought to the job. These qualities were allied to a strong competitive instinct – never conceding defeat in winning a project. Another reason for the IDA's success was the full support and efficiency of the service given to industry. All of these factors played a decisive part in the often finely balanced decisions that multinationals reached in favour of locating in Ireland. The foreign companies themselves have testified consistently and publicly on the positive influence on their decisions of the commitment and efficiency of the IDA staff.

Remarkably little attention is paid in Ireland to the significance of the culture of the agency and the continued motivation of its executives. The original IDA staff suffered

considerable disorientation with the break-up of the organisation into three agencies in 1993. The public-service embargo
on recruitment has restricted the flow of ambitious new
executives, and the incentive to go that 'extra mile' is
diminishing. While the success of the IDA in dramatically
increasing investment since 1994 is unquestioned, only the
return of tougher economic times in the US or Ireland will
really test the continued vitality of the IDA as a 'fighting fit'
agency.

The boom in the Irish economy and the skill shortages have
brought into the public arena for the first time the previously
unthinkable question: do we need to promote foreign investment
any more if the existing companies have difficulty in getting
staff? Maybe a vibrant IDA will no longer be needed. There is
a certain logic in arguing against adding to the annual growth
in demand for skilled staff. Certainly, it is easy to understand
that companies already facing difficulties in recruiting staff
would feel that way. But I have serious reservations about the
danger of ceasing to promote investment. If Ireland Inc is closed
for business, other competitor countries will quickly take our
place. And, as in the case of commercial products, once you cede
market share to a competitor, it is very hard to regain it.

The nature of industry keeps changing – there is a continuous
process of decline in some sectors (for example, textiles and
mechanical engineering) and growth in others (software and e-
commerce). So we can assume that a fair share of the industries
we have today will decline and decay in coming years. Thus, we
need to be continually searching for the emerging star sectors
that are competitive in an Ireland of rising costs compared with
others in an enlarged European Union.

There remains considerable potential for new industries in
modern regional centres linked to the rest of the world with the

most advanced broadband communications. Such enhanced regional centres, like Sligo, have large future flows of native sons and daughters with language and technology skills and still have their own regionally linked diaspora to draw from. As the Northern Ireland and Republic of Ireland economies draw closer together, there will be the opportunity to promote, by cooperation, the entire island of Ireland as a unique 'island of enterprise' in Europe. For all these reasons, continued foreign-investment promotion in tune with the times should remain a central part of Ireland's future economic weaponry.

I have advised many countries on organising their investment promotion: the Baltic states, Hungary, Poland and Croatia in Europe; Venezuela, Paraguay, Bolivia, Ecuador, Peru and El Salvador in South America; Swaziland and Zimbabwe in Africa; and Malaysia in Asia. Usually, I am on assignment for the World Bank's Foreign Investment Advisory Service (FIAS) or the European Commission's PHARE or Lomé programmes. Today, countries starting from roughly the same position Ireland was in some thirty years ago and wishing to copy the successful model of national investment promotion find it virtually impossible to do so. In the course of advising countries on how to organise themselves to attract foreign direct investment and generate desperately needed employment, I find that the odds against them emulating the IDA's success are extremely high. This is the case for a variety of recurring reasons.

First, there is an institutional resistance to creating a government agency like the IDA. Very often, the Ministry of Foreign Affairs resists a new organisation having a foreign presence and insists that the diplomats can be effective promoters of foreign investment. But this apparently logical and cost-effective alternative does not work because foreign-investment promotion is specialist business requiring continuous attention, whereas the diplomat's first priority will always be the demands of his Foreign Affairs masters. Second, if established, the development body finds it difficult to secure the right calibre of proactive people to run it. And third, the government rarely provides it with a clear development mandate or the funds to carry out the mandate. More fundamentally, the mission of the putative investment-promotion agency is not linked clearly to the government's economic or employment agenda. The result is that the promotion agency or unit operates in isolation and is disconnected from the government's priorities. It is marginal to the country's progress. A simple test of a government's commitment to investment promotion is whether they are prepared to fund it.

I became something of an expert in devising slimline promotion organisations costing $1 million a year, but in most cases the government could not muster even this amount of Exchequer funds, or do so with any consistency over a number of years. In Ireland, by contrast, the operating budget of IDA Ireland was some $28 million in 1998. Yet, in all countries the president or prime minister commits considerable personal energy to advocating the virtues of their locale for foreign investment. It is usually a key theme in their foreign travel and missions. They will often participate in the expensive World Economic Forum in Davos, high in the Swiss mountains. The problem is that after the eloquent testimonies for their native land, there is no professional follow-up with prospective investors. And if, perchance, the investor seriously sets about investigating the opportunities in the country itself, he will usually encounter a hostile bureaucracy, particularly if seeking visas or residence permits for key workers.

In every country, the obstacles are different. In some, it is sheer inertia and stifling bureaucracy. In others, it is corruption

and lack of skill or a failure of the required political momentum
and drive to combine all the human and other elements needed
for success. Those requirements include the right people, the
necessary legislation, the agency operating to a clearly defined
mandate and with the drive to innovate. Very few countries have
been able to create the combination of circumstances and people
to forge an effective national investment promotion. In itself
that stands as a measure of the IDA's success.

14

The International
Financial Services Centre
a National Development Dream

Padraic White

The story of how Ireland became an international financial centre in the decade from 1987 is a remarkable case study of how to achieve a national-development dream against all the odds. At the start of that year, the economic background could hardly have been less encouraging. The public finances were in a mess, emigration was on the rise, and the mood in the country was one of deep pessimism. As a result, Ireland was winning increased international media attention, but for all the wrong reasons. The image projected to the world was that of an economy in a downward spiral, and heading towards disaster.

Ireland had a tiny stock market in Dublin, then valued at £4 billion, and exchange controls were still in operation for domestic investors. As a financial market, Dublin was completely over-shadowed by London, one of the top three international financial centres in the world, with a total market capitalisation of £Stg336 billion, more than a hundred times greater. This was hardly the ideal environment from which to launch the dream of creating 'Ireland as an international financial services centre'. Yet that was the ambitious title of a policy document launched by Charles Haughey on behalf of the Fianna Fáil party during the 1987 general election campaign.

It was a specific and technical paper on the specialist topic of international financial services. As such, it was a somewhat unusual policy initiative to launch in the middle of an election campaign. However, the news headline to grab media attention was the target of '7,500 full-time jobs over a period of five years'. The ambitious jobs figure was widely regarded then, and for some years later, as a fantasy figure, or simply dismissed as a piece of political hyperbole. Nevertheless, this slim sixteen-page political manifesto was the genesis of what later became the gleaming new financial centre at Dublin's old docklands area. As 1999 came to a close, some 7,000 people were employed in Dublin's International Financial Services Centre (IFSC), and that original Haughey target will be exceeded during the millennium year. The Centre not only underpins substantial additional jobs in ancillary services such as legal and accounting operations but also provides good business for hotels, restaurants and taxis servicing incoming clients and company executives.

The rationale behind the financial-services policy proposal was clear. The analysis suggested that a combination of factors now created an opportunity for a regional location like Ireland to become a player in the international financial services industry. First, world financial markets had become highly interdependent and operated on a round-the-clock basis. Second, the technology to set up and run international data- and fund-management centres was, in turn, creating an electronic market place, thanks to improvements in international telecommunications. And third, global deregulation of financial services meant that an increasing range of these services were provided from beyond national boundaries.

Ireland was well placed to meet these opportunities, and the national advantages were identified as location, language, education and technology. We were in the same time zone as London. We spoke the language of international finance, namely, English. We had a computer-literate young labour force. And we had a modern digital-based telecommunications network. Most of the guidelines laid down in the document were both streetwise and practical and proved their worth over time. Above all, the proposals were rooted in realism. The document cautioned against a futile attempt to set up international trading activities to compete directly with the big financial centres like London and New York. And it contained a blunt commitment that the new policy was not 'oriented in any way towards the creation of a tax haven'. So from the start, understandably, this led to a justified obsession with avoiding 'brass-plate' operations. Instead, there was an insistence on substantive activity and jobs as the distinguishing features of the Irish version of an international financial centre.

The government was also advised to take four main initiatives in order to build confidence in Ireland as a suitable financial centre. These involved ensuring adequate data-protection laws, supplying top-class telecommunications, but with a competitive cost advantage to attract projects, having Irish regulations based on the European Union's proposals for a single market for financial services and, not least, offering attractive tax arrangements. And, as the years went by, the prescience of those who gave that good advice was fully vindicated.

The central vision and act of faith in the Fianna Fáil financial-services document – handsomely achieved in less than a decade – is worth quoting. It declared that:

With a concerted effort by government, the regulatory authorities, the IDA and Telecom Éireann, and by building on the goodwill of international businesses and institutions already operating here, Ireland can be actively marketed as a highly attractive centre for high-technology international financial services.

But throughout the financial-services blueprint, there is just a brief single reference to what became two of the defining features of the Irish international service centre, namely, its location in a 'specially designated business park' and the need for 'a licence to operate' there.

*

Dermot Desmond has the legitimate claim to having been responsible for the success of the International Financial Services Centre proposal. He had formed a new stockbroking and financial firm, National City Brokers (NCB). There, he gathered together a highly talented group of economists and equity and bond traders and became an innovative and aggressive operator in Dublin's established and traditional stockbroking arena. But, in addition, he had a strong personal interest in exploring business opportunities in the computer, software and communications areas, and he possessed the skills needed to support the rapidly changing financial-services industry. Already, he had set up his own financial-services software company, Quay Financial Software Systems, to develop software and provide computer-based training for financial-trading rooms. He became acquainted with the IDA from 1983 on, having backed a number of high-technology start-up companies, which the IDA was also supporting. I had met him during the final stages of IDA negotiations on a financial package for his own software company, which was designed to support a major expansion of jobs and increased export earnings.

Fully aware of the technology changes in the financial services in the US, his focus was on developing products and services in Ireland which would attract international interest and collaboration. A charmer by nature, he could weave a compelling vision of his financial-software ambitions for his own companies and for the country. In the spring of 1985, at a dinner in Dublin's Shelbourne Hotel, his persuasive portrayal of Ireland's financial services opportunity triggered a sequence of events which would lead to the setting up of the International Financial Services Centre. The host that evening was the Minister for Labour, Ruairí Quinn. As part of his own personal exploration of ways out of the high-taxes and high-borrowing vicious circle, he had asked Greg Sparks, a political associate and accountant, to convene an informal dinner party of business people to discuss their ideas. Dermot Desmond was one of those invited by Sparks, whose own accountancy firm were the auditors for Desmond's business. As his contribution to the round-table discussion at dinner, Desmond suggested that Ireland should follow the French model of concentrating on a small number of sectors. Specifically, he argued that the international financial sector was a great opportunity for Ireland. He listed his reasons: The financial services industry was becoming global, boosted by advances in telecommunications technology. The operating costs in Ireland were cheaper than in London. In addition, there was a plentiful supply of young, well-educated Irish people with the necessary skills to service the sector. And, not least, Ireland could exploit its position in the global time zone, as a link in a twenty-four-hour trading chain. Financial services could be offered from Dublin in the hours after the

Asian markets had closed and before those in the US had opened.

As he drove home that night, Desmond determined to follow through on his dinner-table proposition. Next day, he put his financial-centre concept on paper and sent it to Minister Quinn. When Quinn expressed his strong interest in the idea, Desmond then took it a stage further. He approached Peter Kelly, a partner with Price Waterhouse accountants, to conduct a preliminary and independent evaluation of the financial-centre concept for Ireland. This proved positive and was forwarded to Ruairí Quinn.

Over a number of lunch meetings involving the Minister, Greg Sparks, Niall Greene (a Labour Party activist and then Chief Executive of the Youth Employment Agency) and Desmond, it was agreed to carry out a full-scale analysis of the financial-services proposal. The £150,000 cost of the study was, at the time, significant, and it was funded jointly, and equally, by the Youth Employment Agency, then under the jurisdiction of Minister Quinn, and Dermot Desmond's NCB stockbroking firm. Desmond's share of the cost came to one-third of the firm's annual profits at the time.

The feasibility study completed by Price Waterhouse in 1986 confirmed the considerable potential of an international financial centre, but Ruairí Quinn could not get sufficient backing for the project. The report was pigeonholed and Desmond became frustrated with the failure to capitalise on the financial services opportunity.

In the run-up to the 1987 general election, Charles Haughey, the Fianna Fáil leader, visited Desmond, whom he had befriended in 1985, to learn more about his financial-services proposal at first hand. Haughey came away enthused with the proposition and wanted it included in the Fianna Fáil manifesto. To underline its significance, he also wanted the proposal to be published as a separate document. And so Desmond and his NCB colleague, Michael Buckley, became the anonymous authors of the Fianna Fáil manifesto document 'Ireland as an International Financial Services Centre', unveiled in the run-up to the February 1987 general election.

*

However, the Fianna Fáil policy paper was certainly wrong to claim that no initiative had been taken to create the business environment necessary to attract foreign investment in projects in international financial services. Previously, both IDA-Ireland and Shannon Development had advanced ambitious plans to promote financial services, but these were stymied by official caution. The story of these endeavours and how they were frustrated has remained untold.

In the middle of 1973, the IDA launched international services as its latest product. At the time, this category included both technical consultancy services and computer services. However, within the IDA's own research unit, work continued to identify and analyse other service products, including those in the financial-services area. One of the economists engaged in this task was Ken O'Brien, who later, as founder of *Finance* magazine, would provide specialist coverage of the Dublin financial centre. Our New York office befriended a Wall Street lawyer, Bob Slater, who was familiar with the then-exotic world of offshore banking – the reasons why banks set up in specialist offshore centres, the kind of financial activities undertaken there and the nature and number of jobs created in this developing sector.

As manager of the planning unit, I agreed to take on Bob

Slater, both as a consultant on financial services to IDA and to produce a study of offshore banking centres. This would help identify the employment potential of Irish offshore banking. His report examined the success of Bermuda in creating jobs in financial services, and he was satisfied that Ireland could emulate its achievement. And so in 1978 – innocently, in hindsight – we set out to promote international financial services to the world, and did so on a pilot basis to test-market the reaction. The IDA executives embarked on their selling mission, armed with the expert conclusions of the Wall Street expert.

During that year the IDA team soon landed some big fish in the form of two US banks that had developed specific job-creating proposals. However, the agreement of the Central Bank was first needed. Michael Killeen considered the proposals sufficiently important for himself to go with Jerry Kelly, who was negotiating the projects, and myself to make the case for Central Bank authorisation. The reaction was not encouraging and we left the Dame Street offices feeling rather dejected. We could not give the required assurances or promise of authorisations to our foreign bank clients. The projects died and we ceased to do any more financial-services promotion. Subsequently, it emerged the bank had no stomach for the projects and would not approve them. However, the IDA could never get a clear reason for this. The most authoritative word which came back indirectly was that the Central Bank believed the offshore financial projects 'smacked of a banana republic'.

The IDA decision to broaden the range of international services led to new legislation in 1981. This empowered the IDA, for the first time, to award employment grants to service companies. The Minister could designate specified services as eligible for the incentives. And since we still had hopes of reviving promotion of financial services, the very first list of twelve designated services, announced in 1981 and based on IDA recommendations, included international financial services.

But we hit another brick wall in 1985 following an innovative proposal from a subsidiary of General Electric of America (GE) to develop an international financial centre in Ireland. The GE company had a subsidiary, GE International Services Co (GEISCO), in Dublin. This provided computer services using its global communications network. It was one of the three largest providers of computer services in the world at the time. The IDA's Jerry Kelly was negotiating with GEISCO to expand its small development centre in Ireland so as to develop software for its computer centres in Maryland, Ohio and Holland. Kelly befriended the chief executive of the GEISCO corporation based in Maryland. He was from Northern Ireland and also was convinced that Ireland could emulate Luxembourg and develop a specialist financial service, using the existing 10 per cent tax incentive. A detailed proposal was formulated by GE in which it made a commitment to put a reinsurance project into the proposed Irish financial centre, with treasury operations and asset management to follow. Sadly, the Department of Finance turned down the GE proposal. General Electric was later to prove as good as its word and has three subsidiary companies operating in Dublin's international financial centre.

And thus, the IDA's brave attempts to promote international financial services in Ireland were brought to an end. The file was closed. It was not reopened until Charles Haughey returned as Taoiseach in March 1987. Meanwhile, down in Shannon a parallel plan was in gestation to develop financial services in the Shannon Free Zone. The Free Zone area had a unique freedom from its very start: it could support any type of activity such as manufacturing, trading, transport or financial operations, provided the individual activity was awarded a licence. And if licensed, the company would qualify for the 10 per cent tax rate.

By the mid 1980s, Shannon had attracted a unique cluster of international financial service companies, such as Guinness Peat Aviation, Yeoman Leasing and Minet Insurance. Spurred on by these successes, Shannon Development created an ambitious plan to make Shannon a financial-services offshore centre. After a hard battle, it won official approval, but with a minimum employment requirement of fifteen jobs in qualifying companies. And so in 1986, it printed up its new marketing brochures.

But a year later, when the government chose Dublin as the location of the new International Financial Services Centre, the full weight of the national effort swung towards making this project a success, by attracting the world's leading financial institutions to it. Shannon had lost its unique selling point as the only authorised place in Ireland for offshore financial services with a 10 per cent tax. And while it continued, bravely, to seek financial companies, the action inevitably moved to the new Dublin centre.

The original policy statement had not spelt out where the designated financial centre would be situated. Considerable speculation developed about the likely site, with the Custom House Dock area strongly favoured. A year earlier, in 1986, the outgoing government of Dr Garret FitzGerald had introduced legislation to set up the Customs House Docks Development Authority. The Finance Act of 1986 provided financial incentives (100 per cent capital allowances, double rent deductions and a ten-year remission on local rates or taxes) for building development on the derelict dock site. The new Authority met for the first time in November 1986, as authorised by the Urban Renewal Act 1986, and in January 1987, all the land held by the Dublin Port and Docks Board in the Custom House docks area was transferred to the new Authority. However, given the depressed state of business at that time, there was little confidence that the financial incentives would trigger a wave of building by Irish developers to regenerate the run-down docks site in the north inner city.

But once the dock site, with its range of incentives, was chosen as the location for the new International Financial Services Centre, then in one step, an ideal solution was at hand. A successful centre would ensure property development, economic activity and jobs in the area. For its part, the proposed financial centre would have a ready-made designated area, complete with property incentives, and with an organisation already in place to orchestrate the physical development of the site. It had another critical advantage for a government in a hurry – the Docks Authority had unique fast-track planning permission powers. So, in May 1987, without much ado, the Haughey government selected the twenty-seven-acre Custom House Dock site as the location for the IFSC.

The government decision meant the financial-services project was overlaid on the existing Custom House Docks Authority mandate for urban regeneration. There was no modification of the legislation governing the Authority. Indeed, until its last day in office in April 1997, it never had an explicit legislative mandate to develop a financial-services centre. This omission carried the seeds of trouble in later years.

*

In April 1987, shortly after the formation of the Haughey minority government, I was called to the first meeting in Government Buildings of what was termed the International Financial Services Committee 'to realise the dream of an international financial services centre and fulfilling the commitment to 7,500 jobs in five years', as the Fianna Fáil manifesto had promised.

The meeting had a unique composition. At the head of the table was Padraig Ó hUiginn, Secretary of the Department of the Taoiseach. He was the Taoiseach's right-hand man and had a reputation for getting things done. He was a past master at crafting solutions, but, perhaps most important, he spoke with the authority of the Taoiseach. Although his listeners were often unsure whether his declarations were those of the Taoiseach or his own, it was always prudent to assume he had Haughey's ear and full backing. Ó hUiginn's natural instincts were always developmental and entrepreneurial rather than restrictive and bureaucratic. To any assignment he brought a high intelligence, humour and a mastery of language.

Around the table, the heads of the key government departments, the Revenue Commissioners and the Central Bank sat side by side with the private-sector business chiefs from the leading Irish banks and accountancy and stockbroking firms, including Dermot Desmond, who was the inspiration for the government's commitment to the project.

The composition of the IFSC Committee, its mandate and method of operation were unique. The top people in the public- and private-sector organisations critical to the success of the Centre were all represented However, new policies and proposals present a challenge to the administrative system. Within the public service, new initiatives tend to develop slowly. These are advanced, after much consultation, and refined, usually by committees and through the medium of written documents. So before a policy proposal finally emerges as government policy, it must survive a high degree of scrutiny via the checks and balances that operate at civil-service level. And, invariably, since any new proposal has tax or spending implications, the Department of Finance and the Revenue Commissioners are consulted.

The successful implementation of a major new development

involves treading a perilous path. Proposals for change – such as that represented by the IFSC initiative – may encounter resistance and objections. All too often the objectors can easily kill or mortally wound an initiative that defies the conventional wisdom. Except in this instance, the composition of the IFSC Committee made the vital difference. So when Ó hUiginn turned to any departmental secretary and gently enquired, 'I presume this is possible', there was no place to hide, and there was a presumption in favour of a solution being found.

The approach adopted was also unique in one other respect. Certainly, for the first time in my experience, the heads of the most powerful public-sector organisations in the state were joining together with leaders of the public sector to achieve a common goal. Between them, they were thrashing out in real time the policies to achieve the Taoiseach's urgent commitment to create a world-class international financial services centre in Ireland. But implicit in the whole exercise was the promise that the government would act speedily in taking whatever decisions were necessary to realise that dream. For it was understood that Ó hUiginn would take any committee recommendations directly to the Taoiseach and that it was a short journey from there to the Cabinet table.

At that first meeting of the IFSC Committee on 9 April 1987, the Taoiseach swept in from his nearby office to encourage the members and remind them of the government's absolute commitment to the election manifesto promise of an international financial centre. The Committee met almost weekly in the early months and initially there was much staking out of individual positions by the differing interests: the Irish banks wanted to be fully included, there was opposition to designating one particular site for the financial centre and the Department of Finance was worried about tax losses from the existing bank base.

The key characteristics of the planned financial centre were essentially agreed by the IFSC Committee between April and June 1987. A licensing mechanism would identify the most desirable projects and ensure there was substance in terms of jobs and serious activity. Irish financial companies should have equal access to the Centre, provided they were creating additional international business and related jobs. Indeed, it was accepted that foreign companies might be sceptical of the credibility of the new financial centre if the big Irish banks were not participating in it. But, above all, a tax incentive which matched the attractions of the established and competing financial centres such as Luxembourg and the Channel Islands was also needed. The proposal for a 10 per cent tax for licensed companies was agreed without difficulty by the IFSC Committee, endorsed by the Cabinet, included in the 1987 Finance Act and passed through the Oireachtas by June. There would be no cash grants given. Everyone on the Committee was adamant that the Irish centre would have the highest standards of prudential supervision under the Central Bank and would strive for a reputation of the highest integrity.

One of the most interesting and creative early discussions was about the precise financial services to be targeted. The growing deregulation of financial services worldwide had led to a surge in the financial engineering of new products and services that capitalised on tax, regulatory and cost regimes both within and between countries. However, no one was sure of a satisfactory definition of international financial services. But if the project was to be included in the Finance Bill then before the Dáil, an immediate formula had to be found. There was early agreement on the inclusion of global money management, foreign-currency dealing, equity and bond dealing and insurance activities. Then Pádraig Ó hUiginn crafted a catch-all legislative provision which allowed the Minister for Finance to add services 'similar to or ancillary to' those specified in the Act. And so three months after the formation of the government, the laws were fully in place to promote the new Centre, including the 10 per cent tax incentive and certification or licensing system. Meanwhile, the IFSC Committee members were putting forward their favoured kinds of financial services that could be attracted to Dublin. And these discussions generated a long list of possibilities.

The IDA's role was to refine and add to these categories and bring the results back for further consideration. In truth, we were all speculating. For what Ireland could offer was still only being assembled. At this stage, we were still talking to ourselves rather than to potential international clients. Not surprisingly, there were wildly differing expectations. The job target of 7,500 for an untried programme was a formidable one, and there was talk of relocating large foreign-exchange operations, securities trading or dealing rooms from London with hundreds of jobs in each. Even though the IFSC project was a personal priority of the Taoiseach, and all ministers were expected to support it enthusiastically, it was still only a concept. The ultimate decisions would be made by bankers abroad, cautiously at first and then with increasing confidence as the Irish model proved its'worth and won international confidence.

The eventual success of the IFSC project can be traced back to that unique constellation of forces marshalled behind it in 1987 and its early years. Right from the outset it developed a strong political momentum, since it was born during the general election campaign and was clearly a pet project of the Taoiseach. In the midst of the gloom of the times and the budget cutbacks, there was something daring about embarking on such a dream – or fantasy – project at the same time. The project was driven forward from the office of the Taoiseach and every minister and every arm of government was expected to facilitate and promote it.

Any minister travelling abroad, irrespective of the nature of his or her departmental responsibility, was required to speak about and publicise the new financial centre. The entire evolution and promotion internationally of the IFSC was done in collaboration with the private sector and in a way not achieved with any other project. The initial showpiece seminars during 1988–9 in London, Frankfurt, Tokyo and New York were organised by the IDA jointly with the Financial Services Industry Association (FSIA). The very first seminar was held in the Whitbread Brewery in the heart of the City of London on St Patrick's Day 1988 with an audience of 300 people and exceptional interest in this new Irish product.

The Taoiseach, by his personal involvement in the IFSC project, gave it a high profile and surrounded the entire project with a certain allure which, in turn, attracted the enthusiastic support of leading business people. He signalled his commitment in the case of the established IDA promotion of Ireland for industry and international services. I recall one early dinner where John Gunn, head of the then British and Commonwealth financial group in the UK, was principal guest. He was invited by Dermot Desmond to look at the investment opportunities in Ireland. The dinner party was hosted by Taoiseach Charles Haughey, with Minister for Finance Ray Mac Sharry, Secretary of the Department of Finance Seán Cromien and Padraig Ó hUiginn in attendance. On another occasion, the Taoiseach entertained a group of Swiss bankers in his private dining room. And when the President of Mitsubishi Trust arrived at Dublin Airport, the Taoiseach's office arranged a motorcycle escort for him.

In global terms, it was wholly exceptional for an administration to be able to present such a united and cohesive approach, with the full participation of the private sector. The message to incoming financiers was clear – the financial-services centre was a top priority of the entire government. The unity, consistency and enthusiasm of the Irish approach had a powerful influence on foreign support for the new centre. Investors felt confident that they would get the full assistance of the Irish authorities and that, if they met administrative obstacles, these would be overcome. Again, the Irish regulatory authorities such as the Central Bank and the Revenue Commissioners managed to convey not only a commitment to tough standards of regulation but also a strong sense of commitment to the success of the financial centre project. While doing their regulatory duty, they were also part of the Irish team. Foreign companies were profoundly impressed by this approach.

The debt-management group in the Department of Finance, led by Michael Somers, had regular dealings with foreign banks in the financing and scheduling of Ireland's mountain of foreign debt. The group used their contacts to promote the message of Ireland's new financial centre. As the early marketing of the IFSC gathered momentum, Finance Minister Ray Mac Sharry, together with Somers and his colleague Adrian Kearns, used the annual meeting of the World Bank, held in Berlin in the autumn of 1988, to good effect. In the course of their scheduled face-to-face appointments with over a hundred banks on debt-management issues, they also drove home the Irish financial centre message.

The minister was not averse to using the tactic of putting the banks under some pressure, particularly those financial institutions doing good business from Ireland's excessive foreign debt. When he met the German Commerzbank, he was fully aware it had been the lead bank in arranging a number of bond issues on behalf of the Irish government. But when he pressed the case for the bank participating in the IFSC, the Commerzbank representatives told him the bank was already committed to setting up in a similar type of centre in Spain. Mac Sharry expressed his disappointment and informed them that another German bank (Dresdner Bank, whose identity he did not disclose) was about to set up in the Irish financial centre. After a quick huddle among themselves, the Commerzbank executives did a volte-face and informed the Minister that they would now consider setting up in Dublin. The bank set up a majority-owned subsidiary the following year in conjunction with AIB Bank and later added three more subsidiary companies. Michael Somers later became the first Chief Executive of the National Treasury Management Agency and was joined by his colleague, Adrian Kearns, who heads up the Foreign Currency Debt group. The new Agency continues to advocate the merits of the IFSC to its clients.

*

Gradually during 1987, the incentive package on offer to incoming financial institutions emerged. The 10 per cent tax was intended for licensed financial companies on a twenty-seven-acre designated site in the Custom House Docks in Dublin and required the approval of the European Commission. Finance Minister Ray Mac Sharry twice met the EU Commissioner in charge of state aids, fellow Irishman Peter Sutherland, to make the case for approval. The Commission's assent was secured by November 1987, authorising the certified IFSC companies to enjoy the 10 per cent tax regime until the end of 2005.

One reason for this prompt and hassle-free approval was that at this stage the other member states did not fully realise the extent of the Irish ambitions. Or if they did, then they believed Dublin stood little chance against competition from the already established European financial centres. The Isle of Man, which had created a well-established niche for itself, was openly sceptical of the Irish plans. The island's commercial-development officer then claimed that 'Dublin would be better building on its own resources, which do not particularly include financial services.' By contrast, in later years, winning an extension of the tax regime was to prove a much tougher fight.

Since the licensed companies were expected to locate in the Custom House Dock Area, the early provision of attractive buildings there was essential to the credibility of the project. In June 1987, the Custom House Docks Development Authority launched its planning scheme for the IFSC and a public competition to design and develop it. An exuberant Charles Haughey presided over a gathering of Ireland's great and good of the business community and public sector. His literary instincts were reflected that day in a remarkably apt quotation from James Joyce's *Ulysses*. He reminded his audience that across the road from the Docks site once stood the cabman's shelter. There, Leopold Bloom, the novel's central character, had coffee with his young friend, Stephen Dedalus. Bloom had foreseen the new financial centre, implied the Taoiseach, in the following lines: 'My beloved subjects, a new era is about to dawn. I, Bloom, tell you verily it is even now at hand. Yea, on the word of a Bloom ye shall ere long enter into the gold city which is to be the new Bloomusalem in the Nova Hibernia of the future.' The winning consortium (Hardwicke Ltd, McInerney Properties plc from Ireland and British Land plc from the UK) unveiled their plans and models in November 1987.

The initial marketing of the Centre was based on photographs of the winning design, which were included in brochures and publicity, with a model on display in the offices of the Dock Development Authority. Once work commenced in May 1988 on the previously derelict site, there was at least tangible evidence of the new centre to show incoming groups assessing Dublin's attractions. In September, the Taoiseach laid the foundation stone for the financial centre with full pomp and ceremony, at a memorable public occasion. There, he foresaw the day when the centre would be the 'nucleus of a new neighbour-hood, a place where employees, residents and visitors alike can mingle and socialise'.

Licensed companies were permitted, temporarily, to occupy premises elsewhere in Dublin as a transition measure, while the new buildings at the docks were under construction. This was an imaginative solution. It meant that approved companies were able to begin business and create jobs once they found suitable office space anywhere in the city. Some become so attached to these provisional offices outside the IFSC, usually at much lower rents, that the companies were reluctant to relocate to the official IFSC buildings in later years.

The IDA was assigned responsibility for marketing the IFSC internationally. The organisation had no current expertise in promoting financial services, ever since previous IDA attempts to do so had been blocked. Now it would be very much on trial in this highly visible project, with precise and ambitious targets set, including 7,500 new jobs in five years, and with the Taoiseach's office making the running. One of the traditional strengths of the IDA has been its flexibility, notably the speed with which it could change its internal organisation and move staff to promote new industrial sectors or niches. On 8 April 1987, I extended the mandate of the International Services Division to include financial services and set up a new Financial

Services Unit within it. Dr David Hanna was manager of the division and was the ideal person to drive the new financial-services project. He was soft-spoken and low-key, with an outstanding record of success in persuading companies to choose Ireland. And from his stint as head of IDA's Los Angeles office, he had first-hand international experience.

I selected Brendan Russell to head the newly born Financial Services Unit. He had come to the IDA on secondment from ICC Bank plc to add to our financial-analysis expertise in judging incoming investment plans. His financial know-how, his banking experience and his natural enthusiasm made him a good choice for the new assignment. His unit was complemented by the assignment of Nick Kendellen in Chicago to be our US-based point man on financial services, while in London, Maura Saddington took on a similar role for Europe.

I wanted some first-hand experience of the market reaction to the IFSC concept and so I went with Brendan Russell, head of the Financial Services Unit, on his first marketing mission, to meet three Japanese banks based in London. Being in the City, one of the three world financial centres, concentrated the mind wonderfully. We had a map of the Dublin docks area, the promise of a 10 per cent tax then awaiting European Commission approval and belief in the quality of Irish graduates. Unfortunately, we had no examples of agreed projects to reassure our potential investors. Instead, we had the long list of target financial activities worked out with the IFSC Committee and explored the attractions of these with our Japanese hosts. On that day, the job target of 7,500 seemed a long way off.

The IDA's long experience of promoting Ireland as a location for foreign direct investment in sectors – like electronics – where the country had no previous track record has proved invaluable. In pioneering new investment areas, the organisation acquired the confidence to survive setbacks and developed the skills to overcome the resistance of potential foreign investors. However, no amount of homework or planning in Ireland can substitute for the reactions and feedback IDA staff get from their face-to-face encounters with foreign-company executives in their offices across the globe. The trick is to listen closely, be ready to amend preconceived ideas and refine the Irish package of incentives to meet the market-place reaction. It became evident that in the early stages, the IFSC projects would be in leasing, funds administration and treasury operations and that the typical project would have low job numbers. The international financial companies would first dip their toes in the waters of the Custom House Docks, rather than go for full immersion.

From a standing start in April 1987, the IDA financial-services team, under the overall guidance of Kieran McGowan, the Executive Director responsible for all foreign investment, achieved, straight away, a remarkable momentum. Within three months, the IDA had succeeded in making formal presentations on the embryonic IFSC to twenty big financial institutions in America and Britain. By August the first three formal proposals from companies were received. And, by the end of December 1987, the IDA Board had given approval to eighteen projects for the financial-services centre.

In mid-September 1987, I had a telephone call from Padraig Ó hUiginn in the Taoiseach's office. He told me that the Cabinet had decided to set up a Government Representative Group to market the IFSC at the highest levels internationally. The chairman was to be Tomás Ó Cofaigh, recently retired Governor of the Central Bank of Ireland. He was to be joined by Séamus Páircéir, former Chairman of the Revenue Commissioners, and Maurice Horgan, former Second Secretary in the Department of Finance. The IDA was to be represented on the Group by the Executive Director responsible for the IFSC, Kieran McGowan. The Agency, although previously given the marketing mandate, was now presented with the new marketing group as a fait accompli.

There had been no prior consultation. There was a widespread feeling among staff that the government decision was a kick in the teeth for the IDA. Ó hUiginn, who proposed the idea to the Taoiseach, believed that the financial services were very different from the IDA's traditional areas of expertise and needed the Central Bank imprimatur the former Governor provided.

I decided to keep my silence. I was determined to make the most of the new situation and to manage cooperation between IDA staff and the new Group in the interests of the success of the project. Certainly, the three retired public servants would bring added prestige and contacts to the IFSC's marketing activities. Indeed, quite independently, I had asked Tomas Ó Cófaigh if he could assist the IDA for these very reasons. But this initiative was now superseded by the government decision.

Within the IDA, the three external members of the Group became known colloquially as the 'three wise men'. The Authority was a tightly managed organisation with clear lines of responsibility and accountability. And the insertion of the 'three wise men' into the marketing effort did cause initial confusion among the staff. It raised the obvious question of whether the staff should report to the new trio and take instructions from them, rather than from their own managers. Kieran McGowan, the IDA Director who was a member of the Group, worked hard to eliminate these difficulties. And I chaired regular liaison meetings with the 'wise men' to review the marketing programme and ensure full cooperation all round. In fact, the 'wise men' initiative proved to be an outstanding marketing success. After the initial adjustments, the working relationships with IDA executives in

Dublin and abroad over the next two years were good and highly productive.

The 'wise men' worked out a division of labour among themselves. So in presentations to prospective investors, Ó Cófaigh would handle the overall financial centre concept and the economy, Parcéir would deal with the tax issues and Horgan would cover education and skills. The IDA staff on the ground abroad would arrange all the groundwork for the top-level meetings and then follow up on the initiatives agreed between the 'wise men' and the bankers.

Their first mission was to Asia, where, along with Kieran McGowan, they visited Hong Kong, Taiwan and Korea. It proved to be an inauspicious start. They found themselves talking to banks in Hong Kong about the Irish financial-centre vision on Black Monday, 19 October 1987, the day of the global stock-market crash. They began their series of meetings with a courtesy call on the Financial Secretary (Minister for Finance), Piers Jacob. The Hong Kong Stock Exchange had been closed for the previous five days, and when the market opened on that Monday morning, there was pandemonium. Nevertheless, Piers Jacob kept his commitment to meet the three travelling Irishmen who had come to tell him about the new International Financial Services Centre in Dublin. During the meeting, the Irish delegation could see the monitor on the wall relaying the precipitous share-price falls in the local market. The Financial Secretary remained the very model of professionalism, courtesy and discretion. However, he did, gently, suggest that his Irish visitors might advise their government not to go ahead with a Financial Centre at that time – and that some other sector might be less volatile.

From such a shaky start and such unpromising beginnings did the IFSC develop. Subsequent missions took the trio to

Tokyo, Germany, the Netherlands, Belgium, Sweden, France, Finland, Switzerland, Australia and Canada. In one marketing mission to the US in 1988, they met thirty-seven banks; the three men did not return to America, as they judged that the Irish message by now was sufficiently well known because of the visits of ministers and the IDA presence.

Ó Cofaigh's relationship with Europe's key central bankers proved to be a real trump card. From his six years as Governor of the Central Bank (1981–7) and his previous years as Secretary of the Department of Finance, he had come to know them well. He also had the benefit of a year's stint as chairman of the Committee of Central Bank chiefs of the European Community. So he figured that an introduction from a country's central banker to its leading commercial banks would ensure a good hearing for himself and his two colleagues as they made their pitch for the new financial centre in Dublin.

His first approach, based on a personal friendship, was in December 1987 to Wim Duisenberg, President of the Dutch Central Bank (and later, in 1998, the first President of the European Central Bank). The two men met for dinner, and Duisenberg suggested various changes to the list of Dutch banks that Ó Cofaigh had originally felt merited a visit. Duisenberg then wrote a letter of introduction to all the banks on the agreed list. The Irish group met them in spring 1988 and a number – including ABN–AMRO and Rabobank Nederland – have very successful operations today in the international financial centre.

Later that month, Ó Cofaigh sent a message to Karl Otto Pohl, President of the German Bundesbank and probably the most dominant and influential European banking figure at that time. He sought Pohl's cooperation to secure a meeting between the Irish group and some of Germany's top banks. When the two met in January, Herr Pohl immediately offered to make the necessary introductions. Subsequently, he advised on either additions to or exclusions from the target list. True to his word, he sent a personal note to them on behalf of his Irish friend, Tomas Ó Cofaigh. By the end of February 1988, the Irish marketing group had met ten leading German banks and three insurance companies on an individual basis. By any standards, this was whirlwind top-flight marketing.

The meeting with the Dresdner Bank Group, the third-biggest bank in Germany, illustrates well the inner dynamics of the IFSC success story. On 2 March 1988, Ó Cofaigh and his colleagues had breakfast in Frankfurt with three of the top executives in the bank: Meinhard Carstensen, a main board member; Wolfgang Baertz, head of Dresdner Luxembourg; and Dr Franken, the bank's legal adviser. The timing of the Irish visit was good. Just then, Dresdner had started a strategic review of external opportunities so the Irish potential sounded interesting and could complement its specialist operations in Luxembourg, while the availability of graduate staff in Ireland was a distinct advantage. The breakfast ended with an agreement that the IDA executives in Germany would advance the discussions. Later that year, Dresdner became the first major German bank to locate in Dublin's financial centre. It opened for business in April 1989 with a commitment to employ twenty-five people. Ireland now had its German 'flagship' project. Meinhhard Carstensen, who had participated in the initial breakfast and had been a champion of the Irish case, chaired one of the Dublin companies. The bank brought Ernst Matthiensen from its New York offices to head up the new Irish operation and he, in turn, became an eloquent advocate of Ireland's advantages.

I became a board member of the Dresdner companies in Dublin in June 1990 after leaving the IDA. And there I saw at first-hand its commitment to succeed in Ireland, even in the face of measures by the German Federal Finance Ministry to negate the tax advantages the bank enjoyed in Ireland. In September 1999, Dresdner Bank celebrated its tenth anniversary as an IFSC company at a ceremony in Dublin Castle with Tánaiste Mary Harney in attendance. By then, Dresdner had fifty people employed, double the initial target, and operated banking and fund-management subsidiaries in Dublin. And the chairman of the bank subsidiary was one of the breakfast participants from that first encounter in Frankfurt in March 1988 – Wolfgang Baertz.

Those early Dutch and German initiatives became the template used by the 'wise men' in marketing the IFSC in other countries. Within eighteen months, they had met over a hundred of the largest banks in the world and a hundred other leading financial institutions, such as insurance companies and others engaged in large financial transactions. Increasingly, as they travelled, they found that word of the IFSC's success preceded their arrival and that news of the financial centre was already known to the companies they were visiting. As the first projects were announced, they got international publicity. The continuous public-relations campaign and the promotional seminars all helped to spread the message of the emerging Irish financial centre.

By April 1989, the 'three wise men' felt they had accomplished their mission. They wrote formally to Taoiseach Charles Haughey, requesting that they be 'stood down'. They had carried the message to the world's key financial companies, and some sixty projects had been approved already. Now these, they felt, would serve to attract others. He agreed readily, on the basis of their great success. He delayed their formal dissolution until October 1989, just two years after they had first come together.

Setting up a new financial-services centre at a time when the government, via Finance Minister Ray Mac Sharry, was cutting spending ruthlessly to try and restore balance to the national finances presented its own particular problems. The scale of the cutbacks meant there was no special spending allocation to advertise the planned financial centre in the international media. In fact, the IDA's entire advertising and promotion budget was more than halved from £4 million in 1986 to £1.75 million the following year – when the IFSC was launched. Normally, a new international product launch, in this case selling Ireland as a location for financial services, would require a hefty advertising and public-relations budget. Necessity was to be, yet again, the mother of invention and the IFSC was promoted in ingenious ways that did not require state expenditure.

Instead the marketing exercise was based on a personalised approach to hundreds of target financial companies both by the 'wise men' and by IDA executives throughout the world. In parallel, journalists from the main international media and specialist financial magazines were invited to Dublin to learn about this Irish dream of a new financial centre in a country then enduring painful surgery to rectify the fiscal imbalance in the economy. And as individual project successes for the new centre were announced publicly from late 1987, the IFSC itself became a developing financial-news story. Where newspapers and magazines were prepared to run a specialist supplement on the topic, private companies like Guinness Peat Aviation and the Irish banks willingly took advertising space. The Taoiseach and all his ministers in those early years were also enthusiasts for the IFSC in press briefings, speeches and seminars.

Ireland Inc may never have cooperated better to the benefit of the country than was the case with a series of pioneering seminars organised jointly by the Financial Services Association of Ireland (FSIA) and the IDA. These seminars were organised in the leading world financial centres: London, Frankfurt, New York and Tokyo. Usually, these briefings featured an introduction by the FSIA Chairman, Alex Spain, to be followed by an Irish banker, an accountancy partner such as Ron Bolger or Eoin Clarke, an IDA speaker and a Minister. Then at the close of the seminar, the Irish banks and accountancy and legal firms invited their counterparts and business associates to join them at their corporate table.

The foreign guests were immensely impressed by this experience of private and public sectors working in total harmony with government, and doing so with palpable conviction in the interests of Ireland and its dream of an international financial centre. In truth, as Irish participants, we marvelled at being part of such a united Irish endeavour. I recall in particular the excitement and enthusiasm of the financial-services seminar held in the Park Plaza Hotel in New York during St Patrick's Week in March 1989. It was a sell-out, with over 400 participants. The featured Minister and last speaker before lunch was Albert Reynolds, then Minister for Industry and Commerce. Faced with a full house in the Park Plaza, and imbued with the transforming zeal of the new government, he put his script aside. Instead, he spoke, as a businessman-turned-politician, both of Ireland's commitment to free enterprise, as epitomised by the low 10 per cent tax for business, and of harnessing the energy of the private sector. He capped it by announcing that Chase Manhattan bank had decided to establish another project in the new Irish financial centre and suggesting that other American banks should follow its example. He received a standing ovation. Over lunch I spoke to many invited US company executives. They could scarcely believe a European minister would speak with such passion and conviction for the cause of private sector investment and personal initiative. It was a good day for the gospel of the IFSC in the USA.

By the end of 1987, the IDA board had formally approved eighteen projects for the IFSC. These were then sent for scrutiny by a Certification Advisory Committee, which, when satisfied, recommended to the Minister of Finance that he should sign the final certificate of authorisation. The honour of having the very first IFSC company certified by the Minister for Finance, Ray Mac Sharry, fell to Tim Brosnan. He had been very successful as a dealer with the Irish subsidiary of the US bank Citicorp. And so it seemed in keeping with the daring spirit of the new financial centre that a young Irish executive should have the courage to tap its potential and be able to win financial backing in Ireland for his initiative. His company, Gandon Ltd, has evolved over the years and is now a fund-management company owned by the South African banking group Investec. Kredietbank of Belgium was the first foreign bank to decide in 1987 in Dublin's favour. Its decision was influenced positively by InterContinental Bank of Dublin, in which it had a shareholding and whose chief executive, Paddy McEvoy, was a powerful advocate of the new IFSC.

The marketing pace picked up and in 1988, the first full year of promotion of the centre, an average of fifteen companies visited Ireland to learn about it at first-hand. By the end of that year, the IDA had forwarded over fifty projects for licensing. Most important of all, the international flagship projects, which would give credibility to the fledgling financial centre, were coming through: Chase Manhattan and Citicorp from the USA, Dresdner Bank and Commerzbank of Germany, ABN Bank of the Netherlands and Banque Bruxelles Lambert of Belgium.

The build-up of projects coming into the IFSC accelerated fast. And in less than three years, by the end of 1989, the IDA Board had cleared ninety-five financial projects for admission.

These included two flagship Japanese projects, Mitsubishi Trust and Bank and the giant Sumitomo bank, each illustrating a different approach to banking success. Mitsubishi had a stake in Tony Ryan's GPA company in Shannon, and he became part of the Irish sales effort that culminated in the successful negotiation of the bank's commitment to the Dublin centre.

Sumitomo was the most prestigious bank in Japan. Its capture was regarded as a special prize both in its own right and for its demonstration effect in influencing other Japanese companies to follow its lead. Throughout his political career, Taoiseach Charles Haughey rarely ventured outside Ireland on official missions. But in April 1989, he decided to make the long journey to Japan to promote the IFSC and to encourage a final decision from Sumitomo. Jim Cashman, the IDA's top man in Japan, had prepared the way carefully. So expectations were high as the Taoiseach and the Irish party met with the President of Sumitomo bank and his party. They sat facing each other on the low couches much loved by Japanese corporations. The Taoiseach matched each protocol gesture from his guests and, after the initial verbal skirmishing, we waited anxiously to hear the fateful words. These could only come from the bank President. And they came, eventually, to our great relief – and joy. Yes, Sumitomo would come to Ireland's financial centre.

After the formal announcement, the bank's European chief, Mr Okaba, who was based in London, came over to Dublin to pay a courtesy visit on the Taoiseach at his office. I accompanied him to the meeting. As he was greeted by Mr Haughey, with a smile he told him how earlier that day he had already been welcomed to Ireland. To a puzzled Taoiseach, he relayed the experience of his taxi ride from Dublin airport. The taxi driver was curious about his business and nationality. When Okaba told him he was a Japanese banker, the taxi man responded, 'You must be the Sumitomo Bank – I saw the Taoiseach on TV saying you were coming to the Docks.' Mr Okaba was most impressed with this further example of popular support for the IFSC. For his part, the Taoiseach saw it as further proof of the perspicacity of the typical Dubliner as well as evidence of the public awareness of his pet project. It was a tale he was to retell many times.

The IFSC was on a roll. As 1990 drew to a close, the projects approved for the centre had climbed to 150. Some ninety of these were already in operation and employing 600 people at this early stage. The first building in the IFSC zone, the West Block, acquired by AIB Bank, did not become available for occupation until October 1990. The number and range of approved projects continued to grow in succeeding years. Instead of exhausting the potential of financial services, new areas of opportunity were being discovered continuously and exploited by the IDA under Kieran McGowan, its new chief executive.

And as the 1990s progressed, the reputation of the IFSC was firmly established. American blue-chip financial institutions chose it as the locale to serve the European market in large-scale projects, with a high labour content. In turn, Merrill Lynch, Citibank and Chase Manhattan made commitments involving 800 jobs and over. By the end of 1998, some eleven years since its inception, some 6,500 people were employed directly in the licensed companies in Dublin while many thousands more worked in companies providing services to them, for example, legal, accounting, security, printing and catering services. During the millennium year of 2000, the original vision of Ireland as an international financial services centre will be handsomely achieved, with the original target of 7,500 jobs exceeded, even if a little behind schedule. Today there are over $100 billion of funds under administration or management at the IFSC, and total assets of the foreign companies there come to another $100 billion. This has put Ireland firmly on the world map as an international financial services centre.

*

In May 1987, just six months after the first meeting of the new Custom House Docks Authority, the members and their chairman, Frank Benson, found themselves with a new responsibility. The Haughey government had decided to locate the International Financial Centre on their twenty-seven acre site at the Docks. And in August, the government appointed the Taoiseach's point man, Padraig Ó hUiginn, as a member of the Authority.

The master-project agreement, which the Authority signed in January 1988 with the site developers (the Hardwicke–McInerney–British Land consortium), was to govern the scale and pace of physical development at the docks for the next decade. The scheme provided for a mixed development of 1.6 million square feet of floor space to be constructed over five years. Half the space would be offices for the IFSC companies, and the rest would comprise a hotel, museum, shops and 200 residences. A special marketing centre was opened at the Custom House Quay, complete with the scale models and illuminated photographs. For the hundreds of financial companies investigating the IFSC option, it became a standard port of call.

The Custom House Docks Authority set out to minimise its risk by contributing the site as its capital, while maximising its return by sharing the agreed profit with the developers. The first building to get under way was the West Block, which was constructed to the highest specifications, with provision for high-ceiling dealing rooms and computer-network cabling throughout. The quoted rents of more than £30 per square foot in 1988–89 were by far the highest in the city and reflected the initial high standards of specification then thought necessary for financial services. Few incoming companies from Europe or North America could understand why the rents were so high and the lease terms so long and tough. This issue was to be a constant source of irritation.

The reality was that the IFSC offices had a captive market since incoming financial companies were required to move to the centre as a condition of their licenses. Typically, the individual buildings were bought as an investment by Irish companies, which then sought to select the choicest tenants from among the approved IFSC companies. At the crucial interface between the enthusiastic foreign company seeking to meet its licence obligations by moving into the IFSC and the landlord looking for the most secure rent roll, the key state agencies – the Custom House Docks Authority and the IDA – were essentially onlookers. The total space available for IFSC companies never matched the potential space demands of the approved companies. The rental costs were often twice that of their temporary accommodation in Dublin, and the terms more demanding.

Despite regular cajoling from the Department of Finance and the threat of cancellation of their licence, some 150 companies were still outside the designated financial centre in 1999, paying rents about half the levels in the IFSC. The licence required them to occupy 'reasonable accommodation' in the IFSC. However, given the shortage of space there and the high costs, the Department of Finance would have a weak legal case if it tried to compel the companies to relocate in the Centre.

A new regulatory and tax framework is now emerging that will resolve these frictions. From the start of the new millennium, and as required by the EU, no new financial companies can be granted the special 10 per cent tax rate, but from January 2003 they will be eligible for the low national corporate tax rate of 12.5 per cent on trading profits that will come into effect on that date. The IFSC will have lost its differential tax advantage. Financial-services companies will be free to locate anywhere in the Republic and enjoy similar tax treatment. A sign of the new regime was the decision of a licensed IFSC company, Scottish Amicable, in March 1999 to take a long-term lease on a larger office block (45,000 square feet) in Dublin's Adelaide Street, on the other side of the Liffey river from the IFSC.

As a member of the Customs House Docks Authority for over seven years from February 1990 to its cessation in April 1997, I was a participant in many stormy meetings under Chairman Frank Benson and, subsequently, Séamus Páircéir and Professor Dervilla Donnelly, as the Authority sought to get the physical plan implemented, at rents which would be acceptable. While the master plan provided for completion of the development over the five years from January 1988, it could not force the developers to start a building if they did not want to do so. And since the developers were responsible for raising all the cash funding, they had a strong hand.

The first wave of buildings, the gleaming green-glass curved buildings looking out on James Gandon's Custom House and Michael Scott's Busarus and Harbourmaster Places 1 and 2 were all sold by the developers and completed in 1990–1 – a total of 600,000 square feet of office space. It was a good start, but then came a hiatus in development. A property slump in Ireland and the Gulf War had triggered off instability in international financial markets. And even though the IFSC had a captive list of the world's blue-chip financial clients as potential tenants, the development consortium refused to begin any further construction unless a minimum of 50 per cent of the space was pre-let.

Almost four years were to elapse between the start of construction on the first two Harbourmaster offices in July 1989 and the next building, Harbourmaster 3, in April 1993. This meant there was a serious loss of momentum on the construction side. In between, the Authority signed a new agreement with the developers, setting out a revised building timetable. However, building was required to start only if the planned offices were substantially pre-let. As the general property market recovered and a range of Irish companies (such as solicitors and accountants) sought space in the centre, the development company recovered its nerve and the last phase of building on the original twelve-acre site was completed in record time.

The end result of these frustrations was that when the Authority came to decide on the best way of developing the adjoining twelve-acre site, originally earmarked for a sports centre and outside the remit of its agreement with the Development Company, it issued public invitations to developers in early 1997. The Authority was also strongly supportive of the development by Brian Rhatigan of offices for IFSC clients on the site of the former Post Office sorting office in Sheriff Street.

The new Dublin Docklands Development Authority, the brainchild of Ruairí Quinn, when Minister for Finance, came into being in May 1997 with the much wider remit of rejuvenating economic and social life on 1,300 acres of land on both sides of the Liffey river. It has an explicit legislative mandate 'to facilitate the development of financial services' – a provision missing from the legislation that governed its predecessor. In its first year, the new Authority, under its Chairman, Lar Bradshaw, by opening up the extended twelve-acre site, succeeded in a variety of deals designed to deliver 500,000 square feet of new space by the millennium year for Citibank, MG Insurance, Bank of Ireland and A and L Goodbody, Solicitors. Today, the IFSC is a fine and lively hive of activity, complete with a hotel, apartments, shops, coffee houses, restaurants and pubs. It is an eloquent testimony to the dreamers of 1987.

*

The drive to establish the IFSC was sustained against a difficult background – the real sense of economic crisis that existed in 1986 and 1987. The success of the financial-services initiative stemmed from the powerful support lent both by the office of the Taoiseach and the central IFSC Committee, under the Chairmanship of Padraig Ó hUiginn, from 1987 to 1993. The strong degree of commitment from the top was felt throughout all the agencies of government. But, predictably, that sense of urgency and responsiveness diminished over time and was replaced by a more normal bureaucratic regime. Ó hUiginn's successor as Secretary to the Department of the Taoiseach was Paddy Teahon. He also succeeded Ó hUiginn as chairman of the re-titled IFSC Clearing House Group. This has four working groups reporting to it: Banking and Treasury group, Funds group, Insurance group and Special sub-groups comprising public- and private-sector representatives.

In recent years, there have been two major reviews of the operations of the IFSC: the *Report of the International Advisory Group* (May 1997), which was chaired by Minister Gay Mitchell, and the government's new *Strategy for the Development of the International Services Industry in Ireland* (March 1999), which dealt with an entirely new environment for attracting financial services in the new millennium.

As a result of the agreement between the government and the Commission on the introduction of a low standard tax rate of 12.5 per cent from January 2003 for all trading activities, financial services will be able to establish anywhere in Ireland and avail of an attractive low tax. The last batch of new companies entitled to a 10 per cent rate for financial services were approved in 1999 – thereafter, new entrants will pay the standard tax as it descends from a level of 28 per cent in 1999 to the target of 12.5 per cent. So what would happen to the Dockland financial centre then? And would anyone need to continue promoting Ireland for financial services internationally if the low tax rate was automatically available?

The government's answer was to assert that the Docklands would be the hub for the long-term development of the international financial services industry in Ireland. The new Docklands Authority would provide suitable office accommodation and services for incoming companies. There was a recognition that while the more specialist front-office financial-service activities would be encouraged to locate in the Docklands area, close to the original twenty-seven-acre centre, the other more labour-intensive back-office operations could be located elsewhere in Dublin or in the regions, which are pressing for more inward investment.

In future, financial companies coming to Ireland will not require licences to avail of the low tax regime; they were never eligible for IDA grants. The need to continue marketing Ireland in the more open regime has been recognised, and the IDA has been given the responsibility for devising a new marketing plan. For each financial speciality, a nominated specialist will represent the country internationally and be the 'front person' for the government system at all levels.

Significantly, the government's statement acknowledged the creeping bureaucracy of the Irish administrative approach when it referred to the 'failure of the current structures to deliver results on some issues, for example, the company-law amendments'. Improvements in administrative procedures are promised to restore some of the original enthusiasm that distinguished the Irish approach. There remain unlimited opportunities and niches to add to the impressive foundation of world-class financial companies in Ireland, but only if the political and administrative will is sustained.

15

FROM CELTIC PAUPER TO CELTIC TIGER

Ray Mac Sharry and Padraic White

If countries really can go broke, then by late 1986–early 1987, Ireland, cast in the role of Celtic pauper, was emerging as a prime candidate for bankruptcy. For five years, various governments had tried without any real success to keep fiscal deficits in check and stop the public finances from spinning out of control. Accordingly, the media and the financial markets grew more concerned about the size of the fiscal imbalances and the threat these posed to national solvency. For the second time in thirty years, the viability of the Irish state was at issue. This time the concerns lay with credit risk, or fear of government default on national debt repayments. For the debt had virtually doubled in four years and, by 1986, had reached 129 per cent of GNP. Ireland 'had the statistics of a third world country', as the then Secretary of the Department of Finance, Maurice Doyle, readily conceded some thirteen years later in September 1999, when giving evidence before the Dáil Public Accounts Committee.

In the mid-fifties, a similar crisis of confidence arose in our ability to manage our economic affairs. Between 1953 and 1958, the economy failed to expand and was beset by periodic balance-of-payments difficulties. And while three decades separated these two serious economic setbacks, some of the parallels were striking. In both periods, economic activity was depressed and living standards fell as unemployment rose, despite large-scale emigration. However, in the late 1950s, a sharp reversal of policies and the pursuit of a new development strategy laid the basis for a strong and sustained recovery. Economic isolationism was ended and the goal of self-sufficiency abandoned; free trade was embraced and, gradually, Ireland opened a wider window on the world. Within a generation, the economy moved from being one of the world's most closed economies to becoming both one of the most open and, latterly, one of the most successful.

In 1958, the challenge, as defined by Seán Lemass, was 'to ensure the economic foundation of independence'. Scrapping protection in favour of free trade, while increasingly relying on foreign direct investment to meet the country's employment needs, became the new way forward and the best means of securing that independence. The combination of tax concessions and grants to encourage foreign investors to locate their manufacturing plants here was seen as providing the key to rapid economic development and job creation. This radical change of policy direction marked a major financial turning point in the economic history of the state – perhaps the most fundamental since its foundation.

However, three decades later, the economy was again facing serious difficulties. By the mid-eighties, the government was over-borrowed, the people were over-taxed and the economy was underperforming, as unemployment and emigration again soared. And, as in the mid-fifties, there were renewed doubts about the capacity of the political and administrative system to overcome the fiscal challenges presented. The outlook was bleak indeed.

In August 1986 the Irish pound was devalued by 8 per cent against all other EMS currencies. Living standards had not increased for five years. Nearly one in five people were out of work, and the public finances were in a state of disarray. And then, by January 1987, a measure of political instability was added with the collapse of the coalition government, although the actual break-up between Fine Gael and Labour, which had been pre-arranged, was amicable. The coalition's successor in office was a minority Fianna Fáil administration with Charles Haughey elected as Taoiseach, but only on the casting vote of the Ceann Comhairle.

In absolute terms, if Ireland's vital economic statistics looked unimpressive, in relative terms, international comparisons also failed to flatter the country's economic performance. Debt per head of the population was three times greater than Mexico and, proportionately, among the highest in the industrialised world. At the same time, Ireland had the second-highest unemployment rate (after Spain) among the OECD countries. And, in addition, the country had fewer people at work, as a proportion of the total population, than any other OECD country. This high dependency ratio caused an additional strain on the public finances. It meant that in 1985, every worker supported over two dependants (children, the elderly and the unemployed), and this pushed up public spending, which, in turn, required higher taxes, or increased borrowings, to finance.

In January 1987, just as the general election campaign started, the *Economist* magazine wrote a damning analysis of the management of the economy, under the headline, 'How the government spent the people into a slump'. The text and the accompanying graphs − with slick sub-headings like 'In hock, out of work' − charted a depressing picture of joblessness, indebtedness and growing public disillusionment. It predicted the new government would be formed by 'Mr Haughey and his rural-based Fianna Fáil supporters, longing to hand out money after four years in opposition'. And the article ended by saying that 'Irish bankers fear that, to their shame, the International Monetary Fund may have to step in to impose the stringency that their politicians cannot muster.'

The real question the article raised was whether, as in the fifties, we would be able to rescue ourselves or whether, as almost happened in Britain just a decade before, an IMF lifeline might be needed. The *Economist* may have been right in its analysis, if harsh in its judgement, but it was wrong in its prognosis. The IMF was not called upon to do the 'dirty work' which, the magazine had contended, the politicians 'know is needed, but cannot do themselves'. Instead, the politicians finally rolled up their sleeves.

By March, the first of a series of tough budgets was introduced. The spring seeds of economic transformation were sown and were quick to bear fruit. The switch in emphasis within the budget, towards cutting spending rather than raising taxes to reduce the deficits, helped re-establish greater control over the public finances. And by October, this rigorous approach was underpinned by the Programme for National Recovery, an agreement reached between the government and the social partners, where moderate pay increases were swapped for promised future tax cuts.

The development marked the start of an economic recovery the *Economist* itself was slow to recognise. Just a year later (on 16 January 1988) it published a major thirty-page survey of the economy, under the heading 'Poorest of the rich'. And to illustrate its theme, the cover picture included a woman and child sitting on Dublin's O'Connell Bridge with a begging bowl. Undoubtedly, it was chosen as a metaphor for our economic condition.

Ten years later, in June 1997, the *Economist* returned to examine what by now had been heralded internationally as Ireland's economic miracle. In fact in 1994, Kevin Gardiner, a London-based economist with the US investment bank Morgan Stanley, had first awarded the Irish economy its Celtic Tiger status. But this time, the magazine readily conceded that 'here was one of the most remarkable economic transformations of recent times: from basket-case to "emerald tiger" in ten years'. Ireland had become a shining light and a beacon to the world.

However, on closer scrutiny, it found the economic recovery somewhat easier to explain. Quite simply, it concluded that Ireland, having endured a bad recession in the early 1980s and having later sorted out her public finances, then resumed and improved upon an earlier trend of rapid growth, when the rest of Europe was doing badly. 'This may be less than miraculous,' the *Economist* reported, but 'it is nonetheless an enviable achievement.'

The OECD report on the Irish economy that appeared two years later, in June 1999, was more impressed with the significance of the sustained growth performance and more fulsome in its praise. It acknowledged that:

The Irish economy has notched up five straight years of stunning economic performance. No other OECD member country has been able to match its outstanding outcomes in a variety of dimensions. Output growth has averaged over 9 per cent per year on a GDP basis in the period 1994–8, bringing GDP per capita in purchasing power parity terms to a higher level than the European Union average. Half of that growth has been reflected in considerable employment gains and the rest in impressive labour productivity growth. Despite substantial increases in the labour force, thanks to Ireland's particularly favourable demographics and to an important reversal in migration flows, the unemployment rate has fallen by nearly 9 percentage points.

The OECD had found it astonishing 'that a nation could have moved all the way from the back of the pack to a leading position within such a short period, not much more than a decade, in fact'. But so too did many others, not least in Ireland, who had watched it happen at close quarters.

What explains the remarkable economic turnaround? How does an economy move so rapidly out of the Celtic twilight zone? How does it then manage to emulate the performance of the former high-growth Asian Tiger economies and so, by 1994, merit the Celtic Tiger tag? Certainly, there is no single, or simple, explanation for an economic transformation that none had predicted. However, the sustained nature of that strong recovery after 1987, followed by the record growth levels achieved since 1993, shows that it was less a temporary revival, following years of economic stagnation, than a permanent structural shift in the level of Ireland's economic performance. So what were the agents of change that produced such a remarkable reversal of national economic fortune? The renowned American economist Paul Krugman, writing in *International Perspectives on the Irish Economy*, put it succinctly when he said that Ireland, ' . . . through a combination of good luck, good timing and good policies, has caught the crest of a geographical and technological wave, and has ridden it to a prosperity nobody expected.'

Many different factors contributed to Ireland's accelerated rate of expansion from the late eighties onwards. Some of these helped create the right conditions for economic take-off, while others later acted as the specific drivers that sustained the booming economy in the mid to late nineties, when the rate of growth quickened.

Ever since Ireland's accession to it in 1973, the European Union has exercised a positive influence on the Irish economy, both financially and in other respects, not least in ensuring a longer-term approach to economic planning. This was certainly true after 1987, when the rapid rate of economic recovery, in part, reflected the scale of EU transfers received under the two rounds of Structural Funds (£7.5 billion between 1989 and 2000). In particular, the Delors 1 round (1989–93) helped finance much-needed infrastructural investment. This enabled an increase in capital spending to take place, following earlier years in the eighties when it was restricted by tight fiscal constraints.

The EU transfers meant that as the economy expanded, there were fewer infrastructural bottlenecks to choke off the recovery under way. In addition, the discipline imposed by the Maastricht criteria, as a qualification for membership of the single currency, ensured continuing tight control was kept on the public finances. And that also helped impose an external discipline and checked any regression back to fiscal profligacy.

A further beneficial factor was the change in the population structure, with an expanding labour force boosted by net immigration into the country, and an increase in the rate of female participation in the workforce. The result was a sharp reduction in the dependency ratio – with those at work having fewer dependants to support. This produced both higher tax revenue and lower spending.

Fortunately, both the short- and long-term economic influences and factors operating within the economy came together positively after 1987, at just the right time. Their interaction had a mutually reinforcing effect in releasing the economy's latent growth potential. In addition, the late eighties also saw a sharp improvement in the external economic environment, particularly in Britain. There, the 'Lawson boom', fuelled by tax cuts and lower interest rates after the 1987 stock-market crash, raised demand for Irish exports and facilitated the domestic recovery.

In the early nineties there was a further external stimulus, with the introduction of the single market in 1993. This development encouraged many US multinationals to locate in Europe and produced a significant inflow of American investment to Ireland. The attractions were low corporate tax rates, a ready supply of educated labour, relatively low wages and a good telecommunications system. At the same time, world trade grew very rapidly in our main markets, Europe and the US. This combination of strong external demand allied to the increased level of inward investment helped achieve the record growth rates between 1994 and 1998, the peak years of the Celtic Tiger.

The relative importance of some of these different factors as the drivers of economic growth should be considered. The success that was finally achieved reflected both short- and long-term influences, over different time scales. But successive governments deserve a share of the credit too for taking a single-minded approach to some key aspects of policy-making.

Politicians

Over many years, politicians generally took a long-term strategic view on a number of specific issues, for which they have won too little recognition. These policy decisions were to prove important in shaping the future form of economic development. And in taking them, the politicians combined foresight, in introducing the policy changes when needed, with fortitude in withstanding any short-term pressure to amend or abandon them – as in areas like corporate taxation and investment in education. This combination of continuity and consistency of approach brought clarity and certainty to important areas of economic policy-making. And, in time, this has yielded a significant return to the economy.

Since the late fifties, governments have exploited with great skill the limited policy autonomy a sovereign state can exercise in the economic sphere. The contrasting performance of the two economies on both parts of this island serves to illustrate this point. The Republic's flexibility and capacity for policy innovation contrasts sharply with Northern Ireland's relative rigidity and lack of policy discretion as a regional economy within the UK, even when one allows for the handicap imposed by three decades of civil strife.

Education

The introduction of free secondary education in 1967 became over time an important factor in laying the foundations for future rapid growth, and that too reflected a major political input. It was to have far-reaching economic consequences in later decades. Over time, further educational reforms raised the skills base of the workforce, as third-level education was expanded. This resulted in a major improvement in human capital. The improved levels of educational attainment gave overseas companies, and particularly the major US multinationals operating in the high-technology sectors, a much greater incentive to locate here.

But those higher standards of education also resulted in more women entering the labour market, thereby raising employment, but without generating inflationary wage pressures. The rapid rate of increase in economic growth from 1993 onwards owes a good deal to the investment in education by successive governments over many decades. Since the 1960s, spending on education, as a proportion of national income, has doubled. After 1967, and the introduction of free secondary schooling, major public investment in third-level education followed, with the construction of Regional Technical Colleges, two new universities and an expansion in facilities at the country's existing universities. The result was a sharp increase in participation rates at all levels of education. And today, Ireland has one of the highest tertiary enrolment rates in the OECD area. The consequent availability of a large pool of skilled labour has been critical in winning the high level of overseas investment over the last decade.

An economic study (*ESRI Medium Term Review: 1997–2003*) by Tony Fahey and John FitzGerald showed that, 'At present between 40 and 50 per cent of those leaving the educational system have experienced third-level education and over 80 per cent of the (relevant) population have reached Leaving Certificate standard.' This has raised the skills base of the labour force and made Ireland – with an English-speaking workforce – a more attractive base for foreign direct investment. The outflow from second- and third-level institutions of well-educated people into employment has raised productivity and boosted competitiveness and growth. As the OECD has pointed out, the investment in education and training has been just as effective a form of capital accumulation as physical capital. And in an increasingly knowledge-based economy, a high level of human capital is critical to the achievement of long-term prosperity. The National Competitiveness Council in its annual report for 1999 argued that human capital has become a vital strategic asset for all countries, adding that 'the quality of human resources in the economy is a key determinant of economic success and dynamism given the marked shift over recent years towards the knowledge-based economy.'

In part, the education system is being adapted to meet the needs of enterprise, by strengthening the links between the world of learning and the world of work. In Ireland's case, there has been a focus on education serving the growth areas of the economy, notably in the industrial and service sectors – like electronics and financial services – where a high level of foreign direct investment is now concentrated. Successive governments have recognised the importance of education and training both for competitiveness and to add to the availability of skills in order to secure a continuing flow of new overseas investment.

In 1997, the government announced the establishment of a £250 million Education Technology (Investment) Fund. One quarter of the total will be spent supplying schools with 60,000 computers and training 20,000 teachers. The aim is to have one personal computer for every five secondary students by the end of the programme. The Fund will make a significant contribution to improving the education infrastructure and provide for the creation of a projected 7,000 new third-level college places at degree and technician level in high-technology areas.

As Paul Tansey noted in his book *Ireland at Work*, in summing up the nature of our recent economic success, 'Ireland carved out its niche in the global market for mobile investment by offering a location that was highly profitable, where labour was plentiful, educated and technologically adept.'

Foreign direct investment

In the case of the Republic, nowhere has autonomy in economic policy-making been more apparent, or used to better effect, than in the role played by governments over four decades, both in promoting foreign direct investment and using low corporate tax rates and grants as the key industrial incentives to secure it. At the same time all the main political parties, either in or out of office, have endorsed this approach. The degree of political cohesion established on this issue not only created a greater degree of certainty about the continuity of decision-making at government level, it raised business confidence and made Ireland a more attractive location for inward investment.

After 1987, the sharp rise in foreign direct investment became one of the main drivers behind the Celtic Tiger economy that emerged in the mid-nineties, bolstered by the Partnership agreements, which helped to moderate wage cost excesses. The approach adopted by the 'new IDA' formed in 1970 of identifying both the future growth sectors — such as pharmaceuticals and electronics — and targeting the key companies, like Intel, within each one, created a base of successful international companies.

In population terms, Ireland accounts for just 1 per cent of the European Union. But despite her small size and peripheral location, she secures over 20 per cent of new inward investment in Europe in the combined manufacturing, software, telebusiness and shared-services sectors, according to authoritative surveys. The impact of foreign direct investment on the economy has been substantial, accounting for one-fifth of GDP. Foreign-owned firms now dominate the industrial base, and their arrival since the early sixties has helped to open up the Irish economy. Today, the foreign sector accounts for half the total employment in manufacturing industry, over three-quarters of industrial exports, and two-thirds of the output of the manufacturing sector.

According to the OECD, in its economic survey report (1999) on Ireland, 'the massive inflow of direct investment has been the major positive shock influencing the economy in the 1990s ... Ireland's share of OECD total inflows surged in the 1990s, reaching a level out of all proportion with its GDP share.'

In 1997, the country ranked fifth in the world as a destination for US direct-investment outflows.

IDA-Ireland systematically monitors the total impact of the national foreign-investment programme on the Irish economy. Its 1997 survey showed expenditure of $11 billion, mainly incurred in labour costs and in buying services and components. And so, while the 1,100 foreign companies directly create 116,000 jobs, they generate at least the same volume of employment indirectly via the spin-off in expenditure, through subcontracting, outsourcing and the multiplier effect. Given the growing trend for international companies to focus on their core activities and to outsource other functions, the full national economic benefit of foreign investment can only be seen by tracking carefully both the direct and indirect economic effects of foreign direct investment.

Increasingly, IDA-Ireland has developed the rifle-shot, rather than the scatter-gun, approach in seeking foreign investment. This has proved highly successful to date. It involves identifying the expanding international sectors of industry and targeting niche companies that could operate well in Ireland and could bring with them clear employment and economic benefits. As a result of its continuous interaction with the market place for foreign direct investment, IDA-Ireland regularly adjusts its targeting of sectors and companies, while fine-tuning the range of financial incentives on offer to attract inward investment. More and more, the new foreign-investment locating here has been in the high-technology sectors – electronics, software, pharmaceuticals and financial services – thus matching the improved skills base of the work force and reflecting the higher level of educational attainment of the population generally.

Fiscal adjustment

Unless the two critical pillars – fiscal stability and social partnership – on which recovery was built were firmly in place from 1987, the Celtic Tiger economy would never have materialised in the mid-nineties. Undoubtedly, the main pre-condition for a sustained economic recovery was fiscal stabilisation, given the overall size both of the national debt (£24 billion) and the level of Exchequer borrowing, at 12 per cent of GNP in 1986. So unless, from the outset, progress was made on debt control and lowering the fiscal deficit, any pick-up in economic activity would have been short-lived. It would be little more than a temporary rebound, following the years of zero growth in the early eighties.

Financial shock therapy was the economic cure prescribed. Spending had to be cut in order to stop the national debt rising more rapidly than the economy was growing. But before the debt could be reduced as a proportion of national income, stabilisation first had to be achieved. Once the sharp expenditure cuts in the 1987 and 1988 budgets showed signs of producing greater fiscal balance, however, interest rates fell rapidly in response and business and consumer confidence rose.

Earlier, the social partners had already accepted that tough corrective action was needed. This was reflected in the consensus reached in the NESC report – *A Strategy for Development 1986-1990* – in the autumn of 1986. This provided an inspiring lead for the new Fianna Fáil minority government to follow in March 1987 in its first budget. In the NESC document, employers, trade unions and farmers recognised that sacrifices all round were required in the national interest and had signalled their readiness to make them. By later negotiating a social-partnership arrangement with the government, they showed the measure of their commitment.

Social partnership

The second pillar helping to support economic regeneration was the Programme for National Recovery, which was agreed in the autumn of 1987 and marked a return to centralised bargaining through a three-year national accord. Pay restraint was traded for future tax cuts, while the social partners – not least the trade unions – were given a greater influence over aspects of economic policy. The painful correction in the national finances that finally got under way in 1987, via reduced spending and pay moderation, laid firm foundations for the economic recovery that followed. The combination of budgetary restraint and social partnership added stability to the public finances and certainty of paying costs at a critical time, both for the government and the private sector.

At first glance, the odds in 1987 seemed to be set against government success in regaining control of the public finances. Since the early eighties, different governments had tried, and failed, to reverse the steady deterioration both in the budgetary and debt balances. The newly elected Fianna Fáil government, as a minority administration, lacked a parliamentary majority to implement its proposals.

But undoubtedly, the serious economic difficulties encountered in the early and mid-eighties also had a profound effect in bringing about a change of attitude on all sides. Over the period, politicians, employers, trade unions and others had seen the national debt double, growth stagnate and living standards fall, while undue reliance on higher taxes had failed to cut the fiscal deficit. In part, the political difficulty was compounded by the lack of a broad cross-party consensus on the need for fiscal rectitude.

However, in 1987, all that changed quite dramatically. And it happened at two different levels, at much the same time. In

September, the Fine Gael leader, Alan Dukes, outlined what became known as the Tallaght Strategy. In that speech, he offered the government conditional support on economic matters. As the Finance Minister during most of the coalition's tenure since 1983, no one was better placed than Dukes to appreciate the dimensions of the unresolved crisis in the public finances. He admitted that 'the resolution of our public-finance problems is the essential key to everything that we want to do in the economic and social fields'. In political terms, this amounted to a pledge not to defeat the minority government in the Dáil, where it was attempting to achieve fiscal stabilisation.

The political consensus on the economy provided a spur for the social partners, as they completed their negotiations with the government. A month later they reached agreement on the Programme for National Recovery. At that point a broad national consensus had been established for the first time, both at the political level and also between the social partners, in relation to pay and spending. This suggested a remarkable degree of political and social cohesion in facing the worst economic crisis since the state's foundation.

The degree of resolution shown in addressing the economic crisis was impressive, and produced a faster-than-expected improvement in the economic fundamentals. As fiscal stabilisation was achieved and social partnership was seen to be effective in securing pay moderation, the impact on the economy was positive. This led to a virtuous circle being created where, as the inexorable rise in the debt-to-GNP ratio was checked and reversed and as budget deficits fell, lower interest rates and declining inflation resulted. And these were later followed by increased inward investment, higher growth and a falling tax burden.

The rapid turnaround in the public finances helped ensure

a more competitive economy. But if fiscal stability and social partnership provided the cornerstones of that recovery, other elements came into play subsequently to sustain it. These served as the drivers of the accelerated pace of economic development from 1994, where growth averaged 7.7 per cent annually in GNP terms between 1993 and 1998, and which brought domestic living standards close to the European Union average.

EU support

To many international economic commentators, the high level of EU financial transfers Ireland has received largely explains the 'economic miracle' of recent years. Since, proportionately, the state has been the greatest net beneficiary of Community support, it is all too easily assumed that this flow of funds – via the CAP and particularly the Structural Funds – explains the country's rapid convergence on the average living standard in the EU. In 1987, income per head was two-thirds of the EU average level, and by 1998, the gap was almost closed. However, that strong economic out-performance over the period is not the result of lavish subsidies from the EU alone, although these have been substantial.

The level of EU support needs to be put into perspective. It does represent one of the key elements in the mix of ingredients that underpinned Ireland's two-part economic recovery, first from 1987, when growth resumed, and then, after 1994, when the economy expanded rapidly. But it would be wrong to exaggerate the significance of the Community transfers in securing the transformation of the Irish economy. The OECD, in its annual economic survey on Ireland (1999), estimates that over the past decade, Structural Fund receipts may have raised growth by between one-quarter and one-half of one per cent annually. And in fact the ESRI's own analysis suggests that the single-market initiative was a far more important economic growth promoter, being responsible for three times more growth than the Structural Funds.

Certainly, Structural Fund support raised the economy's productive capacity at a critical time in the late eighties. It did so just when fiscal constraints, and the need to reduce borrowing, might have led to reduced investment in infrastructure, industry and education. The Structural Fund transfers obviated that possibility and left Ireland well positioned to capture an increased share of foreign direct investment as multinational companies established a manufacturing presence here, ahead of the completion of the 1992 single market. This investment, which was 75 per cent financed by the EU, enabled the economy to grow more rapidly without meeting capacity constraints that otherwise could have choked off the recovery at an early stage.

The discipline imposed by the five-year Community Support Framework served as a useful form of long-term planning for the economy. It not only forced the adoption of a series of national development plans as the basis of investment decisions but required that spending be evaluated to ensure the funds used were deployed effectively. But, in particular, it made capital investment less vulnerable to a stop-go approach to economic development, via annual budgetary changes.

Population changes

The rate of increase in overall employment has been the most singular success of the Celtic Tiger economy. In just over a decade more jobs have been created than in any comparable period in the country's history. In 1987, when total employment stood at 1.11 million, there were fewer people employed than in 1926. Then, in just eleven years, quite remarkably, the numbers at work had soared to 1.459 million by 1998 – showing a 32 per cent increase. And over the same period, the rate of unemployment more than halved, dropping to 6.4 per cent of the labour force by August 1999.

The expansion in employment reflected both the strength of the economy and a number of more favourable demographic factors that had developed in the 1990s, as numbers in the working age groups of the population rose. This increase reflected the high birth rates of the 1970s, as more people entered the labour market and fewer emigrated, given the buoyancy of the economy, but also as more women, in particular, opted for employment. All these factors helped increase the labour-force numbers. Other developments, such as a declining birth rate and lower fertility levels, helped ensure an improvement in the unfavourable economic dependency ratio.

In Ireland, the baby boom peaked in 1980, much later than in either Britain or the US. This had contributed to a high rate of economic dependency at a difficult time, just as the economy entered a long recession, and against the background of rising unemployment levels. The downturn was compounded by the size of the dependency ratio – the number of non-workers in the population divided by the number of people employed. By 1987, every ten workers were supporting twenty-three dependants among the non-working population, whether children, the elderly or the unemployed. However, with fewer people at work, the tax take for the Exchequer was lower. But, with more dependants to support, this also meant a heavy tax burden on the working population. This not only helped to keep overall taxes high but helped ensure low growth.

But in the past decade, the combination of a falling birth rate, a rising rate of economic participation among women with a third-level education and the reversal of the historic tide of emigration has produced a fundamental change. The increase in the domestic supply of labour has improved the possibility of sustaining growth over a longer period. And by 1997, every ten workers were supporting just seventeen dependants. So today the tax-revenue base is larger, with a larger working population supporting fewer dependants.

The depressed conditions of the 1980s resulted in a 'brain drain' from the country, as some of the best and brightest emigrated to seek work. At that stage, one-third of all emigrants had third-level education, up from less than a fifth in the 1960s. But later, after 1993, as economic prospects improved, many of these emigrants returned as immigrants, lured by the new job opportunities opening up and the evidence of rising real incomes.

The country's changing demographic structure has meant an expanding labour force, which, in turn, has facilitated the unprecedented level of strong growth recorded from the mid-nineties onwards, without either encountering labour-supply problems or precipitating inflationary wage increases. However, by mid-1999, signs of overheating in the economy were beginning to emerge, with labour shortages in the private sector and a wide range of public-sector pay demands for increases above the terms set by Partnership 2000.

*

Six years of sustained high-level growth since 1994 is unprecedented in Ireland's economic history, and with the economy increasingly facing capacity constraints, the problem is not a scarcity of jobs but a scarcity of workers to fill them. Overcoming that means removing the impediments to employment, whether these be transport congestion, soaring house prices – which reduce labour mobility – or high personal tax rates, which discourage people from moving from welfare to work and depress labour supply. The failure to overcome these difficulties can only mean that labour and skill shortages will increase, thus checking the economy's remarkable progress. We cannot hope to maintain for much longer the growth rates achieved since 1993. That means engineering a soft landing for the economy, which would still allow for sustainable growth of 4 to 5 per cent annually, while also requiring a readiness to adapt to the rapid rate of change in the high-technology sectors.

Success can breed success, or it may well generate complacency, particularly if we forget the lessons of the late seventies and early eighties and take our future economic prosperity for granted. For one cannot simply assume that the strong growth that raised living standards has become self-sustaining. The Celtic Tiger phenomenon was built on a consensus established between the social partners. The partnership was based on clearly defined economic and social objectives, with agreement on how these should be achieved. And the discipline imposed by those agreements was sustained for more than a decade, with great success.

The result has been the most far-reaching transformation of the economy since the foundation of the state. Under virtually every indicator, greater economic progress was made since 1987 than in any comparable period over the previous sixty-four years. Rising real incomes have ensured that living standards have converged on the European Union average, virtual full employment has been reached and the tide of emigration has been reversed. Workers are now returning to take up employment at home, rather than leaving to try and find work abroad.

What has distinguished the approach since 1987 has been the willingness to think about the long term when seeking solutions to our economic problems and the readiness of the social partners to act in a concerted manner to help resolve them. By working together to serve the larger national economic interest, the self-interest of employers, unions and farmers has been best advanced. And by doing so over four different social-partnership agreements, pay restraint has ensured that productivity has risen faster than real incomes. This has enabled the strong output growth to be reflected in a rapid rate of increase in employment, while international competitiveness has been maintained.

Social partnership has indeed been the winning formula. And the challenge for the future is to adapt that highly successful model to changed conditions. This means recognising fully the different set of economic circumstances facing the country in the early years of the new millennium. In this respect, Ireland's membership of monetary union marks a major shift in economic policy. Since the government has lost the use of interest and exchange-rate instruments either to influence demand or to offset any loss of competitiveness, this makes pay moderation even more critical in maintaining competitiveness and employment.

The difference between present and past economic circumstances, as Brian Patterson, chairman of the National Competitiveness Council, noted, is one between necessity and freedom. For in the mid-1980s, when faced with the crisis in the public finances, and later with the need to meet the Maastricht criteria, the choice was stark. If governments failed to rectify the fiscal imbalances, the IMF would almost certainly intervene and dictate the terms of our economic rehabilitation, while failure to stay within the Maastricht guidelines meant Ireland was unlikely to qualify for membership of the single currency. In both instances, the necessary economic discipline was accepted, though partly under the threat of some external sanction.

This time, as Patterson has warned, 'the discipline has to be generated internally – which means we have to manage our affairs in a more mature way', and without that same outside pressure. However, having already met the challenge of 1987, and having made the change so successfully since then, the Irish economy has now come of age. Through that shared experience we have gained the self-confidence and also acquired the self-discipline not to dissipate the gains made but to build on those achievements in the new millennium.

Odd Eikin, the leader of the Swedish Employers Federation, cautioned against complacency after his visit in 1998 to examine Ireland's social-partnership model. Observing the stresses and strains developing between the social partners, he remarked on how much easier it is to achieve national partnership when a country is threatened by economic crisis than once economic success has been achieved. The crucial issue then is how to share the new wealth without destroying the means whereby it was created.

BIBLIOGRAPHY

Barry, Frank (ed.) (1999) *Understanding Ireland's Economic Growth*, London: Macmillan Press.

Brown, Terence (1981) *Ireland: A Social and Cultural History, 1922-79*, London: Fontana.

Budget Booklets 1973-1999: Dublin: Stationery Office.

Cantillon, Sara, J. Curtis, and J. FitzGerald (1994) *Medium-Term Review: 1994-2000*, Dublin: ESRI

Chubb, Basil (ed.) (1992) *Federation of Irish Employers 1942-1992*, Dublin: Gill and Macmillan.

Chubb, Basil and Paddy Lynch (eds) (1969) *Economic Planning and Development*, Dublin: Institute of Public Administration.

Collins, Stephen (1992) *The Haughey File*, Dublin: O'Brien Press.

Congdon, T. (1988) *The Debt Threat*, Oxford: Blackwell.

Connolly, Bernard (1995) *The Rotten Heart of Europe*, London: Faber and Faber.

Culliton Report (1992) *A Time for Change: Industrial Policy for the 1990s, Report of the Industrial Review Group*, Dublin: Stationery Office.

Daly, Mary (1992) *Industrial Development and Irish National Identity*, Dublin: Gill and Macmillan.

Department of Agriculture and Food (1999) *1998 Annual Review and Outlook for Agriculture and the Food Industry*, Dublin: Stationery Office.

Drudy, P. J. and Dermot McAleese (eds) (1984) *Ireland and the European Community*, Cambridge University Press.

Duffy, David, J. FitzGerald, I. Kearney and F. Shortall (1997) *Medium-Term Review: 1997-2003*, Dublin: ESRI.

Duffy, David, J. FitzGerald, I. Kearney and D. Smyth (1999) *Medium-Term Review: 1999-2005*, Dublin: ESRI.

Economic Development (1958) Dublin: Stationery Office.

European Commission, Directorate General for Economic and Financial Affairs (1996) 'The Economic and Financial Situation in Ireland in the Transition to EMU', in *European Economy, Ireland*, Brussels: EC.

European Commission (1997) *Agenda 2000*, Brussels: EC.

Fahey, Tony and John FitzGerald (1997) *Welfare Implication of Demographic Trends*, Dublin: Oaktree Press.

Fanning, Ronan (1983) *Independent Ireland*, Dublin: Helicon.

Farrell, Brian (1983) *Sean Lemass*, Dublin: Gill and Macmillan.

FitzGerald, Garret (1968) *Planning in Ireland*, Dublin: Institute of Public Administration.

FitzGerald, Garret (1991) *All in a Life*, Dublin: Gill and Macmillan.

FitzGerald, Garret (1998) 'Twenty-five Years of EU Membership: Retrospect and Prospect'. Paper delivered at the 21st Anniversary Dublin Economics Workshop, Kenmare, October.

FitzGerald, John (1999) 'Understanding Ireland's Economic Success'. Working paper No. 111, Dublin: Economic and Social Research Institute.

FitzGerald J., I. Kearney, E. Morgenroth and D. Smyth (eds.) (1999) *National Investment Priorities for the Period 2000-2006*, ESRI Policy Research Series No. 33, Dublin: ESRI.

Fogarty, M. P., D. Egan and W. J. L. Ryan (1981) *Pay Policy for the 1980s*, Dublin: Federated Union of Employers.

Forfás (1996) *Dublin, Shaping Our Future*, Forfás.

Gallagher, M. and R. Sinnott (eds) (1990) *How Ireland Voted, 1989*, Galway: Centre for the Study of Irish Elections, University College Galway.

Gibson, Norman and John E. Spencer (1977) *Economic Activity In Ireland*, Dublin: Gill and Macmillan.

Gillespie, Paul (ed.) (1998) *Britain's European Question*, Dublin: Institute of European Affairs.

Gray, A. W. (ed.) (1997) *International Perspectives on the Irish Economy*, Dublin: Indecon Economic Consultants.

Guiomard, Cathal (1995) *The Irish Disease and How to Cure It*, Dublin: Oaktree Press.

Halligan, B. (1998) 'Britain, Ireland and EMU: The Currency Dilemma', in Gillespie, P. (ed.) (1998) *op. cit.*

Honohan, Patrick (ed.) (1997) *EU Structural Funds in Ireland – A Mid-term Evaluation of the CSF 1994-1999*, ESRI Policy Research Series No. 31, Dublin: ESRI.

Horgan, John (1997) *Sean Lemass*, Dublin: Gill and Macmillan.

Hunt, Colin J. (1999) *Eurovision 2006*, Dublin: Goodbody Stockbrokers.

IBEC Technical Services Corporation (1952) *An Appraisal of Ireland's Industrial Potentials*, New York: IBEC.

Industrial Development Agency, Ireland: Annual Reports, various years.

Institute of European Affairs (1999) *Agenda 2000: Implications for Ireland*. Dublin: Institute of European Affairs.

Ireland: National Development Plan 1994–1999 (1994), Dublin, Stationery Office.

Jacobsen, John Kurt (1994) *Chasing Progress in the Irish Republic: Ideology, Democracy and Dependent Development*, Cambridge University Press.

Kennedy, K. A., T. Giblin and D. McHugh (1989) *The Economic Development of Ireland in the Twentieth Century*, London: Routledge.

Kennedy, Kieran A. (ed) (1998) *From Famine to Feast: Economic and Social Change in Ireland 1847-1997*, Institute of Public Administration.

Krugman, Paul (1997) 'Good News from Ireland: A Geographical Perspective', in Gray, A. W. (ed.) (1997), *op. cit.*

Laver, M., P. Mair and R. Sinnott (1987) *How Ireland Voted, 1987*, Poolbeg Press.

Leddin, A. and B. M. Walsh (1998) *The Macroeconomy of Ireland* (fourth edition), Dublin: Gill and Macmillan.

Lee, J. J. (1989) *Ireland 1912–1985: Politics and Society*, Cambridge University Press.

Little, Arthur D., Inc. (1967) *Review of the Structure of the Industrial Development Authority*, Dublin: Industrial Development Authority.

McAleese, D. and A. Foley (eds) (1991) *Overseas Industries in Ireland*, Dublin: Gill and Macmillan.

Mac Sharry, R. (1994) 'The Irish Dilemma: How to Achieve Fiscal Reform', Foundation for Fiscal Studies, Ninth Annual Conference.

Matthews, Alan (1994) *Managing the EU Structural Funds in Ireland*, Cork University Press.

Meenan, James, (1970) *The Irish Economy*, Liverpool University Press.

Murphy, Antoin E. (1994) *The Irish Economy: Celtic Tiger or Tortoise*, Dublin: MMI Stockbrokers.

National Competitiveness Council (1999) *Annual Competitiveness Report '99*, Dublin: Forfás.

National Economic and Social Council (1982) *Telesis: A Review of Industrial Policy* (Report No. 64), Dublin. NESC.

NESC (1986) *A Strategy for Development 1986-1990* (Report No. 83), Dublin: NESC.

NESC (1989) *Ireland and the European Community: Performance, Prospects and Strategy* (Report No. 88), Dublin: NESC.

NESC (1990) *A Strategy for the Nineties* (Report No. 89), Dublin: NESC.

NESC (1993) *A Strategy for Competitiveness, Growth and Employment* (Report No. 96), Dublin: NESC.

NESC (1996) *Strategy into the Twenty-first Century* (Report No. 99), Dublin: NESC.

National Treasury Management Agency (1997) *Annual Report.*

O'Brien, James F. (1981) *A Study of National Wage Agreements in Ireland.* Dublin: Economic and Social Research Institute.

Ó Grada, Cormac (1997) *A Rocky Road: The Irish Economy Since the 1920s,* Manchester University Press.

O'Hagan, J. W. (ed.) (1995) *The Economy Of Ireland*, Dublin: Gill and Macmillan.

O'Mahony, David (1967) *The Irish Economy*, Cork University Press.

O'Malley, Eoin J. (1980) *Industrial Policy and Development: A Survey of Literature from the Early 1960s to the Present,* National Economic and Social Council.

OECD, Economic Surveys: Ireland 1974-1999, Paris: OECD.

Partnership 2000 for Inclusion, Employment and Competitiveness (1996), Dublin: Stationery Office.

Penniman, H. and B. Farrell (eds.) (1987) *Ireland at the Polls: 1981, 1982, and 1987*, American Enterprise Institute, Duke University Press.

Programme for Economic Expansion (1958), Dublin: Stationery Office.

Programme for National Recovery (1987), Dublin: Stationery Office.

Programme for Economic and Social Progress (1991), Dublin: Stationery Office.

Programme for Competitiveness and Work (1994), Dublin: Stationery Office.

Sheehy, S. J. and D. J. O'Connor (1999) *Report on the Future of Irish Agriculture*, prepared for Joint Oireachtas Committee on Agriculture, Food and the Marine. Dublin: Stationery Office.

Sweeney, P. (1997) *The Celtic Tiger: Ireland's Economic Miracle Explained*, Dublin: Oaktree Press.

Tansey, Paul (1998) *Ireland at Work*, Dublin: Oaktree Press.

Teahon, Paddy (1997) 'The Irish Political and Policymaking System and the Current Programme of Change'. Presentation by Secretary General of the Department of the Taoiseach to OECD meeting of senior officials from centres of government, Dublin, September.

Tutty, M. (1994) 'Fiscal Reform in Ireland: A Department of Finance Perspective'. Foundation for Fiscal Studies, ninth annual conference.

Von Prondzynski, F. and W. Richards (1994) *European Employment and Industrial Relations Glossary*, Dublin: Sweet and Maxwell.

Whitaker, T. K. (1983) *Interests*, Dublin: Institute of Public Administration.

Ray McLoughlin's Industrial Development Model

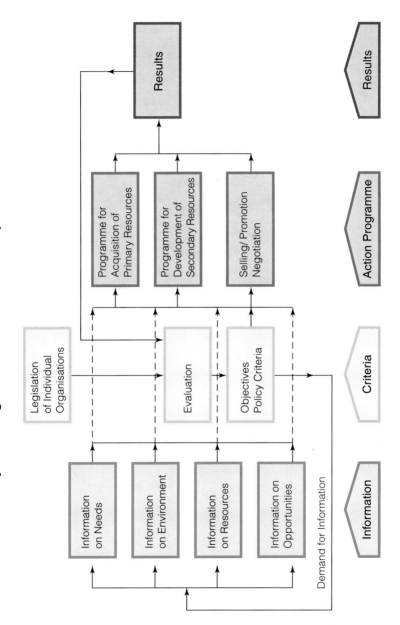

Source: *Administration*, Spring 1972

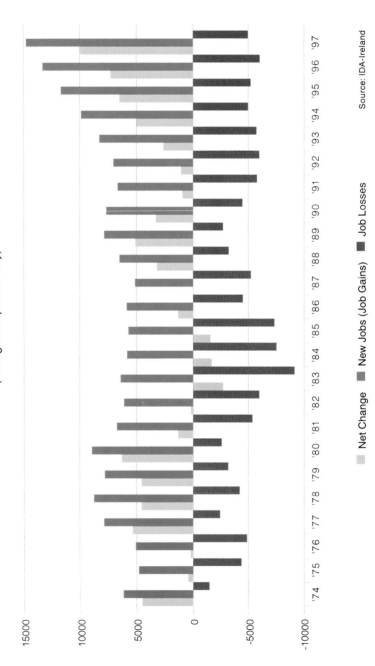

IDA Ireland - Employment 1974–1997
(Foreign companies only)

Source: IDA-Ireland

■ Net Change ■ New Jobs (Job Gains) ■ Job Losses

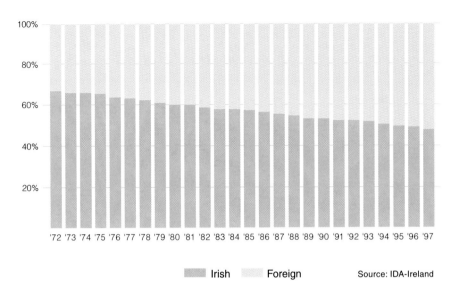

Employment by Ownership 1972–1997
(Forbairt and IDA Ireland companies only)

Irish   Foreign   Source: IDA-Ireland

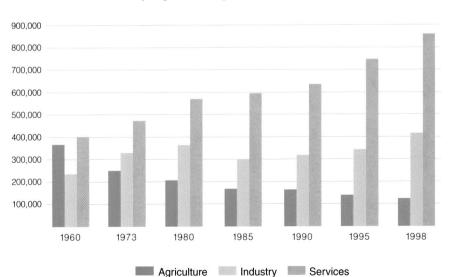

Employment by Sector 1960–1998

Agriculture   Industry   Services

Source: Offical Statistics and ESRI Estimates

Number of Trade Disputes 1960–1998

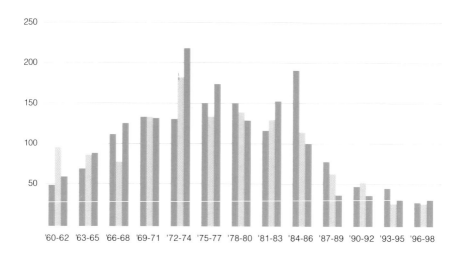

Source: CSO

Unemployment Rates 1988–1999

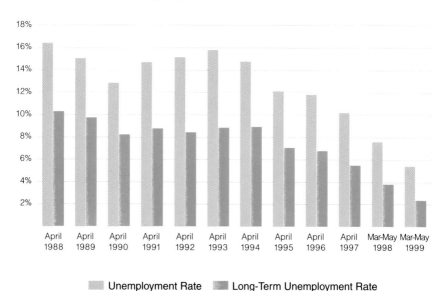

Unemployment Rate   Long-Term Unemployment Rate

Source: CSO

Trend in National Debt 1977–1997

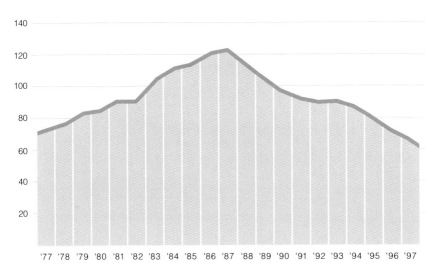

Source: Dept. of Finance

Exchequer Borrowing/Surplus 1977–1998

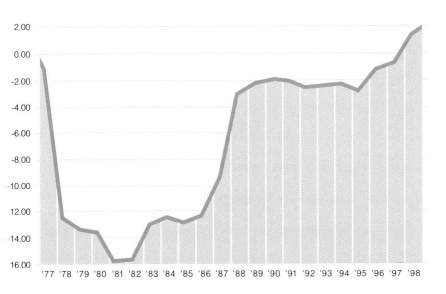

Source: Dept. of Finance

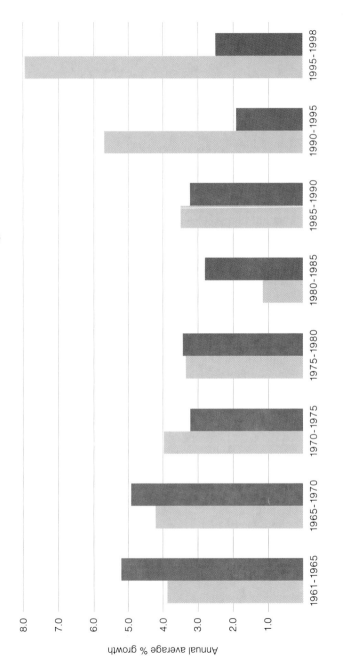

Economic Growth Five-Year Averages 1961–1998

Annual average % growth

8.0
7.0
6.0
5.0
4.0
3.0
2.0
1.0

1961-1965
1965-1970
1970-1975
1975-1980
1980-1985
1985-1990
1990-1995
1995-1998

Ireland   OECD

Source: CSO and OECD

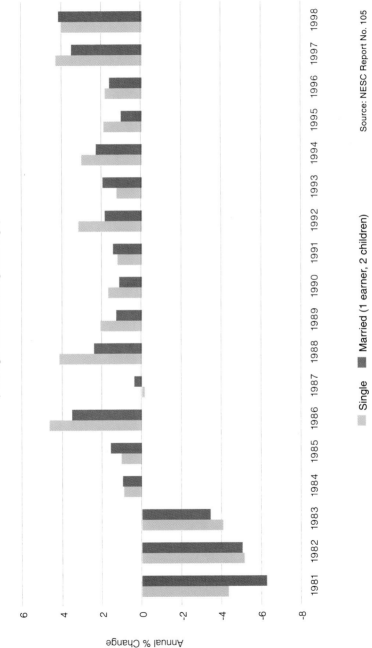

Changes in Real Take-Home Pay 1981–1998
(Average manufacturing earnings)

Annual % Change

Single   ■ Married (1 earner, 2 children)

Source: NESC Report No. 105

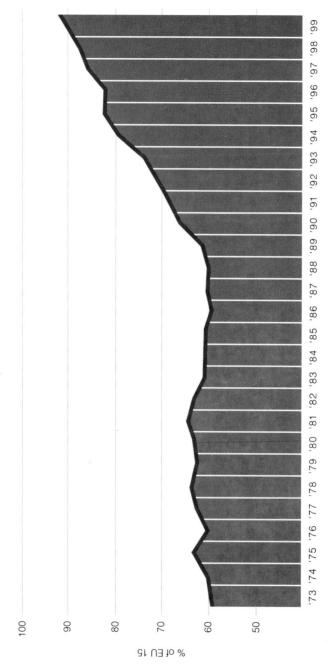

GNP per head 1973–1999

Source: CSO and OECD

INDEX

comparable growth rates, 40

opts out of EMU, 107

attitude to currency devaluation, 108

leaves ERM, 108-9

influence of EU membership on economic dependency on
    Britain, 149-50

'Lawson' boom, 363

British Land plc, 335, 349

Brittan, Leon, 167

Brosnan, Tom, 346

Brussels, 43

Bruton, John, 56, 67, 115, 268

Buchanan, Colin, 197

Buchanan Report, 197, 299, 300, 301, 304-5

Buckley, Michael, 323

Building on Reality, 44, 59

Bundesbank (Germany), 112

Burke, Dick, 250

Burlington Industries, 274

Business Week, 242, 244

C and D Petfoods, 221

Carrick, John, 216

Carstensen, Meinhard, 342

Cashman, Jim, 347

Cashman, Seamus, 258

Cassells, Peter, 128-9

    general secretary of ICTU, 129

Cassidy, Brendan, 196

Cement Roadstone Holdings, 223

Central Bank, the, 54, 59, 65, 86, 324

Chase Manhattan bank, 345, 346, 348

Kredietbank (Belgium), 346

Krugman, Paul, 361

Krups, 189

Labour Party, the, 32, 42, 45, 54, 57, 60-1, 64, 82, 113, 125, 130-1, 358

    holds Finance portfolio in 'Rainbow' coalition, 115

Labour Party (Britain), 109

Lee, J. J. (Joe), 40

Leinster House, 12

Lemass, Seán, 15-16, 61, 150-1, 183, 184, 192, 357

Leneghan, Joe, 61

Leo Laboratories, 275

Liebherr Cranes, 189

Little, A. D., 190-1

Locate in Britain Bureau, 309

Lomé (European Commission), 314

Lotus, 208, 295

Lucent, 290

Lufthansa-United, 226

Lynch, Jack, 51

Lyons, John, 196

Maastricht Treaty, 106-7, 116, 377

McCabe, Frank, 282

McCabe, Joe, 212, 217-8, 222, 252, 273

McCarthy, Charles, 135

McCarthy, Colm, 70

McConnell's Advertising Agency, 209, 239-49, 242

McCreevy, Charlie, 93, 104

    Finance Minister, 117

McEvoy, Paddy, 346

Matsushita (Panasonic), 290

Measurex, 188

medical-devices sector, 279-81

Merck, Sharpe and Dohme, 200, 276
    Hanrahan case, 277

Merrell Dow, 278-9

Merrill Lynch, 348

MG Insurance, 352

Microsoft Corporation, 208, 291, 295-6

Millan, Bruce, 168

Minet Insurance, 326

Mitchell, Gay, 353

Mitsubishi Trust, 332, 347

Moloney, Willie, 197

Moore, Gordon (Intel), 215, 220

Morgan Stanley bank, 360

Morgan, J. P., 100

Morning Ireland, 85, 268

Morrissey, Dan, 183

Mostek, 201, 218, 287

Motorola, 213, 214, 289

Mountbatten, Lord, 202

Mulcahy, Jack, 189, 276

Murphy, Kevin, 70

National City Brokers (NCB), 320, 322

National Competitiveness Council, 365, 377

National Digital Park, 298-9

National Economic and Social Council (NESC), 43-4, 45-6, 62,
    63, 66, 123-7, 129, 132, 140, 143, 144, 369

National Employer–Labour Conerence (NELC), 136-7

National Farm Survey, 174